CROSS-FUNCTIONAL MANAGEMENT

PRINCIPLES AND PRACTICAL APPLICATIONS

Kenji Kurogane, Editor in Chief

Asian Productivity Organization

Published in 1993 by
  Asian Productivity Organization
  4-14, Akasaka 8-chome
  Minato-ku, Tokyo 107, Japan

Distribution in North America, the United Kingdom, and Western Europe by
  Quality Resources
  A Division of the Kraus Organization Ltd.
  One Water Street
  White Plains, NY 10601, USA

Originally published in Japanese under the title *Kinobetsu Kanri Katsuyo no Jissai* by the Japanese Standards Association, Tokyo, Japan. Copyright © 1988 by K. Kuro-gane. All rights reserved. This is an authorized English language translation from the Japanese edition under arrangement with the Japanese Standards Association.

ISBN: 92–833–1117–5 (cloth)
        92–833–1118–3 (paper)

Cover design by Joseph DePinho.

Printed in Hong Kong by Nordica International Ltd., 16 Westland Road, Quarry Bay, Hong Kong.

List of
Contributing Authors

Kenji Kurogane,* Counselor, Japanese Standards Association

Zenzaburo Katayama,** Toyota Motor Corporation

Kozo Koura,** Saitama Institute of Technology

Kanemitsu Tsuzuki, Toyoda Automatic Loom Works, Ltd.

Takeji Uchida, Yaskawa Electric Manufacturing Company, Ltd.

Kiyoshi Yokoyama, Yaskawa Electric Manufacturing Company, Ltd.

Haruki Sugihara, Aisin A.W. Company, Ltd.

Kenichi Sato, Toyota Auto Body Company, Ltd.

Mitsuhiro Ozaki, TAKENAKA Corporation

Takao Okayama, JUKI Corporation

Kenichi Munekata, Toyoda Machine Works, Ltd.

*Editor-in-chief
**Editor

Preface

The year 1980 was a boom year marking the beginning of "TQC fever" in corporate Japan. This phenomenon—total quality control without quality assurance—was criticized by many scholars, who described it by coining the expression "TQC donuts theory."* The feverish trend, however, has cooled down, and Japanese corporations have begun focusing more on the proper TQC activity: customer-oriented quality management.

Quality control was introduced to the Japanese by Americans after World War II. For the next 40 years it evolved and was significantly developed along Japanese lines. As a result, quality control in Japan has received considerable attention from the United States and other countries in recent years. Today's Japanese-style TQC would not have survived without its specifically Japanese development.

Many Japanese industries helped their country's war-torn economy to recover. They helped Japan to achieve its important position in the global economy in spite of adverse conditions such as trade frictions and unfavorable dollar-yen exchange rates. During the process of change, the Japanese created a uniquely Japanese TQC characterized by companywide participation, policy management, quality-control diagnosis, and QC circle activity.

The concept and implementation of cross-functional management are described in this book, which addresses four functions: development of new products, quality assurance, cost management, and delivery control. I consider cross-functional management to be yet another characteristic of Japanese TQC. The concept of cross-functional management was originally formulated by Toyota Motor Corporation in the 1960s, and its specific administrative methodology was introduced later. It caught the eye of TQC-oriented corporations, and its implementation has increased down to the present time.

---

*Translator's note: This refers to a physical phenomenon involving rapid expansion without strengthening the critical core, thus leading to weakness.

The contents of the book are divided into two major parts, dealing with the principles of cross-functional management and with its practical application. The first part is divided into three chapters. Chapter 1, contributed by Kenji Kurogane, describes the principles and history of quality control, promotion of TQC, and the meaning of cross-functional management; Chapter 2, contributed by Zenzaburo Katayama, describes the history of cross-functional management at Toyota Motor Corporation and at Komatsu, Ltd.; and Chapter 3, contributed by Kozo Koura, describes the administrative aspects and key points of cross-functional management, including classification, structure, implementation processes, and results. The second part, entitled "Practical Application of Cross-Functional Management," is divided into four chapters introducing the application of the method by examples from various companies. These examples include the development of new products at Toyoda Automatic Loom Works, Ltd., and Yaskawa Electric Manufacturing Co., Ltd.; quality assurance at Yaskawa Electric Manufacturing, Ltd., and Aisin A.W. Co., Ltd.; cost management at Toyota Auto Body Co., Ltd. and TAKENAKA Corporation; and delivery control at JUKI Corporation, and Toyoda Machine Works, Ltd. These examples are described along with the administration of companywide cross-functional management at each company.

Numerous scholarly articles concerning cross-functional management have appeared, some of which are listed at the end of Chapter 3. However, technical terms used in cross-functional management are not included in the Japanese Standards Association's *Glossary of Terms Used in Quality Control*, JIS Z 8101–1981. The interpretation of "function" in cross-functional management varies from company to company, as noted in Chapter 3. In other words, cross-functional management plays a fluid, flexible role within the world of quality control. The authors hope that this volume will effectively demonstrate how cross-functional management should be applied during TQC promotion in a manner tailored to each company's individual circumstances.

Many thanks are due to Mitsugi Iizumi, director, and Tatsu Sawada of the Publication Department of the Japanese Standards Association for their valuable assistance.

Kenji Kurogane,
on behalf of the editors and contributors

Contents

       Cross-Functional Management
       Kozo Koura   **33**

       Corporate Needs and Identification of Policy   33
       Classifications of Functions   34
       Structural Organization of Cross-Functional
           Management   37
       The Cross-Functional Management Committee: Its
           Tasks, Structure, and Administration   42
       Steps for Cross-Functional Management Deployment ·
           and Implementation   46
       Cross-Functional Management, Management by
           Department, and Management by Product Line   54
       Cross-Functional Management, Policy Management,
           and Day-to-Day Management   56
       Effects of Cross-Functional Management   56
       Key Points in the Promotion of Cross-Functional
           Management   57
       Cross-Functional Management and Standardization   62
       References   66

Part II   Practical Application of Cross-Functional Management

4   **Development of New Products and Cross-Functional**   **71**
       Management

       Development of New Products and Cross-Functional
       Management at Toyoda Automatic Loom Works, Ltd.
       Kanemitsu Tsuzuki   **71**

       Introduction   71
       Cross-Functional Management at the Company   72
       Policy Management at Toyoda Automatic Loom
           Works   75
       An Example of New Product Development   85
       Concluding Remarks   97

       Development of New Products at Yukuhashi Plant,
       Yaskawa Electric Manufacturing Company, Ltd.
       Takeji Uchida   **97**

       Introduction   97
       Overview of Cross-Functional Management   98   New Product Development   104

Figures

Tables

I
Cross-Functional Management

TQC Promotion and Cross-Functional Management

Kenji Kurogane

PRINCIPLES OF QUALITY CONTROL

Quality Control Fundamentals

Quality control is defined in the Japanese Standards Association's *Hinshitsu-Kanriyogo (Glossary of Terms Used in Quality Control)*, JIS Z 8101, published in 1981, as "a system whereby the qualities of products or services are produced economically to meet the requirements of the purchaser."

Quality control is sometimes called QC. Since modern quality control applies statistical techniques, it is also sometimes referred to as *statistical quality control* (SQC).

Effective implementation of quality control embraces all phases of business activity, including the following: market survey, research and development, product planning, design, production preparation, purchasing and subcontracting, manufacturing, inspection, sales, after-sales services, financing, personnel affairs, and education. It requires total participation and collaboration of all employees, from executives down to managers, foremen, and workers.

Quality control activities conducted in such a way are referred to as *zenshateki hinshitsu kanri* (companywide quality control, CWCQ) or *sogoteki-hinshitsu-kanri* (total quality control, TQC).

Products and services provided by corporations are designed for customers to purchase and to use. If the quality is inferior, customers will walk away no matter how low the price may be. In fact, customer confidence, which may require ten or more years to build, can be destroyed in a day if products and services trigger mistrust. Business prosperity is based upon fundamental quality management attitudes, the ideal expressed by the motto "quality first," quality-focused management, and continuous quality improvement. Quality control and TQC clearly must be accompanied by quality; however, we tend to be nearsighted in our efforts to ensure short-term gains.

The judgment as to whether quality is good or inferior is made by customers who buy and use products or services. Respecting the voice of the customer, or cultivating a customer-oriented business attitude, is a must. However, customer orientation often becomes secondary while production orientation, or a self-serving business attitude, become the primary concern.

For corporate prosperity, it is critical that there be a sense of crisis vis-à-vis the problems faced, that all departments collaborate systematically under the executive managers' leadership, and that total employee participation be achieved by applying all statistical tools, including scientific management improvement techniques. In promoting corporate growth, industries consider respect for humanity and human development to be important. Treasuring employees is considered to be one of the characteristics of Japanese quality control. (See Figure 1.1.)

It is necessary to develop corporate business activities based upon the principles of quality control. If true quality, customer orientation, and

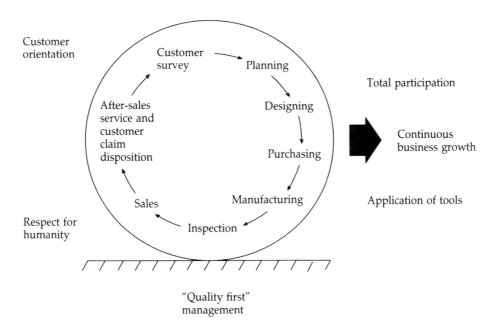

FIGURE 1.1
Principles of quality control

respect for humanity are disregarded, TQC tends to become a superficial and ritual activity.

The History of Quality Control in Japan

Some fundamental ideas of quality control have been discussed in the previous section, but the perception of quality control varies with businesses and individuals. Quality control includes testing and inspection within the company; QC circle activities, which are characteristic of Japanese QC; application of statistical methods utilizing control charts and sampling inspections at manufacturing plants; and methods to improve the quality of businesses and their management.

Each of these four concepts represents a phase of quality control. As Japanese QC evolved over 40 years, beginning with its introduction by Americans after World War II, changes have occurred that are discussed below.

Introduction of Quality Control: The Era of SQC (1949–54)

In 1946, immediately after World War II, the occupation forces of the United States taught Japanese telecommunication manufacturers and associated businesses how to apply American methods of quality control. In addition, QC research groups, consisting of Japanese scholars and engineers, began research on quality control, a new American management technique. Both the Japanese Standards Association and the Union of Japanese Scientists and Engineers (JUSE) began sponsoring quality control seminars in 1949. They greatly contributed toward a foundation for the future Japanese quality control movement. During the same years, the Japanese Industrial Standardization Act established quality criteria for JIS Mark products and provided an incentive for industries to be concerned with improvement of quality. Some believe, in view of these facts, that authentic Japanese quality control began in 1949.

Dr. W. E. Deming (b. 1900) came to Japan in 1950 and introduced SQC, which had been effectively implemented in the United States during World War II. In particular, he introduced statistical techniques such as control charts and sampling inspection methods. He also lectured on the principles of quality control, including the Deming cycle. (See Figure 1.2.)

The Deming Prize was established in 1951 to commemorate Dr. Deming's contributions. It has become a motivating factor in the development of the Japanese corporate quality control movement.

In the 1950s, defect reduction and quality assurance activities were developed by applying statistical methods, predominantly in the manufacturing plants of industries such as steel, pharmaceuticals, and chemicals.

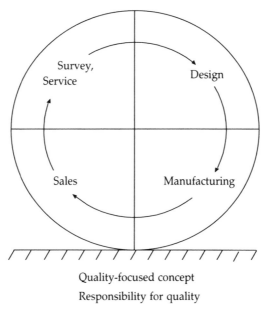

Quality-focused concept

Responsibility for quality

FIGURE 1.2
The Deming cycle

Since statistical methods were the core tools applied, particularly by quality control engineers, this period was referred to as an era of statistical quality control. However, the application of statistical methods was overly stressed at this time and regarded as the only way to ensure quality control.

Building a Solid Foundation for Japanese-Style TQC (1955–69)

Dr. J. M. Juran (b. 1904) visited Japan in 1954 and stressed the importance of quality control as a means of management. The seeds of the unique Japanese quality control movement were sown at this time. The movement was headed by executives and absorbed by managers and supervisors, and eventually matured into a companywide movement.

Quality control activity expanded from the process industry sector to the assembly industry sector, including automobiles and household electric appliances. In order to upgrade the quality of the assembly industry's products, the quality of both assembly work and components became an issue. Suppliers of components for the assembly industry joined in the quality control movement within their umbrella group.

At the same time, in order to create quality in the manufacturing process, the importance of the engineers' and workers' quality awareness and skills was recognized. A monthly journal for supervisors and workers, *QC in the Field* (later renamed *FQC* and ultimately *QC Circle*), was first published in April 1962. It promoted QC circle activity and helped a group of core workers learn and demonstrate quality control. Results of these improvement activities were recognized through QC presentation meetings for foremen and for QC circle members. These opportunities contributed to the self-development and mutual development of workers and supervisors. QC circle activity is regarded as one of the significant characteristics of Japanese quality control, and it has been cited as a contributing factor to much of the global recognition of the quality of Japanese products. Simple and effective tools, such as the Seven QC Tools, were frequently applied by QC circle members.

Concurrently with existing quality-assurance plant inspections, other activities were developed to create a built-in quality system during the 1950s. These activities addressed the quality of manufacturing, including how to manufacture with a minimum of quality dispersion and how to reduce the number of defects. With the higher standard of living and a market flooded with competitive products, customers became more selective in their purchasing. This trend forced manufacturers to become concerned about more than the quality of the manufacturing process itself. Consequently, the importance of a quality plan and of quality design gradually gained recognition in the 1960s through attempts to identify what products and quality the customers demanded under a more intensely consumer-oriented economy.

Along with quality improvement activities in the planning and design departments, quality assurance activities in the market were stressed, including product quality after shipment; higher quality of service in case of quality problems with shipped products; and timely, accurate service in response to customer claims. At the same time, the importance of departmental activities in service and sales began to be better recognized because those involved were the very people who had the most firsthand feedback from customers regarding products on the market.

Thus, Japanese quality control activity developed significantly in the 1960s, transforming itself from traditional SQC into total quality control (TQC). It expanded to include companywide activity and all departmental activities, including not only manufacturing but also planning, design, service, and sales. In addition, in order to align these activities in the same direction, the importance of policy management began to be stressed. Each department, therefore, began to establish its plan of action according to policies and goals set by management. It tracked the results monthly or quarterly, and continued all of the above activities after evaluating the checked results. In the policy statement concerning improvement issues, industries started addressing the improvement of cross-functional management so that activities would not be confined within a single department. These corporate activities included quality assurance, cost control, and delivery control. Specific improvement goals were presented to all of the departments involved, not just to engineering or manufacturing. With this backdrop, quality management diagnosis was conducted by an executive team including the president. This type of executive involvement in quality control activities created yet another distinctive characteristic of Japanese quality control.

Following the years of SQC, Japanese TQC (or CWQC) grew and solidified. Japanese quality control attracted global attention when the First International Conference of Quality Control was held in Tokyo in 1969.

Establishment of TQC in the Manufacturing Sector (1970s)

The economic growth rate was high in the early 1970s. The Japanese economy weathered the storms of a volatile world economy, foreign exchange rate shock waves, and two OPEC price increases. Subsequently, the business environment deteriorated as it was exposed to waves of slow growth and recession. Internally, rising consumerism, public concern over environmental issues, and heightened demand for product safety raised product liability issues with which industry had to cope.

Under the slow-growth economy, many efforts were made to increase business through the development of new products, which required the following: active assessment of the quality demanded by customers; quality deployment for planning and design based upon quality tables; application of design evaluation systems in the development stage; failure-mode-and-effect analysis (FMEA) as a technique to upgrade product reliability; and the application of fault tree analysis (FTA). These efforts were made in order to overcome the harsh business environment through development of new products while strengthening reliability and quality control activity in the departments involved in the early phases.

In order to prevent the manufacture of defective products, management leadership undertook efforts to include environmental protection and in-depth product liability prevention (PLP) by giving due consideration to product safety. The results were clearly significant.

Many corporations experienced a domestic slump and unfavorable foreign exchange rates. They addressed these problems by engaging in long-term TQC activities, which included flexible and strong corporate quality, streamlined management, production rationalization, conservation of resources and of energy, cost reduction, and improvement in the quality of routine work. As a consequence, significant results were realized.

Japanese-style TQC had matured in the 1960s. TQC was not confined within the manufacturing department but was coordinated through companywide activities involving all departments. These activities were not exclusively those of a special professional group of staff members but were carried out by people at all levels. Policy management activities were promoted by executives, managers, and supervisors while QC circle activities were promoted by the rank-and-file QC circle members. Together, they solidified Japanese TQC in the 1970s. Various small-group and QC circle activities played an especially important role, attracting greater attention both domestically and internationally.

Expansion of TQC from the Manufacturing Sector to Other Sectors and the Globalization of TQC (1980s)

The quality control movement gradually expanded from the manufacturing department to departments throughout the company, including development, management, and sales. This movement later developed into groupwide activities, encompassing subsidiaries and vendors. Along with this, TQC activities began gradually expanding from manufacturing to other businesses. This movement slowly grew to include construction, hotel, banking, and financial service industries during the second half of the 1970s, and rapidly accelerated in the 1980s. Several construction companies and the Kansai Electric Power Company were awarded the Deming Application Prize in recognition of their TQC implementation. However, many construction and utility companies still remain at the QC circle level. One of the important challenges for these industries in the future will be to create a suitable TQC for themselves, building upon the existing base in much the same way that has already been demonstrated by the manufacturing industry.

As to the tools applied, as the quality-control movement expanded from the manufacturing sector to other sectors, effective use of verbal information, based on past experience, was emphasized and applied to establish plans of action for improvement. The Seven New QC Tools were promoted and have become widely used.

An early sign of the global quality control movement appeared in the 1960s. The liberalization of trade increased the export of Japanese products, which later led to trade frictions. In due course, the development of quality in new products and the improvement of the service system were required by foreign customers. Along with the global quality control movement, many issues still required solutions in the areas of plant management and promotion of QC circle activities for employees in foreign countries.

The Japanese way of management gained global attention as the country worked to overcome the worldwide recession of the 1970s. Japanese TQC and QC circle activities attracted an increasing number of foreign visitors who wanted to study the Japanese way of quality control.

To promote the international exchange of quality control information, quality control staff and QC circle team members visited foreign countries annually, gaining knowledge for their own future development and stimulating their hosts through the presentation of Japanese quality control cases. Opportunities for international information exchange have been expanding every year. Also, international conferences on quality control and QC circles have begun to be sponsored frequently and to be well attended by representatives of many countries.

One prime example is the International Conference on Quality Control held in Tokyo in 1987. It took place when Japan was faced with a harsh economic environment that included wide disparity in foreign exchange rates against the dollar; but nevertheless, it was attended by 886 participants, including 423 visitors from 43 foreign countries. The conference is held every three years, and once in nine years in Japan. Ten items were presented as characteristics of Japanese quality control during the conference:

1. Thorough prioritization of quality in management
2. Quality assurance from planning and development to sales and service
3. Quality control through participation of all departments and employees, with management taking the lead
4. Policy deployment and management
5. QC diagnosis and application
6. QC circle activities
7. Education and training for quality control
8. Development and application of QC techniques
9. Expansion of QC from manufacturing to other sectors
10. National promotion of QC activities

With these events taking place, expectations for Japanese contributions to the global quality control movement are increasing every year, and there is a continuing call for increased research.

INTRODUCTION AND PROMOTION OF TQC

Issues relating to the introduction and promotion of TQC vary from company to company. If, for example, the president believes there is a need for the introduction of TQC and demonstrates his leadership, an ideal atmosphere for promoting TQC develops. On the other hand, if the president is a mere spectator, the promotional work will not be so simple. The common promotional methods applied in many companies are discussed below.

Understanding TQC and Creating a Companywide Mood for Its Introduction and Promotion

In order to introduce TQC, a proper companywide mood must be created. If the majority of employees are indifferent toward their jobs, introduction will be very difficult. First, top management must recognize the need for TQC and demonstrate its commitment to TQC in order to promote it convincingly. For that to occur, the president must clearly state the introduction and promotional policy to all employees and create the necessary mood for TQC throughout the company.

It is incorrect to assume that TQC has been successfully introduced simply by appointing an office in charge, guaranteeing the budget, and adding QC circle activities. As commonly described, TQC is "QC for top management," and the president must demonstrate his leadership in promoting it. Top executives should create the necessary mood companywide so that every employee will realize the importance of TQC. Executives should communicate to their employees through every possible means, including a company bulletin, brochures, and meetings. Through these means, they can inform employees of the importance of TQC and demonstrate the corporate attitude toward its implementation. The presentation of clear policies and their departmental deployment and the implementation of the presidential diagnosis as a checking mechanism represent some of these steps.

Building the Structure for Promotion and Promotion Plans

Talk alone does not advance the deployment of companywide TQC. It must be accompanied by the identification of specific activities and structures to support a promotional plan, including deployment activities; a structure to promote such activities; an executive-level core person who, as a minimum qualification, must be able to take full charge of TQC; systematic companywide implementation; policy management; QC circle activities; groupwide activities involving vendors and contractors; enhancement programs for the development of new products in conjunction with all of the above activities; quality assurance and quality improvement; and the support of QC education.

Depending upon the size of the company and the stage of TQC promotion, additional structural organizations may be necessary at plants and division offices. These structures may be regarded as substructures in relation to the companywide structure. They will review and establish TQC promotion plans for each structural organization. Subordinate structures for cross-functional quality control—which include a QC circle promotion committee, a quality assurance committee, a cost management committee, and a delivery control committee—can be gradually formulated and re-structured.

Implementation of Education and Training for Human Development

The importance of TQC education cannot be overemphasized, as is expressed by the statement "QC begins and ends with education." Japanese quality control education is unique, and includes the following:

1. Awareness of the importance of quality, and enhancement of problem awareness and willingness to improve
2. QC tools, including statistical methods, and application of the tools to problem solving
3. Practical application of quality control.

Education is implemented companywide on all levels, from executives to workers. However, the process of education varies from level to level because of the differing degrees of responsibility.

Educational seminars on quality control, offered by the Japanese Standards Association and many other institutions, provide opportunities to learn about quality control in a systematic way, starting from the basics. Some seminars provide additional learning opportunities in which participants from different companies meet and exchange ideas.

In-house seminars dealing with similar subjects have been gaining popularity. The advantages of such seminars include mass education of employees, clarifying of corporate objectives for TQC and of problems, and serious group discussion regarding specific themes made possible by employee awareness of the problems.

Many QC presentation meetings and lectures are offered for executives, managers, staff members, foremen, and QC circle members. Participation in these meetings provides learning opportunities based upon case studies from other companies, a chance to compare one's own case studies with those of others, confidence, and, consequently, additional motivation. In order to further promote TQC maturity, it is important to expand educational programs by involving subsidiaries and associated companies.

Many companies are adopting and developing their own curricula and texts for in-house education programs. To maximize the benefits of these sessions, some companies are devising ways of training in which knowledge gained in the classroom is applied to specific problems at work locations. Other educational activities, such as the presidential diagnosis and QC circle activities, may be interpreted as on-the-job training.

Policy Management and Promotion of Problem Solving through Implementation of QC Diagnosis

After identifying current problems, policy statements concerning goals and major plans of action for the company or plant are presented at the beginning of each quarter. Taking these policies into consideration, each department develops specific plans of action. Results are checked on a monthly basis, and plans for the subsequent month are reviewed. At the end of each quarter, the implementation or its results are checked through a presidential QC diagnosis or manager's audit.

In this manner, a company or plant can identify major internal issues that urgently need solutions. Some representative areas include the development of new products, quality improvement, cost reduction, and production and contract quantity. Identification of policy, expressed by quantified goals, enhances the promotion of companywide administrative group or team activities. At the same time, companywide restructuring of management and standardization can be implemented through reviews and reestablishment of a system for developing new products; a quality assurance system; and the identification of areas of responsibility, functions, and control items. Practical training and human development programs for top executives, senior managers, and middle managers can likewise be implemented.

Implementation of QC diagnosis by executives is extremely important because it enhances internal attitudes about quality control, motivates human development for managers, and ultimately shows favorable policy results. As a company matures in TQC, it should upgrade corporate quality gradually by striving to meet more difficult challenges, such as those promoted by JIS (Japanese Industrial Standards), the MITI (Ministry of International Trade and Industry) Award, the Director of MITI's International Trade and Industry Bureau Award, and the Deming Application Prize.

Introduction and Promotion of Small-Group Activities, Including QC Circle Activities

Policy management existed and was maintained through a process of establishing implementation plans based on upper-management policy and utilizing a horizontal administrative structure. Along with this policy management activity, many corporations had small-group activities that were variously called QC circle activity, *Jishu-Kanri* (self-management) activity, and the Zero Defects program. Motivation and human development at work locations depended upon whether the groups were active and autonomous. Activities by these small groups are drawing worldwide attention as characteristically Japanese aspects of quality control.

Japanese QC circles were begun in 1962. Dr. Juran was impressed with the activities in Japan a few years later and predicted that Japan would soon become a world leader in quality. Indeed, the QC circles continued to grow steadily and contributed much to the improvement of quality in Japanese products. Universally recognized were their cost reductions, improvement of quality of work, and improvement of corporate culture. Consequently, many corporations were prompted to introduce QC circles not only for manufacturing departments but also for management, "indirect" staff, and sales departments. Ultimately, the boom expanded from the manufacturing industry to include the banking, hotel, service, and distribution industries.

General principles of QC circles are clearly defined in the *QC Circle Koryo*. It states that the QC circle is a small group voluntarily performing quality control activities within the same workshop. Utilizing quality control techniques, this small group functions continuously, with all members participating, as a part of the companywide quality control activities, with the aims of self-development and mutual development, control, and improvement within the workshop. That the groups are voluntary does not mean that superiors leave them alone; rather, it means that superiors provide subordinates with support and guidance, not direction.

In addition to the above activities, more creative ideas may be needed. Listed below are some of the activities required to further expand and strengthen TQC:

1. Deployment to distribution, sales, and service activities
2. Diffusion of TQC to subsidiaries and vendors, and establishment of a Quality Award
3. Participation in and/or presentation at QC presentation meetings, and exchange of information with other companies.

CROSS-FUNCTIONAL MANAGEMENT AND ITS NECESSITY

Needs for Interdepartmental Cooperation in Quality Improvement and Cost Reduction

When vertical strata of a corporation, such as divisions and departments, deploy activities for quality improvement and cost reduction based on policy, the need for interdepartmental problem solving becomes evident.

Let us take a look at initial production of new products at a plant. At this transitional step from the research and development department to the manufacturing plant, the quality of new products is often inconsistent, with varying degrees of problems. Subsequently, design modifications become necessary. If the production process is not in a stable state, immediate action by the special task team during this time of "initial flow control" is required. If problems with new products are addressed only by the manufacturing plant, action tends to be technologically insufficient, temporary, and slow. Appropriate action requires the cooperation of the research and development group or of originating departments, such as design and engineering. Participation by the originating departments is important not only so that they can resolve problems in the early stages but also so that they can improve development activity step by step. In this way, they can prevent the recurrence of similar problems in the next developmental stage.

The same principle can be applied to new products that are shipped. All is well if there are no customer complaints regarding the new products. However, in spite of thorough advance evaluation of design reviews, new products tend to reveal their deficiencies after they are shipped. The quality assurance department alone cannot easily reduce customer complaints despite these efforts. The sales and service departments must take immediate measures, and research and development and manufacturing must cooperate to take appropriate measures—including design modifications—to prevent recurrence.

The need for interdepartmental cooperation in problem solving relating to the development of new products has been emphasized thus far. In reality, however, sectionalism still prevails strongly in the vertical strata of a corporation, and cooperation among the horizontal units remains a challenge. The importance of improving interdepartmental cooperation and corporate team dynamics will be recognized as TQC progresses. Improvement applies not only to the development of new products but also to the three major function areas of quality assurance: cost management, delivery control, and those functions common to all departments, such as education, human development, assurance of contract quantity, and subcontracting management.

What Is Cross-Functional Management?

As already stated, the vertical strata of a corporation are tied together, but strong sectionalism exists in departments such as manufacturing, sales, and others and impedes communication horizontally. In order to solve interdepartmental problems, committees or councils have been formed to address quality assurance, cost management, and other functions. These bodies actively work with each department on management and improvement of functions. This "cross-functional management" has been devised and administered by Toyota Motor Corporation since the 1970s.

In order to fulfill departmental roles and policies, vertical units of the corporation, such as design, engineering, manufacturing, subcontracting, sales, and others, deploy management improvement activities on a department-by-department basis. This is referred to as "departmental management." "Cross-functional management" has often been used recently in the context of TQC and in contrast to "departmental management."

Committees for quality assurance, cost management, and delivery control are generally headed by the executives responsible for each function. Each committee is composed of representatives from the existing vertical units or related departments of quality assurance, accounting, and production control. They meet on a monthly basis and form additional supporting organization on a lower level if necessary. The functions of each committee, citing quality assurance as an example, are to establish a system to identify responsibilities for each department of the vertical units and to provide departmental directions for quality assurance based upon the results of the committee's monthly reviews of quality assurance and claim disposition. Execution and responsibilities of the quality assurance activity must be borne by each department or vertical unit; the committee's role should be limited to strengthening companywide quality assurance activity. Perhaps this can be described as "weaving the corporate threads," both vertically and horizontally.

The three major functions—quality assurance, cost (or profit) management, and delivery control—should be considered first when selecting the corporate functions. Others, such as contracted orders management, subcontracting management, and personnel management, may also be considered.

The development of new products and the major functions will be discussed in Chapter 4 and subsequent chapters of this book.

2

History of Cross-Functional Management

Zenzaburo Katayama

THE HISTORY OF CROSS-FUNCTIONAL MANAGEMENT AT TOYOTA MOTOR CORPORATION

Anticipating international trade deregulation, Toyota Motor Corporation, Ltd., decided to introduce and implement TQC in 1961 so that corporate quality would be upgraded. A companywide audit, conducted on a department-by-department basis by an executive team at the time TQC was introduced, revealed that each department's management and improvement were based on its own policy, and that departmental activities lacked companywide cooperation. Consequently, the audit team determined that there was a need for improvement of interdepartmental activities.

The team determined that the focal point of TQC promotion was to be the improvement of interdepartmental activities. It identified policies so that quality objectives were clearly spelled out and thoroughly understood by all employees, and it fostered an effective system to facilitate interdepartmental cooperation. To accomplish this, the TQC promotion plan was established for each item to be promoted, as shown in Table 2.1, and activities to initiate the Deming cycle of PDCA—(Plan-Do-Check-Act)—for each item began in April 1962.

In order to follow up on the results of these activities, corporate policy for 1963 was redefined, and the second companywide audit was implemented. Items of this audit are described in Table 2.2.

TQC activities for the audit items were initiated by major coordinating departments through drafting the control system chart for each related department. This chart was studied and modified, problem areas were further identified, and system reorganization was promoted throughout the company.

TABLE 2.1
Items of the TQC promotion plan

1. Development of new products
2. Production preparation for new products (includes decisions about internal or external production)
3. Initial flow control
4. Full-scale production (i.e., production for sales) control (includes inventory and purchased material management)
5. Manufacturing quality control
6. Management of quality information
7. Cost management
8. Clarification of responsibility for senior managers and managers
9. Work standards
10. Management standards for design and research
11. Management of equipment maintenance
12. Establishment of control items
13. Education

} 14. Standardization

In February 1963, the planning committee was initiated as a new corporate decision-making body, and the planning office was established to provide staff support for the committee. Policy management using a system based upon corporate policy was discussed, and the existing system of vertical departmental assignment was abolished. A new cross-functional management system emphasizing assignment by cross-functional areas was discussed and ultimately implemented in March 1963.

The president assigned a group of executives to each cross-functional area, and these executives acted as staff to support the president. They

TABLE 2.2
Items of the second companywide audit

1. Development of new products and design for quality
2. Manufacturing preparation for new products
3. Initial flow control
4. Production quantity control
5. Material management (purchasing management for parts and material and subcontracting management)
6. Manufacturing quality control (includes research on process capability)
7. Product-quality information management
8. Work standardization
9. Machine and equipment control
10. Cost management
11. Organization and areas of responsibility
12. Education

carried out the necessary auditing, coordinating, and advising in their respective areas and reported directly to the president.

Under the traditional departmental management system, executives tended to represent their own departmental interests, and consequently interdepartmental cooperation was not always realized. To solve this problem, companywide system reorganization was put into effect. In this system, executives were assigned to multiple cross-functional areas in such a way as to promote the analysis of activities from a companywide point of view. With the new system in place, effective management was expected, thanks to the opportunity the new system afforded to study various cross-functional management areas from a broader perspective and to concentrate upon system organization without the burdens imposed by old departmental responsibilities.

In order to accelerate promotional activities for system reorganization and to enhance the new cross-functional management, a revised TQC promotion plan was established in May 1963. New and challenging activities were conducted according to the plan in the following cross-functional areas.

1. Long-range planning, production planning, and general coordination
2. Information analysis
3. Product planning
4. Equipment planning
5. Research and development
6. Process design and reorganization
7. Purchasing
8. Sales
9. Design quality management
10. Manufacturing quality management
11. Registration issues management
12. New product facilitation
13. Production and inventory control
14. Cost control
15. Cost maintenance
16. Cost improvement
17. Process analysis improvement
18. Public relations
19. Organizational and administrative management

Items 9–11: Quality control
Items 12–13: Production control
Items 14–16: Cost management

20. Personnel and education

21. Safety and hygiene

The primary objectives of the second stage of the TQC promotion plan were reorganization and enhancement of major areas. In September 1963, manufacturing and equipment maintenance were added to the existing functions. Executives responsible for cross-functional management were assigned to the 11 areas listed below. The third companywide audit stimulated improvement of each function and helped broaden the executive point of view and interdepartmental cooperation.

1. Planning

2. Marketing

3. Engineering

4. Cost management

5. Internal and external products

6. Equipment manufacturing

7. Financial research

8. Purchasing

9. Quality control and auditing

10. Related companies

11. Tokyo branch office

TARGETING FOR THE TOTAL CONTROL SYSTEM

In order to fine-tune and implement promotional activities in wider areas, Toyota Motors Corporation established the QC promotion office in September 1964. Chairman Eiji Toyoda (then vice president) was named director of the office, and President Shoichiro Toyoda (then executive vice president) and Toyota Research Center adviser Hanji Umehara were named associate directors. At the same time, standing committee members were selected from the general office, the promotion office, and each department. The committee held numerous meetings to identify problems, to revise TQC promotion plans, and to discuss the concept of functions. After much discussion, a conceptual function chart was drawn, as shown in Figure 2.1.

In this conceptual chart, functions are not listed in a parallel fashion but are diagrammed according to analytical principles to indicate their interrelationships.

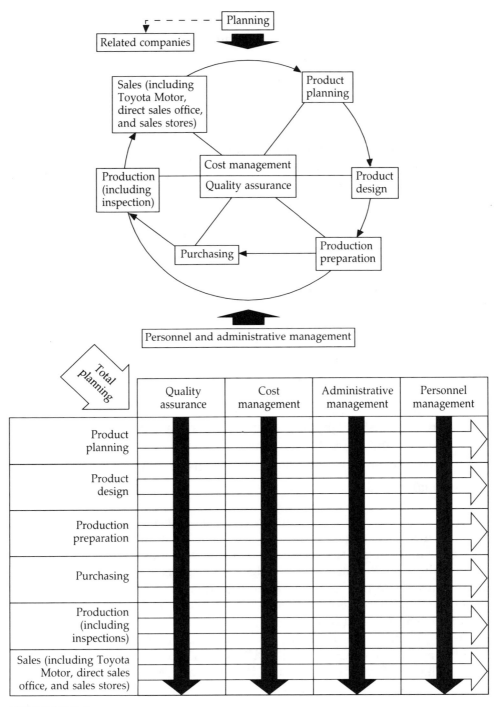

FIGURE 2.1
Conceptual chart for functions under cross-functional management

1. Overall company planning
2. Functions to facilitate the setting and achieving of corporate targets, such as quality assurance and cost management
3. Line work (or process), from product planning and design to sales
4. Personnel and administrative management

According to the quality control concept, quality of the product is to be realized during the line work (or the line process), ensuring quality for the subsequent worker (or the subsequent process). In Figure 2.1, quality control was listed as quality assurance. The QC promotion structure, as shown in Table 2.3, was based on the same concept.

Specific activities were implemented by each promotional organizational unit. Activities under the quality assurance function that were clarified during promotional processes are explained below.

STREAMLINING QUALITY ASSURANCE FUNCTIONS

In order to achieve quality assurance, its definition was reviewed on the basis of the quality assurance system chart. Quality assurance was defined as "ensuring that products are satisfactory, reliable, and economical for users." Quality assurance is achieved through the following:

1. Activities to build quality within the process (product planning, product design, manufacturing preparation, full-scale production, purchasing, sales, and service)
2. Activities to ensure quality through inspection
3. Quality audits.

The idea was to provide quality assurance for customers by ensuring quality during each step of the process, from beginning to end. The ideas, steps, assurance items, necessary work, responsible parties, areas of responsibility, and related major rules were reviewed. The results of the review were summarized in the table of quality assurance activity. This table was standardized to provide guidelines for quality assurance. A sample is shown in Figure 2.2.

Fine-tuning of these quality assurance activities was steadily implemented as part of TQC support, and Toyota Motor Corporation undertook the challenge of competing for the 1965 Deming Application Prize.

Cost management activities at every step of the process, ranging from product planning to sales, were likewise reviewed and revised after assessment of the actual situation.

TABLE 2.3
QC promotion organization

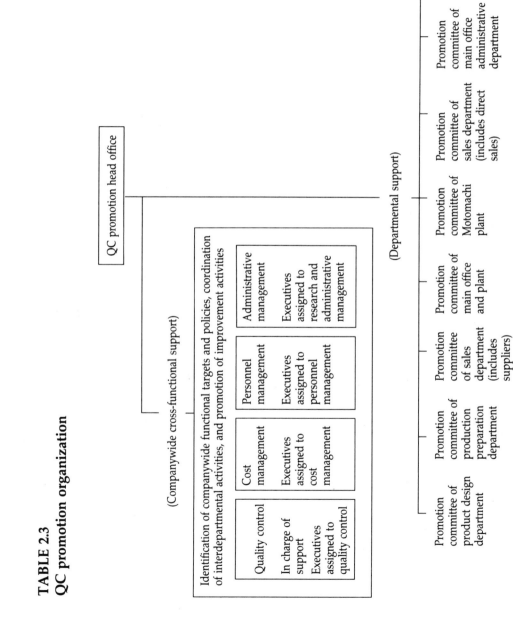

QC promotion head office

(Companywide cross-functional support)

Identification of companywide functional targets and policies, coordination of interdepartmental activities, and promotion of improvement activities

Quality control	Cost management	Personnel management	Administrative management
In charge of support	Executives assigned to cost management	Executives assigned to personnel management	Executives assigned to research and administrative management
Executives assigned to quality control			

(Departmental support)

Promotion committee of product design department

Promotion committee of production preparation department

Promotion committee of sales department (includes suppliers)

Promotion committee of main office and plant

Promotion committee of Motomachi plant

Promotion committee of sales department (includes direct sales)

Promotion committee of main office administrative department

Promotion committee of Tokyo branch office

Step	Assurance items	Necessary work	Responsible parties	Areas of responsibility	Related major rules	Remarks
General planning	General usefulness of planning for new products	1. Projecting demand and market share	Senior project manager Senior overseas project manager			
		1. Predicting competitors' strategies 2. Drafting and evaluating long-range management plan	Manager of general planning office		Rules for drafting a long-range plan (Aa 301)	
General long-range planning for new products	General usefulness of planning by product groups	1. Reviewing fitness of product groups in response to predicted demands and requests for new products	Senior project manager Senior overseas project manager	Product Planning Office Manager	Rules for developing new products (Hb 02)	
		1. Engineering projection and review of adjustment in new-product-development items 2. Review of validity of model-change plan with respect to market share 3. Review of general capability balance for development of new products	Engineering planning office manager Product planning office chief			
Planning for individual new products	Conformance to targeted demand trend	1. Confirmation of conformance to demand trend 2. Confirmation of price competitiveness	Senior project manager Senior overseas project manager Engineering planning office manager			
		1. Review of engineering competitiveness 2. Verification of application of R & D results 3. Confirmation of new-products development capability 4. Conformance to targeted model durability 5. Drafting cost target	Engineering planning office manager Product planning office chief			
Basic plan for individual new products	Quality expected by market	1. Establishment of correct quality target 2. Confirmation of development capability and production capacity 3. Development schedule plan 4. Distribution of predicted costs 5. Prevention of recurrence of major quality problems (applicable to same or similar line of vehicles)	Product planning office chief		Committee rules for new products (Hb 06)	

Product planning

FIGURE 2.2
Sample table of quality assurance activity

The picture of cross-functional management became clearer after going through these processes. Management problems detected were fed into the cross-functional committee composed of the executives in charge of each cross-functional area.

Along with the enhancement of cross-functional management, company policies were analyzed according to each function. Upon careful review of each area by the cross-functional committee, the policies were incorporated into companywide policies, a practice that became routine.

SUBSEQUENT DEVELOPMENT AT TOYOTA MOTOR CORPORATION

In March 1965, Toyota Motor Corporation revived and added the departmental system for accelerating daily work to the existing cross-functional executive assignment system. In principle, the original idea of cross-functional management—as a part of TQC promotion—remained; however, cross-functional analysis methods were revised and improved to respond to corporate needs. The divisions of cross-functional areas were revised in February 1967, in response to the existing TQC promotion plan, as shown in Table 2.4. Subsequently, the corporate TQC Office succeeded in reorganizing cross-functional areas.

Because of revisions in commerce regulations in 1974, the management committee (composed of all senior vice presidents and senior advisers) was established as an executive branch of the company. With its installation, the existing cross-functional committee was made to report to the management committee and was required to audit, to investigate, to advise, and to make substantial decisions for cross-functional affairs. Figure 2.3 shows the Toyota Motor Corporation's top management structure.

TABLE 2.4
Cross-functional areas at Toyota Motor Corporation

Planning
Quality control
Cost management
Personnel management
Administrative management
Engineering and product design
Production preparation and full-scale production
Purchasing
Sales
Related companies

The cross-functional committee was charged with six areas: quality, cost, personnel and administration, engineering, manufacturing, and sales. Its decisions were to be submitted formally to the management committee for approval. However, the cross-functional committee's decisions were likely to become effective for all practical purposes from the time they were first made, since the management committee was apt to endorse them and to incorporate them into companywide decisions unless there were specific reasons to reject them. The cross-functional committee members were selected from those executives concerned with each functional area, and decisions therefore were quickly disseminated in all departments concerned. The cross-functional committee and the general committee have a parallel relationship; however, the latter operates as a committee for implementing the former's decision.

Currently, the cross-functional committees are working on the areas shown in Table 2.5.

In anticipation of more staff activities, the cross-functional committee has been placed under the direction of the executive committee since 1983.

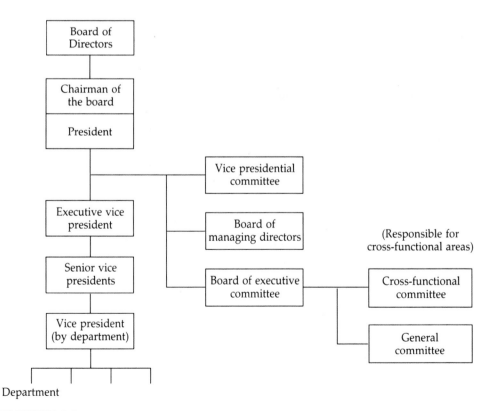

Department

FIGURE 2.3
Top management structure, Toyota Motor Corporation

TABLE 2.5
Current cross-functional
committee areas

General planning
Quality
Cost
Personnel and administration
Product planning
Production
Sales
Residential business

The structural reorganization, involving the division of functions and makeup of committees, has been revised every year after the annual review. (See Figure 2.3.)

After Toyota Motor Corporation's receipt of the Deming Application Prize, member companies of the Toyota Motor Group began corporate quality improvement through TQC. Member companies of the group introduced cross-functional management as one of the priority issues and worked for its integration. The format of cross-functional management varies, depending upon the needs of a particular company, and the division and structure of cross-functions are determined according to individual situations.

Chapter 3, "Administrative Aspects and Key Points of Cross-Functional Management," introduces sample activities of the Toyota Group companies, Toyota Auto Body Company, Ltd. (recipient of the 1980 Japan Quality Control Medal) and Toyoda Automatic Loom Works, Ltd. (recipient of the 1986 Deming Application Prize). The focal point of cross-functional management at the Toyota Auto Body Company, Ltd., is the cross-functional committees on quality, manufacturing, cost, and personnel affairs, while Toyoda Automatic Loom Works, Ltd., deals with TQC promotion focusing on the functions of quality-cost-delivery, at the same time pursuing the functions of personnel affairs, education, safety, hygiene, and information systems.

Actual work of the cross-functional committee continues in each functional area and, if and when necessary, the committee expands its membership.

CROSS-FUNCTIONAL MANAGEMENT
AT KOMATSU, LTD.

Cross-functional management at Komatsu, Ltd. is structured for four cross-functional committees: a quality assurance committee, a delivery control committee, a profit management committee, and an industrial-machine project committee. These report to the TQC promotion committee. The committees are expected to improve interdepartmental functions through organic management and operation.

The Quality Assurance Coordinator Conference was initiated in 1978, and its membership included an executive for quality assurance as a core member and senior managers from concerned departments as additional members. In 1980, the conference was renamed the Quality Assurance Function Committee, with membership consisting of an executive for quality assurance as chairman and concerned executives as members. The new committee is responsible for establishing, evaluating, and implementing long-range plans for quality assurance. It acts with the guidance of the TQC promotion committee, which is headed by the company president. All activities of the committee are undertaken as major corporate activities in the four cross-functional areas. (See Figure 2.4.)

The quality assurance committee consists of a chairman and five members nominated by the company president. Committee members include one or two executives who are relatively free to speak up on issues. The objective of this committee is to improve the quality-assurance system, including all steps from product design to sales and service. In order to achieve this objective, the committee is required to formulate and submit recommendations to the TQC committee on the following:

1. Companywide quality assurance plan
2. Program content and items for improving quality assurance, and designation of coordinating departments.

The cross-functional committee's structure is shown in Figure 2.5. Topics for discussion by the committee are submitted after a thorough review by the coordinating cross-functional center, a substructure of the committee. A working team is chosen according to the difficulty of the topic, and the team reports and makes recommendations to the committee.

Members of the coordinating cross-functional center are senior managers of research, production, domestic and overseas sales, plants, and related companies. The subcenter serves as coordinator for the department to which it reports.

When control points indicate abnormal values, the subcenter initiates a problem submission, stating what system defects create the problem. Following the submission, the quality assurance function committee and the quality assurance department, the support office for the coordinating cross-functional center, file reports. These reports are submitted to the coordinating cross-functional center, reviewed for possible adoption as activity themes, and then turned to the quality assurance function committee.

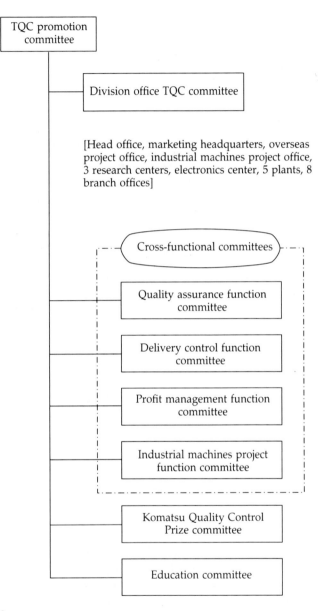

FIGURE 2.4
Promotion system for cross-functional management at Komatsu, Ltd.
Excerpted from "Cross-functional Management Through Quality Assurance,"
Quality, 14, no. 14 (1984): 63–69.

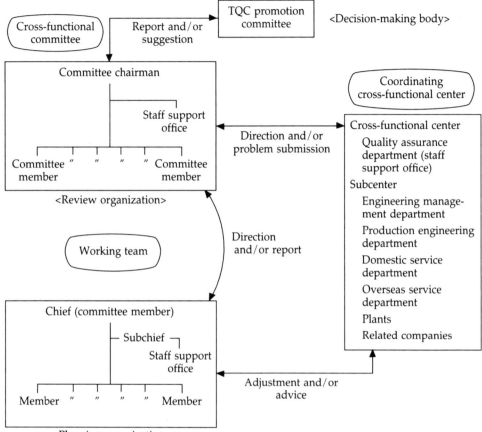

FIGURE 2.5
Current cross-functional committee

The quality assurance function committee reviews activity themes and assigns them to subcenters. Based on reviews by the subcenters, a summary improvement plan is submitted to the coordinating cross-functional center for feasibility review, then returned to the quality assurance function committee for executive reviews and modifications.

Once a final and formal approval is made by the quality assurance function committee, the quality assurance department, a staff support office, communicates the committee's approval for implementation in the line departments and provides support in the implementation.

Under this structure in 1979, Komatsu, Ltd., began a user satisfaction survey, which included questions about quality, service, and parts. Taking the survey results into consideration, quality function deployment was developed and long-range quality assurance indicators were established.

Quality assurance control points were established during this process. Current or future quality assurance issues were determined on the basis of those points. Priority items were identified, and relationships between primary and related departments were clarified according to priority item themes. These themes are reviewed annually, and the results are incorporated in the activity plans for the subsequent year in order to improve cross-functional management.

Because of the activities of the quality assurance function committee at Komatsu, Ltd., the control points were redetermined so that any and all quality assurance activities could be quantified by means of a consistent measurement scheme. The achievement status, problems, and improvements relevant to these control points are determined twice a year by simultaneous checking of all business offices. Results of the check are reported to the quality assurance function committee so that future directions can be determined. There is also a system for reporting important control points for management to the executive committee.

Of the many problems discovered during simultaneous checking, those important for the quality assurance system are reported to the quality assurance department, a staff-support office. Then improvement plans are submitted to the quality assurance function committee, and some aspects of the plans are consolidated into a long-range plan for quality assurance. Plans approved by the quality assurance function committee are implemented by the appropriate line departments.

The activities of the quality assurance function committee are summarized and reported to the TQC committee every six months. Also, a presidential QC audit is conducted at the end of each year for each functional unit at the corporate level. With this system, general evaluation and auditing are implemented and cross-functional management is integrated into corporate activity.

PROSPECTS FOR PRACTICAL APPLICATION

Thus far, the developmental history of cross-functional management at Toyota Motor Corporation and Komatsu, Ltd. has been discussed. However, the approach to cross-functional management varies from company to company, depending upon each firm's situation. This is clearly shown by the companies that competed for the Deming Application Prize and the Japan Quality Control Medal. Dealing with cross-functional management remains one of the most difficult issues for each company.

It is the writer's hope that in some small way he can help those companies facing the same challenges, and it is his wish that the introduction of case histories of cross-functional management will prove to be especially enlightening.

When each department makes an effort to solve problems, the creation of departmental group dynamics and their alignment become critical matters. Cross-functional management requires that everyone ponder how and what group dynamics are necessary for the logical management of a particular company.

It is further hoped that functional objectives will be clarified, specific measures will be deployed, and further corporate prosperity will be realized through the practical application of these means.

3

Administrative Aspects and Key Points of Cross-Functional Management

Kozo Koura

CORPORATE NEEDS AND IDENTIFICATION OF POLICY

When a company introduces and promotes cross-functional management, it must thoroughly identify cross-functional problems and company needs. Let us consider companies that have received the Deming Prize, such as Komatsu, Ltd., which won the prize in 1964. In 1963, Komatsu needed to expand existing plantwide quality control to include cross-functional activity and complete QC activity. This was accomplished through total employee participation, applying the Deming management cycle. In another case, Toyota Motor Corporation was rapidly expanding its business in 1961, but it could not balance quality improvement and production efficiency, and suffered from a lack of interdepartmental cooperation. In response to these conditions, Toyota introduced cross-functional management in 1962 and announced in its 1963 presidential policy statement the intention "to reorganize the corporate management system through cross-functional management."

It recognized the existence of the following problems.

1. Interdepartmental communication and cooperation were poor. Departmental group dynamics were not aligned toward the resolution of companywide problems.

2. For a single function, such as quality assurance, a given department's areas of responsibility were not clear, and the department lacked authorization to act.

Toyota concluded that in order to survive in the severe economic climate of deregulated trade and open-market competition, it was necessary to introduce cross-functional management as part of a TQC program to strengthen corporate quality. Therefore, a presidential policy announcement of the introduction and promotion of cross-functional management was a must.

The business environment was difficult at that time because of trade friction, unfavorable exchange rates against the yen, and competition from newly industrialized countries. Under such conditions, the importance of cross-functional management in a management system improvement program was constantly increasing.

CLASSIFICATION OF FUNCTIONS

The first step of cross-functional management is to select a method of analyzing cross functions that is consistent with the corporate situation. The definitions and classification principles for cross functions vary. Dr. Kaoru Ishikawa identifies primary and auxiliary functions.[1] At Toyota Motor Corporation, where cross-functional management has been highly developed, functions are divided into four groups: overall planning, objective functions, means functions, and service functions.[2] Toyota Auto Body, a company related to Toyota Motor Corporation, recognizes two functions: primary functions and step-by-step management. Table 3.1 shows representative examples of cross-functional division. Table 3.2 shows cross-functional division in companies promoting cross-functional management that won the Deming Application Prize from 1964 to 1986. There is some duplication in Table 3.2 because the 82 companies include division offices, business offices, and recipients of the Japan Quality Control Medal.

Komatsu, Ltd. (1964), Toyota Motor Corporation (1965), and companies related to Toyota Motor Corporation (1965 through 1970) used the term "cross-functional management" in their documentation. Most other companies did not use that term until 1980, even though they were implementing cross-functional management. The term came to be used by all companies after 1981. Table 3.2 is a compilation of functions based on information gathered over the period from 1964 to 1986. Cross-functional designations such as "contract acquisition activity management" and "process schedule management" were used first by Takenaka Corporation—the company that received the 1979 Deming Prize—and are used exclusively in the construction business. Function divisions are based on the individual corporate situation; however, the majority of companies view quality assurance, cost (or profit) management, delivery control, and personnel management as primary functions, and new product development as an auxiliary function. Significantly, from management's point of view, each function is not necessarily ranked at the same level of importance and

TABLE 3.1
Examples of function analysis and its terminology

Category	Kaoru Ishikawa[1]	Toyota Motor Corporation[2] (function)	Toyota Motor Corporation (description)	Toyota Motor Corporation (detail)	Toyota Auto Body[3,4] (function)	Toyota Auto Body (detail)	Komatsu, Ltd.[5]	Japan Steel Works, Ltd.[6]
		Overall functions	Companywide planning function	General planning		Overall management		
Primary functions	Quality assurance; Cost management (profits); Delivery control	Objective functions	Function to establish and achieve corporate targets	Quality assurance and cost management	Primary functions	Quality; Cost; Production quantity	Quality assurance; Profit management; Delivery control	Quality assurance; Profit management
Auxiliary functions	Development of new products; Subcontracting management; Sales management	Means functions	A series of functions from product planning to sales	Engineering: Product planning, Product design; Production: Production preparation, Production; Marketing: Purchasing, Sales	Step-by-step management	Technology development; Product planning; Production preparation; Full-scale production	Industrial machines project	Research and development
Primary functions	Personnel management	Service functions	Support functions for the above three functions	Personnel management; Administrative management	Primary functions	Personnel and environmental affairs		
	Functions are divided into two types—primary and auxiliary. Personnel management is considered to be a primary function.	The question of what functions are necessary to achieve corporate objectives was considered. The above functions were not listed in the same or parallel fashion but were arranged according to the "analytical principle." This principle is considered practical because it is based on corporate needs.			The company modeled its program after that of Toyota Motor Corporation, distinguishing its own program by adopting "means functions" as "step-by-step management."		"Industrial machines project" function is equivalent to Toyota Motor Corporation's "means function."	The research and development function is equivalent to Toyota Motor Corporation's "means function." It is an important function from the "management-by-products" point of view.

TABLE 3.2
Functional division of companies receiving the Deming Application Prize

Primary grouping	Cross functions	Functions that are similar or equivalent	Number of companies	Remarks
Primary function	Quality assurance	Quality control Quality improvement	59	*Term used in construction business to designate functions
	Cost management	Profit management Expense control Cost reduction	54	
	Delivery control	Production quantity control Delivery date management Production system management General construction management* Process schedule management*	39	**Term used at Komatsu, Ltd.
	Personnel management	Human development Education Work morale enhancement	11	
Auxiliary function	Information management	Administrative management Information systems management	3	***Term used at Texas Instruments, Japan
	New product development	Research and development Technology development Production technology	22	
	Sales management	Marketing Sales activity management Contract acquisition activity management* Sales expansion	14	
	Purchasing control	Subcontracting management*	6	Companies surveyed: The 82 companies receiving the Deming Prize and/or the Japan Quality Control Medal that implemented cross-functional management; there is some duplication.
	Safety management	Safety/hygiene control Labor safety control Environmental control	7	
	QC promotional support	QC circle Standardization	3	
	Other	Industrial machines** Future plans***	2	

Source: JUSE, *Summary Report by the Deming Prize Recipient Companies* (Tokyo: JUSE, 1964–86).

significance. Let us look at Toyota Motor Corporation's initial trial-and-error cross-functional management process. There were 13 functions in April 1962, 12 in January 1963, 24 in May 1963, 10 in February 1964, and 11 in November 1964. The number of functions has stabilized at 11 today. Primary functions do not change; auxiliary functions change according to conditions and corporate needs.

STRUCTURAL ORGANIZATION OF CROSS-FUNCTIONAL MANAGEMENT

Top management identifies structural organization clearly and specifically in order to promote cross-functional management. Studies on the structural organization of cross-functional management include the study of cross functions according to each key management area (e.g., quality, cost, delivery, personnel management). A study by Professor Masao Kogure[7] on the grouping of functions in cross-functional management includes their implementation formats. In this study, grouping of functions by implementation format resulted in four categories—type 0 to type III—based on the size and structural complexity of the companies involved. The existence of departments having primary responsibility for each and every function is a prerequisite. Taking this methodology into account, organizational structures of the companies receiving the Deming Prize were grouped roughly into three types: simple, general, and advanced.

Simple Structure

In a simple structure, the TQC promotion committee promotes cross-functional management. Uchino Construction Company, which exemplifies the simple structure, has assets of approximately ¥150 million and employs approximately 150 people. Its TQC promotion committee administers three subordinate committees: quality assurance, cost control, and sales activities (see Figure 3.1). Generally, a company with approximately ten executives can best be managed through this structure.

General Structure

The organization of the construction company Hazama-Gumi, Ltd. is representative of a general structure. Its main office and its branch office each has its own TQC promotion committee with three subordinate functional committees: quality assurance, awarded contract management, and profit management. The main office has two additional functional committees: subcontracting management and technology development. Figure 3.2(a) shows the structure at Hazama-Gumi.

Many companies have this type of structure, in which the TQC promotion committee is served by cross-functional committees (as substructure organizations). Komatsu, Ltd. has additional committees, such as a coordinating-function center and a working team. (See Figure 3.2(b).)

The quality assurance committee is composed of executives who review matters that have been thoroughly studied by the coordinating function

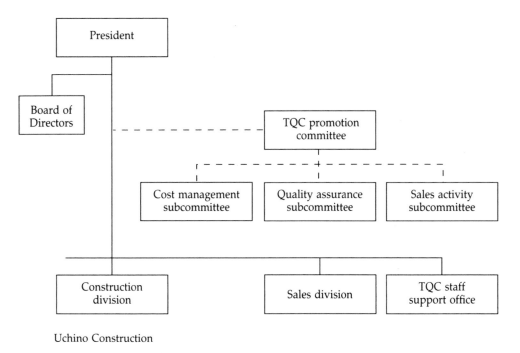

Uchino Construction

Company receiving 1985 Deming Prize,
small/medium-sized company category

FIGURE 3.1
Simple structure

center. The coordinating function center is manned by representatives of the quality assurance department as a staff support office for the center and by senior managers of the engineering control department, production engineering department, domestic service department, overseas service department, plant, and the quality assurance departments of related companies as subcenters. A working team is organized if and when an activity theme is chosen.

Advanced Structure

The advanced structure was established by Toyota Motor Corporation and has been widely applied in Toyota Group companies. In an assembly business without divisions, each and every function of quality, cost, delivery, and personnel management is applied horizontally to each step of the process: product planning, design, test production, production preparation, full-scale production, sales, and service. A structural organization to

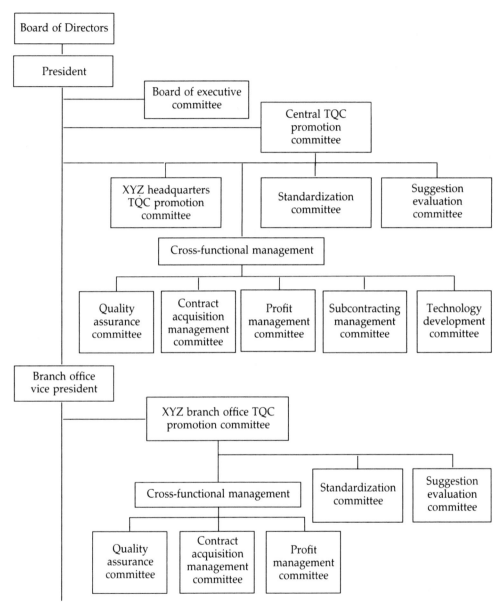

Hazama-Gumi (construction business)
  Company receiving the 1986 Deming Application Prize

Similar structure is found at
  Shimizu Construction Company, Ltd.
  Kajima Corporation
  Matsumoto Plant of Fuji Electric Company, Ltd.

FIGURE 3.2(a)
General structure

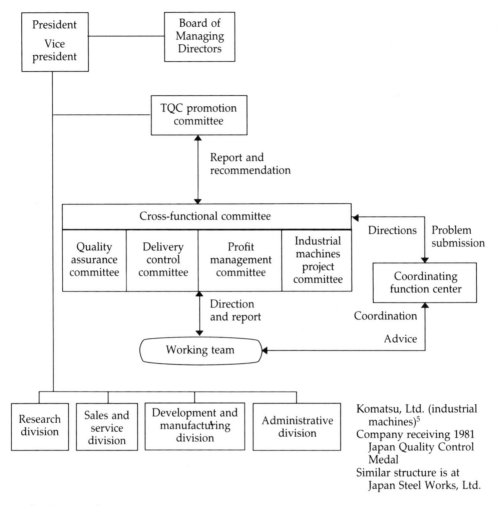

FIGURE 3.2(b)
General organization

facilitate such consistent management is shown in Figure 3.3(a), using Toyota Auto Body as an example.

In this instance, the general committee and the cross-functional committee serve the executive committee. Each functional committee is composed of the executives concerned and is responsible primarily for the "plan" stage. Each department in charge of every step is responsible for implementation ("do"); major issues emerging between the "plan" and "do" stages are reviewed by the cross-functional committee. The "step-by-step" committee is composed of executives in charge of each step as well as executives and senior managers of the departments concerned. It coordinates targeted items for each function with action items, and checks the

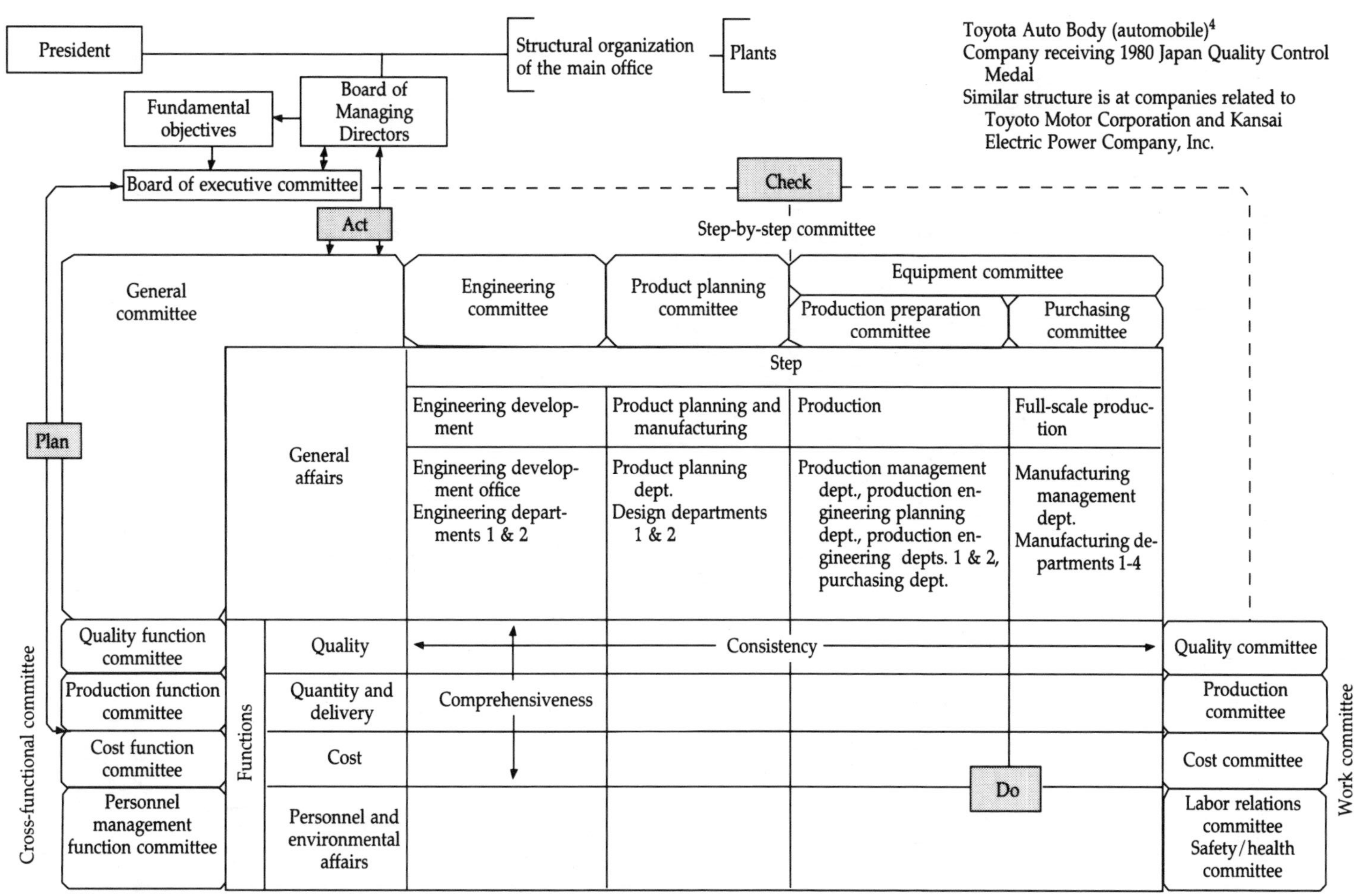

Toyota Auto Body (automobile)[4]
Company receiving 1980 Japan Quality Control Medal
Similar structure is at companies related to Toyota Motor Corporation and Kansai Electric Power Company, Inc.

President

Fundamental objectives

Board of Managing Directors

Board of executive committee

Structural organization of the main office — Plants

Cross-functional committee

Plan · Act · Check · Do

General committee

Quality function committee
Production function committee
Cost function committee
Personnel management function committee

Step-by-step committee

Engineering committee
Product planning committee
Product planning committee
Production preparation committee
Purchasing committee
Equipment committee

Step

Step →	Engineering development	Product planning and manufacturing	Production	Full-scale production
	Engineering development office, Engineering departments 1 & 2	Product planning dept. Design departments 1 & 2	Production management dept., production engineering planning dept., production engineering depts. 1 & 2, purchasing dept.	Manufacturing management dept. Manufacturing departments 1-4

Comprehensiveness ←→ Consistency

Functions:
- Quality
- Quantity and delivery
- Cost
- Personnel and environmental affairs

General affairs

Work committee

Quality committee
Production committee
Cost committee
Labor relations committee
Safety/health committee

FIGURE 3.3(a)
Advanced structure

41

assurance status of the development process. The work committee for senior managers is convened by an executive who is responsible for a given function. This committee is in charge of deploying corporate functional policy and is responsible for coordination and checking during the deployment stages.

The structural organization under a division system is shown in Figure 3.3(b), using Toyoda Automatic Loom Works as an example. In this case, the management committee reports to the senior executive committee and acts like a function committee for the overall corporate decision-making body. It fulfills functions in nine areas: quality, cost, production engineering, purchasing, personnel, education, safety and hygiene, information systems, and TQC promotion. An executive of the main office is assigned as chairman, and senior managers of the division offices are committee members. Together, they establish objectives for each function, confirm achievement status, and assume the responsibility for consolidation, coordination, support, and information exchange for the division offices. Corresponding committees established at the division level include those on quality, cost, TQC promotion, and safety/hygiene. The president convenes management committee meetings that involve the development, production, and sales committees. Division offices have equivalent committees on development, production, and sales and profit.

THE CROSS-FUNCTIONAL MANAGEMENT COMMITTEE: ITS TASKS, STRUCTURE, AND ADMINISTRATION

Generally speaking, the cross-functional management committee or conference is established to support cross-functional management. Examples of the committee's structure and administration, derived from the research of Professor Kaoru Ishikawa, Toyota Motor Corporation and Komatsu, Ltd. are provided in Table 3.3.

Responsibilities

The primary responsibilities of the cross-functional management committee are the establishment, maintenance, and improvement of a cross-functional management system for quality, cost, profit, and delivery. The committee is also responsible for addressing other issues related to improvement.

1. Improvement and maintenance of a cross-functional management system in areas other than specified above

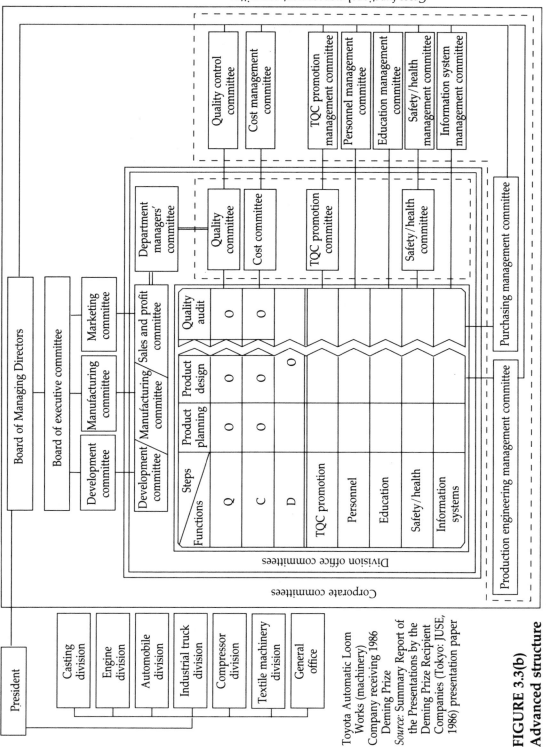

FIGURE 3.3(b)
Advanced structure

Toyota Automatic Loom
Works (machinery)
Company receiving 1986
Deming Prize
Source: Summary Report of
the Presentations by the
Deming Prize Recipient
Companies (Tokyo: JUSE,
1986) presentation paper

TABLE 3.3

Organization and administration of cross-functional management committee meetings

Items	Kaoru Ishikawa[1]	Toyota Motor Corporation[2]	Komatsu, Ltd.[5]
Organization	Cross-functional committee	Quality function and cost function committees	Quality assurance function committee (as example)
Reporting role	Report to board of executive committee	Report to board of executive committee	Report to TQC promotion committee
Responsibilities	Responsible for dealing with cross-functional matters in all departments, assigning responsibilities, and establishing system rules and audits	Same level of responsibility as Board of Directors or Board of Managing Directors; serves as a practical decision-making body	Responsible for improvement of the quality assurance system—which includes all processes from product planning to sales and service—and for upgrading the level of quality assurance
Areas of work		Planning, auditing, coordinating, and recommending	
Composition	Committee chairman: executive with the rank of senior vice president or executive vice president who is in charge of functions Committee members: about 5 executives with the rank of director or higher, 1 or 2 executives from other areas, and a facilitator Staff support office: each department concerned	Chairman: generally a senior vice president of a department to which a particular function is closely linked Members: executives of functionally related departments Facilitators: about 10 executives with the rank of vice president or senior vice president who report directly to the chairman	Committee: quality assurance managing executives Committee members: about 5 related executives Staff support office: quality assurance department
Additional items	[Example] quality assurance 1. Monthly status of quality assurance and investigation of claims status 2. Establishment and revision of departmental assignments concerning areas of cross-functional responsibilities	1. Establishment of objectives; 2. Plans and policies to achieve targeted objectives; 3. Plans concerning new products, equipment, manufacturing, and sales; 4. Important bottom-up items; 5. Measures to eliminate barriers to implementation; 6. Action necessary as a result of checking; 7. Checking performance results of corporate policy and the plan for subsequent year; 8. Other necessary items for cross-functional management	In order to carry out its objectives, the committee reviews and makes recommendations to the TQC committee on the following: 1. Plan concerning corporate quality assurance 2. Concerning quality assurance: a. Improvement plan for the system and the improvement program b. System improvement items and departments responsible
Meeting frequency	Regular and monthly	Once a month, as a rule	Once every other month, as a rule

44

2. Review of basic cross-functional management policy and structural organization

3. Drafting and promoting long-range and annual cross-functional management programs

4. Problem-solving support for the principle cross-functional management areas

5. Review and coordination of items linked with other functions

6. Companywide horizontal deployment of results of cross-functional management

7. Planning and implementation of cross-functional audits

Organization and Administration

The organizational and administrative aspects of the cross-functional management committee are listed below.

1. The committee chairman should be an executive with the rank of senior vice president or vice president in charge of a function. Committee members should be executives in a related department with the rank of director or higher. The number of members should be kept to a minimum, without representation of all departments. Involvement of an executive from an unrelated area is useful. A facilitator should be an executive who is in charge of a function and reports directly to a senior vice president. The staff support office should be maintained in the department responsible for the function.

2. As stated above, executives for the cross-functions (or committee members) are selected from among the various department heads, who are simultaneously responsible for multiple functions.

3. The committee is permanent and formal. It should be given decision-making responsibility and should report directly to the highest decision-making bodies, such as the executive committee and/or management committee.

4. The committee should play a role in planning and checking. Implementation should be carried out by line departments through their management.

5. To address administrative problems, a meeting of combined cross-functional committees or an expanded cross-functional committee meeting can be held. Otherwise, special project teams, working teams, professional teams, or ad hoc committees can be formed.

STEPS FOR CROSS-FUNCTIONAL MANAGEMENT DEPLOYMENT AND IMPLEMENTATION

Fundamentals

Cross-functional management integrates vertical management (or departmental management) with horizontal management. Therefore, it requires that managers, who are used to the departmental management system, recognize the needs and the importance of departmental cooperation. Thus, companywide consensus on fundamentals is ultimately necessary, as described below.

1. Reach a consensus on organization: *consider only the function, and organize a companywide system or design without undue concern for the existing organizational structure.*
2. Reach a consensus about and establish a methodology for the evaluation of objectives and results of every function.
3. Necessary activities will be assigned to existing organizational units in order to achieve objectives; if necessary, organizational changes may take place.
4. The decision-making structure for top management will be revised to ensure functionality.

Steps for Deployment

There are three types of deployment:

1. Companywide system improvement by a cross-functional management committee
2. System improvement by project teams
3. Cross-functional work improvement in the line departments.

Companywide System Improvement by Cross-Functional Management Committee

1. Identification of a subject process, division of the process, and management objectives. Figure 3.4 shows how the processes relating to the quality assurance function were clearly explained.[8]
2. Discovery of system problems through the establishment of a management system chart. Table 3.4 gives symbols for a management

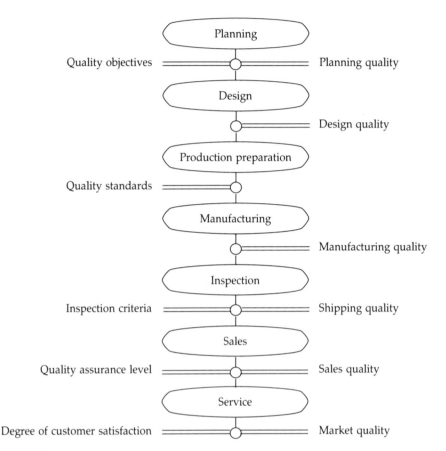

FIGURE 3.4
Clarification of processes showing items subject to control
Source: Toyota Motor Corporation[8]

system chart; Figure 3.5 gives an example of a quality assurance system chart.[10]

3. Drafting a cross-functional management activity table (for example, a table of quality assurance activities). For every process, select line functions and staff functions, and assign a responsible professional staff. Based upon the concept of quality assurance for the subsequent process, determine quality assurance items and the work necessary for the process. Table 3.5 shows quality assurance activities from the appendix of Toyota Motor Corporation's Quality Assurance Rules.

4. Determination of items and the decision-making process that must be implemented by the president or board of directors.

TABLE 3.4
Symbols for management system chart (draft plan)[9]

Process Chart Symbols (Japanese Industrial Standards)			Management System Chart Symbols		Remarks
Symbols for Basic Charts	processing	○ (functional symbols)	□	work, jobs, function items, policies, and plans	1. The name of a function, a work situation, or a condition may be entered in the symbol. In this case, work symbols may be omitted
			⬭	committees, demonstration meetings, and presentation meetings	
			⬡	environmental situations, issues, and problems	
	transportation	○	○	drafting, directions, and commands	2. If necessary, an explanatory note may be entered in a work symbol.
	delay — storage	▽	△	discussion and participation	
	delay — holding	⬠	▽	storing information and documents	3. Numbers to indicate orders should be entered inside a symbol.
	inspection — quantity inspection	□	□	receiving communications and reports	
	inspection — quality inspection	◇ (work chart symbols)	◇	evaluations, reviews, tests, and inspections	
Compound Symbols	quality inspection (principal) quantity inspection (subordinate)	◈	◈ or ◧	decision or determination	4. A major job should be placed outside the compound symbol; a subordinate job should be written inside the symbol.
	quantity inspection (principal) quality inspection (subordinate)	◨	◉	receipt of reports and/or approval	5. A coordinated effort within a principal department should be indicated as shown below.
	processing and inspection	⊡			
	processing and transporting	⊖			⬭ ⎯ ⎯
Symbols for Auxiliary Charts	flow lines	│ (route symbols)	⟶	main route and/or parties to contact (original)	Efforts involving no direct participation/no coordination within a principal department should be indicated as shown below.
			- - →	feedback route, contact parties (copy)	
			- - →	route specifically agreed upon	⎦ ⎯ ⎯ ⎣
	divisions	∿∿∿	⇄	} mutual adjustments	
	abbreviation	⎓ (supplementary symbols)	≋ or = abbreviation		6. If necessary, new additional symbols may be created. If this is the case, provide explanatory notes.
			bold frame	subjects of company-wide management	Example:
			dotted-line frame	subjects of voluntary departmental management	Bidirectional feedback or consensus-making (catch ball)
			⬡No.	To be placed with reference and/or rule materials under this number	←⊘→

5. Establishment of cross-functional management rules (for example, quality assurance rules). According to this procedure, assign the contents of 3 and 4 above to each department.

6. Verification and adjustment of 5 with work assignment regulations.

7. Addition of other important staff functions.

8. Reorganization and establishment of an important subsystem. Take an important quality assurance activity within a quality assurance system as a subsystem, and establish it as a system. Japan Steel Works[11] succeeded in drafting a quality table after establishing quality assurance rules. Subsequently, it adopted an ambitious goal-seeking activity system, an engineering bottleneck registration system, and a design review and evaluation/approval system for sales preparation.

System Improvement by Project Teams

If and when it becomes necessary, the cross-functional management committee authorizes the formation of a project team or working team, depending upon the system improvement review theme. The team reports back to the committee with recommendations based on its findings. At Komatsu, Ltd., the chief of the working team is selected from among the members of the cross-functional management committee (e.g., quality-assurance committee members), and the subchief of the working team is selected from subcenter representatives of the coordinating cross-function center (e.g., departments of technology management, domestic service, overseas service, and quality assurance at plants).[5] Chiefs of working groups provide office work support, and staff from the related departments join the teams as members.

Typical themes for the project team include the following.

1. Quality Assurance
   - Establishment of a quality information system
   - System reorganization for gathering and analysis of claim information

2. Delivery Control
   - Establishment of a classification system for models and parts
   - Reorganization and improvement of order entry system

3. Cost Management
   - Establishment of a system for measuring quality loss
   - Development of a system for new-product cost planning

This is a quality function deployment (QFD) process flowchart.

Step	Function	Customers	Board of Managing Directors	Committees	Marketing	Engineering	Research and development	Production control	Production technology	Material purchasing	Manufacturing	Quality assurance	Quality information	Related regulations and guidelines
Sales/service	Information gathering	Customer trends in the market			Market research		Study of technology and competition							Regulations for data collection and analysis
					Data gathering, analysis, and prediction 1								1. Required-quality deployment table	Regulations for market research
Planning	Planning for new products		New product planning determination	New product development conference		Drafting and recommendation for new product planning 2,3							2. Table of planning quality	Regulations for the new product development conference
													3. New product planning document	Regulations for research and development
Development and design of new products			Determination of new product development	New product development conference		Drafting and recommendation for new product development 4								Regulations for quality analysis
						Development and design (value engineering) 5							4. New product development plan	Design review management regulations
Evaluation of pilot products						Early design review 6								Drawing management regulations
Design						Process design for mass production 7							5. Parts deployment table	Quality assurance regulations
													6. Quality evaluation test data	FMEA implementation guidelines
													7. Process deployment table	Guidelines for standards/criteria management
														Implementation guidelines for process evaluation
														Initial flow control regulation

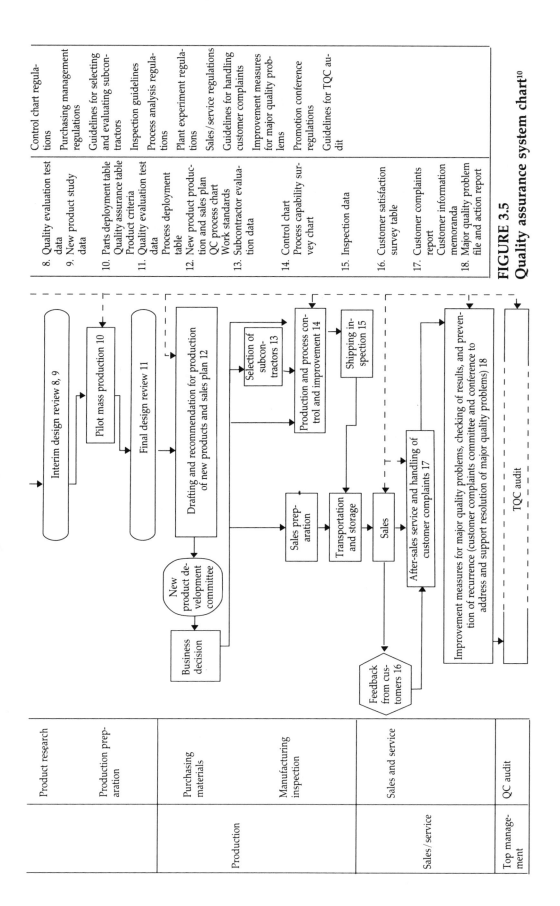

FIGURE 3.5
Quality assurance system chart[10]

TABLE 3.5
Table of quality assurance activites[2]

Step (process)	Assurance item	Work for assurance	Person responsible for assurance	Assurance areas	Related major rules	Remarks

Source: Toyota Motor Corporation

Cross-Functional Work Improvement in Line Departments

Work improvement by the project team and working team becomes a basis and prerequisite for system improvement, and is promoted by the line department in charge. Typical activities in the promotion of fundamental work improvement at Tokyo Juki Industrial Company, Ltd. include reduction of lead time for parts and internal and external manufacturing and improvement of inventory control of manufactured goods.[12]

Implementation Steps

It is commonly recognized that the introduction of cross-functional management should take place after the establishment of policy management, because interdepartmental problems surface only after significant improvements in departmental management are achieved. These improvements reveal hidden needs for interdepartmental cooperation, which, in turn, enhances policy management problem-solving techniques. Therefore, it is generally recommended that implementation steps be carried out through the policy management system. In their article "Establishment of Targets and Policy in Cross-Functional Management,"[13] Professors Yoji Akao and Yuichi Iijima recommend reorganization of departmental problems into the cross-functional areas of quality, delivery, and cost; establishment of cross-functional objectives and policies; target deployment by a system of indicators; an implementation plan; formation of project teams; and a 13-step process.

Mr. Akira Iijima describes policy deployment through linkage of a given target with appropriate means in his article "Managerial Control Items at Toyota Auto Body."[14] He includes discussions of the steps for the deployment process, among them establishment of cross-functional policy, step-by-step policy, departmental policy, and control points for managers and supervisors. Taking the above information into consideration, the general steps required can be described as follows.

Step 1. Establish fundamental corporate objectives.

Step 2. Establish a cross-functional committee to achieve fundamental objectives, delineate function-by-function objectives in each functional area, and assign implementation activities. Items include discovery of cross-functional problems in each department of the corporation; stratification of the problems into departmental and interdepartmental levels; clarification of cross-functional problems through the application of cause-and-effect diagrams and establishment of control characteristics as targets; subsequent decisions on policy; target deployment through a system of indicators and target system charts; and submission of expected target values to line departments.

Step 3. Integrate cross-functional objectives and policies into line departments' objectives and implementation items, based on a consensus. Begin by reviewing departmental objectives and implementation items based upon expected targets for the line departments and the results of the evaluation from the previous year. General consensus-building will be pursued by coordinating with the cross-functional management committee in a way similar to that described in step 2.

Step 4. Establish objectives and implementation items for cross-functional management in line departments.

Step 5. Deploy objectives and items for departments and subdepartments. Bidirectional feedback among senior managers, managers, and supervisors is achieved by using control points included in the implementation plan. At this stage the project team or working team is formed and the project objectives and implementation items for the team are established.

Step 6. During target deployment, develop control items simultaneously for steps 1 through 5 and objectives for each employee level.

Step 7. Implement cross-functional objectives and implementation items defined during the line departments' policy deployment process.

Step 8. Based on an analysis of the degree of success in realizing cross-functional objectives and implementation items, the cross-functional groups evaluate the objectives and items from a companywide perspective and provide feedback for the subsequent year.

Step 9. The cross-functional committee conducts cross-functional audits on line departments' objectives and implementation items one or more times per year. An applicable cross-functional management system is reviewed at that time, and necessary action is taken for improvement. This audit is normally conducted in the format of a presidential or committee audit. An effective way to conduct the audit is to limit the presentation theme to an interdepartmental problem, thus eliminating departmental problems.

The simultaneous checking system for quality assurance at Komatsu, Ltd. is an example of corporate-level quality assurance in which 41 items are determined as corporate-level control points.[5] Breakdown of the 41 items reveals that 20—called market-performed control points—are result-oriented and 21—called quality assurance activity control points—are cause-oriented. Of the 41 items, 16 items (15 market-performance control points and 1 quality assurance activity control point) were of particular importance to management and were reported to the board of directors. These 41 control items are simultaneously checked companywide twice a year, and important problems are reported to the staff support office of the committee. This office then submits improvement plans to the quality assurance function committee. A part of the plans is ultimately reflected in a long-range quality assurance program. Final plans are implemented in the line departments upon proper authorization.

Implementation steps at the plant level have been established at the Muroran Plant of Japan Steel Works.[15] Quality assurance activity evaluation there includes an audit by a quality assurance committee. The format is that of a mutual audit by a group of core committee members and department managers. For audit purposes, a 20-page quality assurance activity evaluation checklist is prepared for use each quarter. An improvement request form is issued when problems are found, and submission of improvement plans in response to the request is required within 15 days. Results are evaluated at the subsequent audits.

CROSS-FUNCTIONAL MANAGEMENT, MANAGEMENT BY DEPARTMENT, AND MANAGEMENT BY PRODUCT LINE

In TQC, there are other ways to enhance interdepartmental cooperation besides cross-functional management. These include task force organizations—represented by project teams, task force teams, and QC teams—and matrix organizations—represented by product management and management by product line. Table 3.6 compares such organizations.

TABLE 3.6
Comparison of horizontal structures[16,17]

Type	Name	Explanation	Permanent structures	Nonpermanent structure
Task force organization	Project teams Task force teams QC teams	A group of talented people who concentrate on and effectively solve problems relating to specific issues, such as research and development, production, business, and quality	Some QC teams are permanently established	O
Matrix organization	Matrix organization	An organization that facilitates the cooperation and interaction of individuals in a departmental setting (such as a research and development department) to work as members of horizontal, vertical, and diagonal project teams	O	
	Product management	An organization responsible for development of products, production, and after-sales services; it is responsible for all phases of planning and coordination necessary for product growth and profits	O	
	Cross-functional management	A horizontal organization to improve management efficiency through enhancement of cross-functional activities	O	
	Management by product line[6]	Interdepartmental organization based on division system; units responsible for individual products in both the marketing department (of the general office) and the manufacturing division (of the local plants) are linked. This type of organization is referred to as an SBU (strategic business unit).	O	

General issues concerning interdepartmental cooperation are addressed by nonpermanent organizations such as project teams and QC teams, and results are standardized and subsequently integrated into departmental management and day-to-day management systems. However, some interdepartmental problems concerning issues of quality, cost, and delivery remain at the corporate level even though support departments exist for each function.[18] For this reason, cross-functional management was introduced. Management by product line was introduced to address strategic issues as well as interdepartmental cooperation in terms of product/marketing research and development. Departmental management is carried out through the use of a basic management system, that is, by vertical management as opposed to horizontal management. In the application of cross-functional management, cross-functional units are responsible for the planning and checking stages of management, while departmental units are responsible for the implementation stages. Nevertheless, there are vested individual and departmental interests that are always favored by their proponents. Strengthened cross-functional management is required so that the cross-functional committee's plan can be executed for the overall betterment of the company and not jeopardized by special departmental interests.

CROSS-FUNCTIONAL MANAGEMENT, POLICY MANAGEMENT, AND DAY-TO-DAY MANAGEMENT

It is highly desirable that system improvement for cross-functional management be promoted by policy management. As described above in the subsection on implementation steps, cross-functional management policy should be established before departmental policy, and should be implemented after the integration of departmental policies. Standards are established after evaluating the success of improvement activities, and assigned cross-functional tasks are implemented as part of a day-to-day management system. At this juncture, the management cycle moves from PDCA (plan-do-check-act) to SDCA (standardization-do-check-act). The implementation status of cross-functional management in line departments is reported monthly to cross-functional groups by filing a cross-functional management report.The cross-functional groups collect all such reports and submit a summary to the cross-functional committee. The cross-functional committee reports twice a year to the top management committee or executive committee.

Normally, a presidential audit and/or committee audit checks a cross-functional management system and its activity status. However, there are other ways of checking, including the simultaneous checking of quality assurance control points at Komatsu, Ltd. and quality-assurance activity evaluation as is done at the Muroran Plant of Japan Steel Works. Table 3.7 shows the correlation of departmental management, cross-functional management, management by product line, policy management, and day-to-day management.

EFFECTS OF CROSS-FUNCTIONAL MANAGEMENT[1,2]

The effects of cross-functional management are listed below.

1. Decision-making and implementation are accelerated with respect to quality assurance, cost/profit management, and delivery control; companywide management becomes flawless and vitalized.

TABLE 3.7
Relationships of departmental management, cross-functional management, management by product line, policy management, and day-to-day management

Classification	Policy management	Day-to-day management	Correlation	
Departmental management	◎	◎	Implementation	Implementation
Cross-functional management	◎	◎	Plan and audit	Plan and adjustment
Management by product line	◎	○		

◎ Greater correlation   ○ Moderate correlation

2. Greater awareness of cross-functional management reaches bottom-level workers, and brings improved departmental cooperation and relationships as well as improved human relationships.

3. Since problems are addressed cross-functionally, the number of departments or sections does not increase.

4. Suggestions from employees below the senior manager level are facilitated.

5. Managing directors are likely to become true managers, not just representatives of their departmental interests. With mental flexibility, they become promoters of greater corporate vision.

KEY POINTS IN THE PROMOTION OF CROSS-FUNCTIONAL MANAGEMENT

Fundamental

1. Introduction and promotion of cross-functional management should be undertaken as a long-range plan. The introduction and promotion of TQC are undertaken to improve corporate quality. Cross-functional management, along with policy management, is a means to improve corporate management. Therefore, it is not going to be a success overnight but must be realized through long-range plans. Let us take a look at cross-functional management at the Toyota Motor Corporation. The company introduced cross-functional management in 1962. Since then, it has undergone a process of trial and error

to become the great corporate entity it is today. During the same period, Toyota-related companies adopted the same management system and realized group-wide quality control.

2. Cross-functional management should be introduced after the establishment of departmental management and policy management. The first stage of TQC introduction requires PDCA through work improvement activities and mastery of problem-solving through QC story techniques. The next stage involves promotion of policy management and departmental management for companywide PDCA. Only if and when interdepartmental problems are discovered are the need for and importance of cross-functional management recognized.

3. Application of cross-functional management varies depending upon company size. A slogan conveying the need for the cross-functional committee is acceptable. However, three separate cross-functional committees for quality assurance, delivery control, and cost management in a company of fewer than 100 employees may be excessive because of the duplication of committee members. Such superficial committee arrangement for the sake of formality must be carefully scrutinized. In this case, one organization, either a TQC promotion committee or an executive committee, should address problems by stratifying quality, cost, and delivery issues.

4. Thinking in terms of cross-functional management is good, but the idea that departmental management is unnecessary is not. Departmental management is the basis on which cross-functional management is built.

5. Cross-functional management is a constant activity, and a cross-functional committee is a constant organization.

The Role of Top Management[20]

1. The role of top management is to understand the needs and importance of cross-functional management and to support its introduction and promotion. Cross-functional management through employee consensus, for example, must be supported as a basic rule. For a long time, company employees have lived with the concept of vertical management. Since it is necessary to integrate the concept of horizontal management with existing concepts, strong support and leadership from top management are essential. Professor Kaoru Ishikawa states that "in order to be called a fabric, both horizontal and vertical threads need to be woven together, and only when hori-

zontal threads—or cross-functional management threads—are woven together with vertical threads can a company be considered similarly cohesive."[19]

2. The structure for decision making and job assignments at the top level should be as cross-functional as possible. If and when a department head is assigned to a cross-functional committee, he should not be a spokesperson for the department but should work for corporate betterment and growth through functional system activities.

3. Attention should be paid to operational aspects. It is highly desirable to operate according to final decisions, because these are based on the coordinated efforts of cross-functional groups and the review and decision-making process of the cross-functional committee. Therefore, the committee's decision should be considered final and, practically speaking, of the highest level.

The Cross-Functional Committee[21]

1. Grant the cross-functional committee the highest possible decision-making power.

2. Committee members should be executives only. Not all professional staff and departmental representatives need be involved. Approximately five members will be sufficient for review meetings.

3. The cross-functional committee is not an executive branch but a unit responsible for planning and checking. For example, the profit control committee should not assign profit goals to departments and work expressly to achieve such goals. The latter are matters to be addressed through departmental policy management.

4. Operation of the cross-functional committee should be flexible. For example, if and when a significant quality assurance issue is discussed by the profit management committee, the issue is first presented to the quality assurance committee ("catch ball," or bidirectional feedback, between the cross-functional committees); then combined committee meetings or expanded committee meetings can be held if necessary.

5. Initially, committee members tend to represent departmental interests. However, they should proceed with companywide management vision. Cross-functional topics should not be mixed with departmental topics. For example, a meeting to discuss the problems of a companywide quality assurance system should not deal with departmental improvement measures or customer claims.

Operation of Cross-Functional Management

1. Establish a long-range plan, and administer it under a policy management system. For example, the number of themes adopted by the quality assurance committee at Komatsu, Ltd. from 1981 through 1983 was 32. Of these,
   - Adopted themes in the quality assurance long-range plan accounted for 75% of the total
   - Temporary themes, assigned by the cross-functional committee, represented 15%
   - Ongoing themes, adopted on an annual basis, made up 10%.

   Sample themes included the following:
   - The long-range quality assurance rolling plan
   - The annual cross-functional committee activity plan
   - A QC audit and QC training meeting plan.

   Also established was an indicator for long-range quality assurance objectives based on user satisfaction.

2. The number of cross-functional divisions should not be too large. The larger the number, the greater each division's independence and the possibility of subsequent interference. Toyota Motor Corporation, for example, had as many as 24 divisions at one point; however, it ultimately reduced these to 11.

3. The means of assigning functions should be determined by system design, leaving aside any consideration of existing organizations while reorganizing the entire company in order to realize overall corporate objectives. Necessary organizational revision should be implemented at the time cross-functional management activities are assigned.

4. Care must be taken not to create an overly controlled system in an attempt to establish a total system at the corporate-level planning stage.

5. Each function requires clear objectives and measuring methods. Each microprocess establishes control items based upon the concept of quality assurance for the next process. The quality assurance control points at Komatsu, Ltd. will serve as an example. Survey results of the main office, related companies, and eight division offices on quality assurance control points and control points dis-

covered by the quality function deployment process identified a total of 119 points. Each of these 119 points was further evaluated to determine its relative importance as a control point and its usefulness in problem identification and data collection. Of the 41 items selected, 21 were quality assurance control points (cause series) and 20 were market performance control points (effect series). Sixteen items were control points for the executive report; of those, 15 were market-performance control points.

6. In cross-functional management activity, interdepartmental overlapping cooperation, referred to as "reaching out," is necessary to deal with barriers between departments.

7. Cross-functional management audits by the president or a committee, or simultaneous checking of control items, is useful. In conducting simultaneous checking, only interdepartmental problems should be discussed, not the problems of a specific department.

8. As part of the routine management system, an information system should be established to facilitate gathering information about cross-functional management in line departments.

The Staff Support Office

1. The majority of cross-functional management problems are long-range. As noted earlier, 75% of the themes adopted by the cross-functional committee at Komatsu, Ltd. were long-range quality assurance problems. Therefore, committee members need long-term assistance from a staff support office to clarify their needs and provide help.

2. Initiative for problem solving must be taken by a staff support office in charge of functions. The office confirms the themes and contents of the plan with the departments concerned, and provides information necessary for the departments to draft their own voluntary plans. The office also coordinates and supports activities to avoid wider gaps between feasible and idealistic goals.[22]

3. The staff support office should thoroughly understand the intentions and directions of top managers and the committee chairman, and collect and analyze problems and data through audits, diagnostic meetings, and committee activities. In so doing, the support office should note any inconsistencies in the department's delivery control and quality of information. In analyzing the information, the office should pick up new ideas and problems and report these to the committee.[22]

CROSS-FUNCTIONAL MANAGEMENT AND STANDARDIZATION

Cross-functional management must uncover companywide and cross-functional problems, resolve them, and carry out improvement measures while promoting interdepartmental cooperation within a departmental management setting. However, there are some problems, as listed below.

1. Consensus must be reached at the highest level of authority because of the need for companywide application.

2. Existing regulations and guidelines, prepared by the department, include many procedures. The specific contents of these documents need to be reviewed, applying the quality assurance concept.

3. In order to further advance cross-functional management, a management system flow chart is drafted and used to discover problems related to system standardization. However, the chart alone cannot include specific implementation information concerning the 5W/1H.

4. Departmental regulations define areas of responsibility; however, there are no documents defining areas of cross-functional management.

5. Cross-functional management audit or checking methodology has not yet been clearly established to verify whether cross-functional management is being executed as standardized, whether the system is functioning correctly, whether the level of quality evaluation is adequate, and so on.

In order to resolve these issues, standardization of systems is necessary. Standardization as a primary function at Toyota Motor Corporation is evidenced in quality assurance regulations and cost management regulations. For cross-functional management relating to policy management, companywide policy management regulations have been prepared. Table 3.8 describes the general contents of quality assurance regulations and cost management regulations.[2] The latter regulations include four subregulations.

Specific items requiring departmental action are summarized separately and checked for consistency, as shown in Table 3.5, and in the "Work-assignment regulations for cost management, attached table," mentioned in Table 3.8.

Table 3.9 is based on summary reports by the Deming Prize recipients and other publications.[23] Items in the dotted box indicate regulations related to cross-functional management.

TABLE 3.8
Cross-functional management regulations, Toyota Motor Corporation[2]

Kinds	Quality assurance regulations	Cost management regulations
Objectives	Objectives are to identify the principal responsibilities of the departments for quality assurance at all stages—from product planning to sales/service—in order to assure users of product quality, to upgrade management efficiency, and to contribute to corporate prosperity.	Objectives are to identify principal responsibilities of the departments for cost management and to execute all necessary work flawlessly.
When	(1) Product planning, (2) Product design, (3) Production preparation, (4) Purchasing, (5) Full-scale production, (6) Inspection, (7) Sales/service, (8) Quality audit	Cost management system — Cost planning, Equipment investment planning, Cost maintenance, Cost improvement
Where	Related departments	
Who	Department head (person responsible for quality assurance)	
How	Formal text from the regulation: Each and every person responsible for quality assurance "works for quality assurance," thus fulfilling duties given in the "assurance item" description and making the necessary decisions	Regulations: 1. Implementing regulations for cost planning 2. XYZ department budget control regulations 3. Cost improvement regulations 4. Work assignment regulations for cost management
Attached table	Quality assurance activity table	Work assignment regulations for cost management, attached table

TABLE 3.9
Table of regulations and guidelines[8]

Kinds of regulations	Subcategory	Items	Similar examples
Basic regulations	Relevant to organizational management	Description of management vision; Corporate charter; Board of directors regulations; Organizational management regulations	• Executive committee regulations
	Relevant to areas of responsibility and authority	Regulations concerning areas of responsibility; Regulations concerning limitations of responsibility; Regulations concerning administrative structure; Executive endorsement regulation; Decision-making standards	• Work assignment regulations • Description of organization and limitations of work responsibilities
Organizational regulations	Relevant to conferences and committees	Meeting regulations; Meeting regulations for cross-functional committee; Meeting regulations for quality control committee; Meeting regulations for new products committee	• Administrative regulations for subcommittee on profit management • Product criteria conference regulations • Administrative guidelines for engineering evaluation • Conference regulations for test-model evaluation prior to mass production
	Relevant to administration and areas of responsibility of quality control organizations	Regulations concerning TQC promotion organization and administration; Regulations on common QC work	
Management regulations — General management	Relevant to policy management	Policy management regulations	• Basic regulations for quality assurance • Basic regulations concerning product criteria • Delivery control regulations • Computation guidelines for standard costs • Guidelines for cost planning
	Relevant to cross-functional management	Cross-functional management regulations; Quality assurance regulations; Production control regulations; Cost management regulations; QC cost management regulations	
	Relevant to system charts	Policy management system chart; Quality assurance system chart; Delivery control system chart; Cost management system chart	
	Relevant to education	In-house education management regulations	• Education regulations • Implementation guidelines for executive visits to plants
	Relevant to QC audits	Regulations on top management's QC audit	• Regulations for in-house QC audit
	Relevant to standardization	Standardization regulations; Management regulations concerning regulations; Management regulations concerning regulations and standards	• Basic regulations for standardization • Revision regulations for the regulation program • Manuals for standardization and for drafting regulatory documents • TQC rules
	Overall quality control	Quality control regulations	
Work regulations — Planning/design/development	Prediction survey	Demand prediction regulations; Market survey handling regulations	• Market quality (including engineering) • Control regulations for research/development • Design review implementation guidelines
	Information gathering	Regulations for information gathering about quality; Information-gathering system regulations	
	New product development management	New product development management regulations; Development-budget control regulations	

Legend:

- - - - Indicates regulations relevant to cross-functional management

Quality assurance

- Quality analysis
  - Competitive quality survey regulations
  - Quality analysis regulations
- Initial flow control
  - Initial flow control regulations
- Drawing management
  - Drawing management regulations
    - Survey regulations for quality of competitors' products
    - Implementation guidelines for FMEA
    - Regulations for introduction of new products
    - Regulations for drawings
    - Drafting guidelines for design drawings
    - Handling guidelines for design records
    - Drafting guidelines for construction drawings
    - Drafting guidelines for drawing records
- Purchasing and subcontracting
  - Purchasing regulations
  - Subcontracting management regulations
  - Subcontractor evaluation regulations
  - Manufacturing regulations
  - Process control regulations
  - Early-stage control regulations
  - Regulations relating to standard time
    - Team formation work guidelines
    - Construction scope criteria for subcontractors
    - Material purchasing regulations
    - Quality assurance steps for vendors and supporting plants
    - Quality control regulations for parts and subassemblies
    - General construction management guidelines
    - Process capability surveying guidelines
    - Implementation steps for prevention of problem recurrence
- Process control
  - Control chart regulations
  - Abnormal report program regulations
  - Plant experiment regulations
  - Work audit regulations
    - Operation criteria for handling abnormalities
    - Process review implementation guidelines
- Inspection
  - Regulations for inspection work
    - Regulations concerning receiving, processing, and final inspection
    - First-product evaluation guidelines
- Stock management
  - Material stock management regulations
  - Products stock management regulations
  - Standard inventory control regulations
- Equipment, measuring instrument, and energy control
  - Equipment control regulations
  - Experimental and measuring instruments management regulations
  - Energy management regulations
    - Machinery and tools maintenance regulations
    - Tool-and-die maintenance regulations
- Sales, marketing, and quality assurance
  - Regulations concerning sales planning and surveying
  - Sales regulations
  - Management regulations for product maintenance
  - Product shipment regulations
  - Long-range quality survey regulations
  - Engineering services implementation manual
    - Domestic sales regulations
    - Contract sales implementation guidelines
    - Building ownership transfer guidelines
    - Management regulations for shipping quality level
    - Product quality auditing regulations
    - Product quality inspection regulations
- After-sales service and complaint handling
  - Customer complaints manual
  - Recall regulations
  - Critical accidents handling regulations
    - Regulations for after-sales services
    - Hidden claims regulations
    - Regulations for claims on raw materials
- Quality inspection
  - Key quality problem-solving regulations
    - Quality inspection implementation guidelines
    - Regulations for registered quality problems
- Environmental protection
  - Environmental management regulations
  - Safety and hygiene management regulations
    - Pollution control regulations
    - Accident prevention drafting guidelines
- Suggestion system and administrative management
  - Suggestion system regulations
  - Administrative management regulations
    - Regulations for QC improvements and suggestions
    - Regulations for confidential documents

Sources: JUSE, *Summary Report by the Deming Prize Recipient* (Tokyo: JUSE, 1978–1982); JUSE, *In-House Standards for Quality Control* (Tokyo: JUSE, 1970); JUSE, *Quality Assurance Guidebook* (Tokyo: JUSE, 1974); Japanese Standards Association, *Revised Quality Control Handbook* (Tokyo: JSA, 1977); Japanese Standards Association, *Techniques for In-House Standardization at Plants* (Tokyo: JSA, 1959); and Japanese Standards Association, *Work Standardization* (Tokyo: JSA, 1982).

REFERENCES

1. Kaoru Ishikawa, "Is the Japanese Way of Management Revolutionary?" *Quality* 10, no. 4 (1980): 3–11.

2. Shigeru Aoki, "Cross-Functional Management for Top Management," *Quality Control* 32, no. 2 (1981): 92–98; no. 3 (1981): 66–71; no. 4 (1981): 65–69.

3. Kaoru Ishikawa and Shinji Isotani, "Introduction and Promotion of TQC (Part Five): Cross-Functional Management," *Quality Control* 32, no. 11 (1981): 88–96.

4. Kenichi Sato, "Cost Control at Toyota Auto Body," *Quality* 14, no. 4 (1984): 70–76.

5. Kaoru Shimoyamada, "Cross-Functional Management in Quality Assurance," *Quality* 14, no. 4 (1984): 63–69.

6. Toshiyuki Mochimoto, "Product-by-Product Management and Cross-Functional Management," *Quality* 14, no. 4 (1984): 9–14.

7. Masao Kogure, "Cross-Functional Management," *Quality Control* 37, special issue (November 1986): 253–59.

8. Soji Mizuno, "Cross-Functional Management," *Standardization and Quality Control* 31, no. 5 (1978): 1–9.

9. Kozo Koura, *Planning Methods for In-House Standardization* (Tokyo: Association of Tax Accountants, 1985), p. 60.

10. Kozo Koura, *Planning Methods for In-House Standardization* (Tokyo: Association of Tax Accountants, 1985), pp. 68–69.

11. Toshiyuki Mochimoto, "Cross-Functional Management and Quality Assurance," *Standardization and Quality Control* 39, no. 8 (1986): 13–20.

12. Takao Okayama, "Delivery Control at Tokyo Juki," *Standardization and Quality Control* 39, no. 8 (1986): 21–27.

13. Yoji Akao and Yuichi Iijima, "Establishment of Targets and Policy in Cross-Functional Management," *Quality Control* 16, special issue (Spring 1965): 109–16.

14. Akira Iijima, "Managerial Control Items at Toyota Auto Body," *Quality Control* 32, no. 8 (1981): 27–32.

15. Shoichi Shikano, and Sadao Hara. "Vitalization of Cross-Functional Management Through Evaluation of Quality Assurance Activities." *Quality Control* 33, special issue (June 1982): 323–26.

16. Toshiyuki Mochimoto, *Development of Management Strategy Through TQC* (Tokyo: JUSE, 1986).

17. Toshiyuki Mochimoto, *Policy Management for Environmental Affairs and Administration of Strategic Management* (Tokyo: Aoba-Shuppansha, 1983).

18. "Administration of Cross-Functional Management." Sixteenth Symposium Proceedings of the Japanese Society for Quality Control, 1984. *Quality* 14, no. 4 (1984): 53–62.

19. Kaoru Ishikawa, "Management in Vertical-Threaded Society," *Quality Control* 32, no. 1 (1981): 4–5.

20. Soji Mizuno, "Cross-Functional Management," *Quality* 9, no. 4 (1979): 25–30.

21. Yoji Akao, "Organization and Administration for Companywide Quality Control," *Organizational Science* 16, no. 3 (1982): 42–50.

22. Hiromichi Noda and Tadayuki Tetsuhashi, "Cross-Functional Management in Delivery Quantity," *Quality* 14, no. 4 (1984): 77–85.

23. Kozo Koura, *Planning Methods for In-House Standardization* (Tokyo: Association of Tax Accountants, 1985), pp. 204–05.

II
Practical Application of Cross-Functional Management

4

Development of New Products and Cross-Functional Management

Development of New Products and Cross-Functional Management at Toyoda Automatic Loom Works, Ltd.
Kanemitsu Tsuzuki

INTRODUCTION

Toyoda Automatic Loom Works was established in Kariya City, Aiichi Prefecture, in 1926 to manufacture automatic looms invented by the company's founder, Sakichi Toyoda. Since then it has upheld the corporate motto: "To promote research and creative ideas, and to be the leader in the industry at all times." In the spirit of that motto, it has been actively expanding its business activities through research on and development of new products, including domestic production of spinning machinery and automobiles, and development of forklifts and automobile air-conditioner compressors.

At the present time, the company has six divisions: (1) textile machinery, (2) automobile air-conditioner compressors, (3) industrial trucks, (4) automobile assembly, (5) automobile engines, and (6) casting. Through its successful operations, the company contributes to the local community.

Toyoda introduced TQC in 1982 in order to become flexible in response to the business environment, improve corporate culture, and resolve management issues. In recognition of its improvement of corporate culture through successful quality assurance activity—with a focus on new product development as its main theme—the company received the 1986 Deming Application Prize.

Improvement in cross-functional management and the development of a new product, the forklift X300, in the industrial truck division, are discussed in this chapter.

CROSS-FUNCTIONAL MANAGEMENT AT THE COMPANY

Division Management

Toyoda introduced the division system in 1971 to foster autonomous management and management efficiency. After several changes, in 1986 a management system was introduced with the six divisions listed above, each responsible for securing profit while implementing all the vertical activities of product planning, production, sales, and service under its division head manager.

The operation system of each division varies, depending on its character. The industrial truck division's operation management system is shown in Figure 4.1. Here, the annual plan is deployed cross-functionally as a part of policy management to ensure development of a long-range business plan. The division management committee, the inspection committee, and the department managers' committee are responsible for follow-up and decision-making.

Table 4.1 shows the relationship between major committees and review items.

Operation of Main Offices

Prior to the introduction of TQC, companywide management was weak in the areas of distributing corporate resources, setting goals, checking and following up on goals, and addressing major companywide issues.

During the early days of TQC promotion, general and company-specific issues of personnel, production engineering, education, and safety and health were addressed by a cross-functional committee, while issues of quality, purchasing, and manufacturing were addressed by a coordinating committee. As the promotion of TQC progressed, changes were made so that the cross-functional management committee and its subordinate general committee administered interdivisional office coordination, adjustment, support, corporate planning, and TQC promotion, and reported to the board of managing directors and the board of the executive committee. The cross-functional management committee identified ten functions: (1) quality and (2) cost as "basic functions"; (3) research, (4) production engineering, and (5) purchasing as "step-by-step functions"; and (6) personnel, (7) education, (8) safety and health, (9) information systems, and (10) TQC promotion as "auxiliary functions." Departments or offices of the general office were responsible for administering each functional area, and a department head was assigned to chair each to address these functional areas.

Figure 4.2 shows the relationship between committees and organizational units, while Figure 4.3 shows the relationship between the division

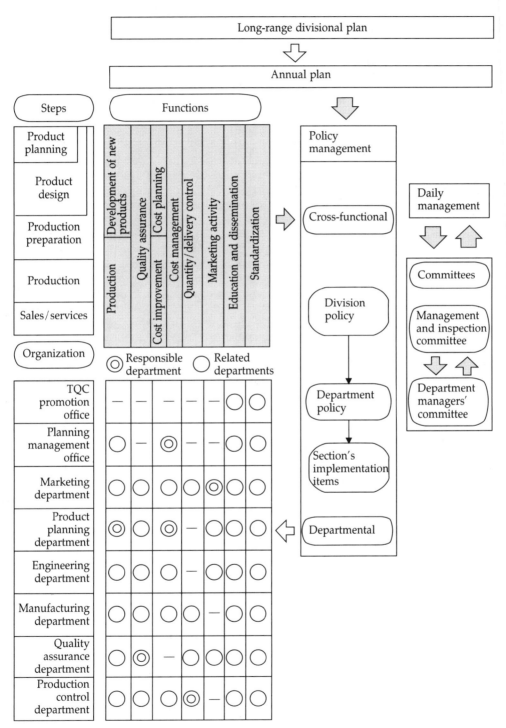

FIGURE 4.1
Divisional operation system

TABLE 4.1
Major committees and review items

Committees	Major review items	Frequency of meetings	Principal committee members (in addition to chairman)
Department managers' committee	Review and decide on major division management problems	Once a month	Division vice president, managing director, and associate manager
TQC promotion committee	Report on TQC promotion and approve activity plan	Once a month	Division vice president, managing director, and associate manager
Operation committee — Quality committee	Review and determine major quality problems	Once a month	Division vice president, quality assurance department manager, engineering department manager, and manufacturing department manager
Cost committee	Review, approve, and coordinate major cost-related items	Once a month	Division vice president, planning management office manager, manufacturing planning office manager, and sales department manager
Research and development committee	Review and approve research and development	Once a month	Division vice president, research department manager, product planning office manager, and engineering department manager
Safety and health committee	Confirm safety and health program, and approve activity plan	Once a month	Division vice president, manufacturing department manager, and safety/health/environment department manager
Inspection committee — Manufacturing quality committee	Promote early intervention in case of major manufacturing quality problems	Once a month	Inspection department manager, manufacturing department manager, and section managers of the manufacturing department
Cost planning committee	Review and coordinate major cost planning items	Once a month	Product planning office manager, planning management office manager, sales department manager, and engineering department manager
Cost improvement committee	Promote cost improvement	Once a month	Associate vice president for division office, engineering department manager, manufacturing department manager, and purchasing department manager
Production planning committee	Review production and sales plan quarterly (quarter includes month of committee meeting)	Once a month	Associate vice president for division office, production management department manager, and manufacturing department manager
Computerization promotion committee	Review and approve major computer system development	Once a month	Associate vice president for division office, production management department manager, parts department manager, and engineering department manager
QC circle promotion committee	Promote QC circle activities	Once a month	Division office vice president, quality assurance department manager, manufacturing department manager, and facilitators from all departments

office committees and the management committee, which includes the cross-functional management committee. Table 4.2 shows the major corporate committees and their responsibilities.

As indicated earlier, each division office formulates its policies according to function and implements them departmentally. However, functional areas such as quality and cost are managed cross-functionally in the case of new-product development.

The cross-functional management system has been gradually enhanced through continual trial-and-error research so that it closely links the roles of the top corporate management committees with the division offices' functions. This continuing effort is one of the characteristics of Toyoda's system of cross-functional management.

POLICY MANAGEMENT AT TOYODA AUTOMATIC LOOM WORKS

Characteristics of the Policy Management System

In order to achieve the "TOPS 70" corporate vision, the company drafted a long-range business plan—with a new product development program as its core—and a long-range cross-functional plan. The first-year plan was deployed as the annual policy for that fiscal year; the PDCA cycle was rotated by the combined efforts of all employees, including top managers; and policy management was implemented to achieve corporate goals.

The key areas of policy management since the introduction of TQC in 1982 are listed below.

1. Identifying the corporate vision, and drafting and improving the long-range plan.

    *   TOPS 70, a ten-year management goal and strategy, was put together to clarify future corporate direction and vision.

    *   In order to realize the corporate vision, a long-range business plan with new product development as the core program was drafted by the division offices, and a long-range cross-functional management plan was drafted by the cross-functional interface office in the general office. The plan was drafted as a five-year rolling plan, including the first year as the initial implementation year. It is revised annually, based on an evaluation of the results of the previous year's performance, on changes in the business environment, and on top management's needs.

2. Linking annual policy with the long-range plan and improving consistency in the deployment process.

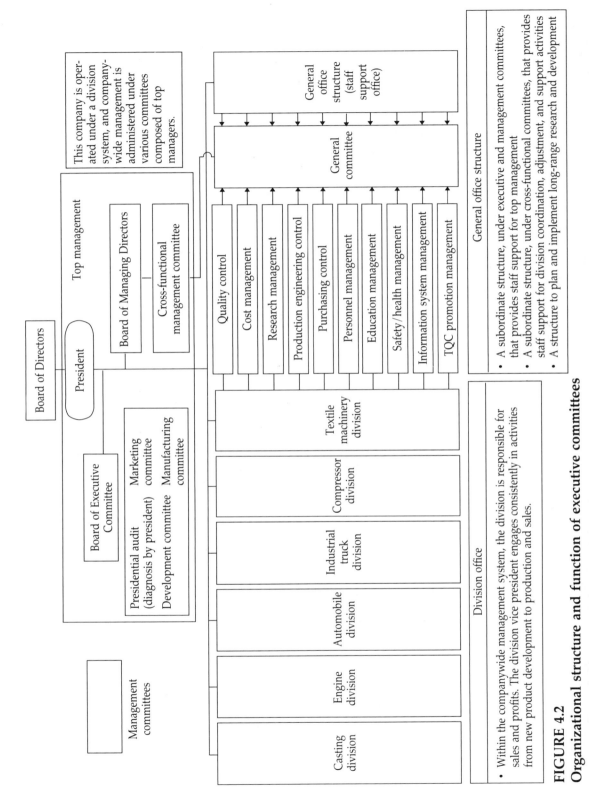

FIGURE 4.2
Organizational structure and function of executive committees

Management committees

Board of Directors

Top management

This company is operated under a division system, and company-wide management is administered under various committees composed of top managers.

President

Board of Executive Committee

Presidential audit (diagnosis by president)

Development committee

Marketing committee

Manufacturing committee

Board of Managing Directors

Cross-functional management committee

Casting division

Engine division

Automobile division

Industrial truck division

Compressor division

Textile machinery division

Quality control

Cost management

Research management

Production engineering control

Purchasing control

Personnel management

Education management

Safety/health management

Information system management

TQC promotion management

General committee

General office structure (staff support office)

Division office

- Within the companywide management system, the division is responsible for sales and profits. The division vice president engages consistently in activities from new product development to production and sales.

General office structure

- A subordinate structure, under executive and management committees, that provides staff support for top management
- A subordinate structure, under cross-functional committees, that provides staff support for division coordination, adjustment, and support activities
- A structure to plan and implement long-range research and development

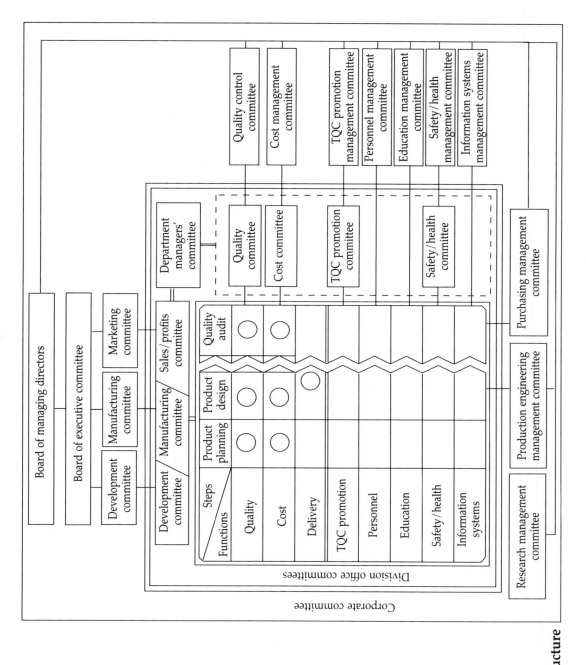

FIGURE 4.3
Committee structure

TABLE 4.2
Major corporate committees

Committees	Responsibilities
Board of Managing Directors	1. Review and decision-making on major management issues 2. Review and decision-making on issues presented by the cross-functional management committee
Board of Executive Committee	Review, check, and follow up on major management issues
Cross-functional management committee	1. Establish, check, and follow up on long-range cross-functional plan 2. Establish, check, and follow up on annual cross-functional plan 3. Conduct division office audit concerning functions
General committee	As a subordinate unit of the cross-functional management committee, the committee provides administrative and staff support in preparing, planning, and adjusting

- The first year plan of the long-range plan was designated as an annual plan, and it ensured an entire system for development, implementation, checking, and follow-up, from drafting policy to departmental policy deployment to specific implementation items. (See Figure 4.4.)

- The policy deployment process was reorganized through presidential diagnosis. The purpose of this was to improve interdepartmental cooperation and thereby ensure consistent policy deployment throughout the process, from establishment of the annual policy—a part of the long-range plan—to sectional implementation.

- Forms and tables were improved, and standardization was promoted so that the process could be drafted, developed, and reviewed in an accurate and timely manner. (See Table 4.3.)

Annual Policy of the Division

Each division's annual policy is based on management vision, fundamentals, long-range priority policy, corporate policy, target values, and long-range division planning. Annual division policy encompasses high-priority concerns in cross-functional areas (e.g., sales, engineering, manufacturing, quality, cost, and purchasing) and spells out control items, measurable goals, durations, and departments for each area.

Annual corporate policy is augmented by general office policy and is fed into the departments so that departmental policy and a section's implementation items can be established. (See Table 4.3.) However, there is also a need to integrate overall division office policy when departmental policies are drafted. Therefore, the company developed Table W, a matrix table that coordinates interdepartmental efforts. (See Table 4.4.) Table W is applied to major new and existing product developments. It lists quality, cost, and delivery along the vertical axis and departments along the horizontal axis. The department(s) concerned with division office policy, indicated by function, are shown within ovals; representatives of the initiating department write in departmental policy below the ovals. As a result, the matrix table provides a user-friendly format to see whether a division policy is being addressed by all departments concerned and whether the level of activity is consistent. Figure 4.5 shows the annual policy statement structure.

At the stage of reorganization of the policy (structure), the division office vice president and president conduct audits focusing on the contents of the policy and the consistency of its deployment—from long-range plans to section implementation items. Once approved by the board of directors, in-house announcement and presentation meetings take place, followed by a 12-month implementation period beginning on 1 April.

At fixed intervals during this period, supervisors assess performance on given control items, and appropriate measures are taken based on their assessment. After six months, audits are conducted by the president and the vice president. Based on performance assessment, analysis, and identification of problems remaining at the midpoint, specific measures are established. At this point, a long-range business plan for the subsequent year starts to roll. The process itself is repeated, while activities are upgraded every year.

Main Office Annual Policy

In the initial stages of TQC, main office policy was established as a long-range business plan encompassing three-year goals and policies concerning departmental responsibilities. Also included was the annual policy, which primarily described departmental responsibilities.

As described in the section "Cross-Functional Management at the Company," subsection "Operation of Main Offices," the role of cross-functional

	President (top manager)	Managing director in charge / Division office vice president	Department manager	Section manager	Assistant manager and rank and file	Related standards
Plan — Formulation	Management vision → TOPS 70 vision (motto) → Long-range plan (management, business, and cross-functional) → Annual policy draft → Board of Managing Directors → Internal presentation of annual policy					Annual policy management regulations / Policy management manual Management regulations for long-range plan Board of managing directors' regulations Management regulations for annual policy forms
Plan — Deployment		Main office policy / Division office policy [W] (a)	Departmental policy [A] (b) → Implementation items [B]			(Forms and tables) (a) Table a: Policy setup table (b) Table b: Departmental policy setup table [B] Table B: Implementation program and management table for implementation items [A] Table A: Corporate policy and table of control items [W] Table W: Corporate policy and table of departmental themes

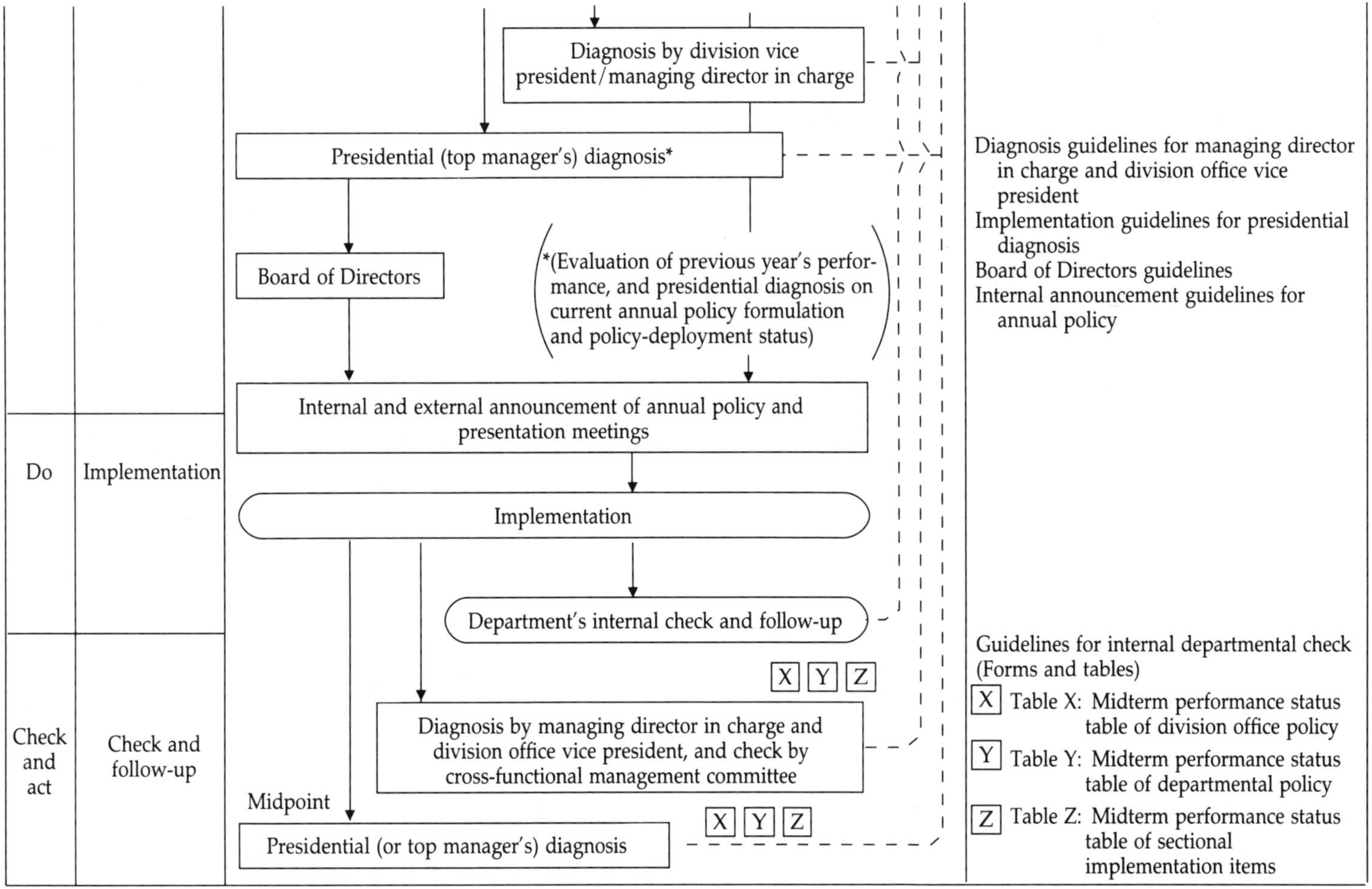

Diagnosis by division vice president/managing director in charge

Diagnosis guidelines for managing director in charge and division office vice president
Implementation guidelines for presidential diagnosis
Board of Directors guidelines
Internal announcement guidelines for annual policy

Presidential (top manager's) diagnosis*

*(Evaluation of previous year's performance, and presidential diagnosis on current annual policy formulation and policy-deployment status)

Board of Directors

Internal and external announcement of annual policy and presentation meetings

Implementation

Department's internal check and follow-up

X Y Z

Diagnosis by managing director in charge and division office vice president, and check by cross-functional management committee

X Y Z

Midpoint

Presidential (or top manager's) diagnosis

X Y Z

Guidelines for internal departmental check (Forms and tables)

X Table X: Midterm performance status table of division office policy

Y Table Y: Midterm performance status table of departmental policy

Z Table Z: Midterm performance status table of sectional implementation items

Do — Implementation

Check and act — Check and follow-up

FIGURE 4.4
Policy management activity system

TABLE 4.3
Forms and tables for annual policy management and their objectives

Names	Titles	Major objectives for forms and tables (year of introduction)
Policy setup table	Table ⓐ	Forms and tables (for fiscal year 1985) to establish division office (or general office) policies and to justify such policies
Departmental policy setup table	Table ⓑ	Forms and tables to input upper-level management policy and to output departmental policy (for fiscal 1984)
Table for the implementation program and implementation item control	Table B	Forms and tables (for fiscal 1984) to draft implementation program, to check and follow up on section's implementation items
Table of corporate policy and control items	Table A	Forms and tables (for fiscal 1985) to clarify and confirm direct linkage between policy and control items at various management levels
Table of corporate policy and departmental themes	Table W	Forms and tables (for fiscal 1985) to confirm and to prevent omissions and duplication, to ensure interdepartmental cooperation
Table of division office policy and midterm performance status	Table X	
Table of departmental policy and midterm performance status	Table Y	Forms and tables (for fiscal 1985) to evaluate and analyze performance results at midterm and to help meet underachieved goals by year-end at various levels: division policy, departmental policy, and section's implementation items
Table of sectional implementation items and midterm performance status	Table Z	

management began to be understood clearly. Staff support departments, which report to the cross-functional management committee, started addressing issues of quality and cost from a companywide viewpoint. A long-range cross-functional plan and annual policy began to be established, and the idea that division office activities should be supported companywide was promoted. With this, linkage between the main office and the division offices was strengthened.

Policy setting, presidential diagnosis, policy deployment, policy checking, midpoint checking, and follow-up activities are implemented in the manner described in the section "Policy Management at Toyoda Automatic Loom Works," subsection "Annual Policy of the Division."

TABLE 4.4
Sample table W **—XYZ year, XYZ division office policy, and summary of departmental policies (XYZ product)**

Department / QCD	Marketing department	Research department	Product planning department	Development department	Experiment department
	Engineering #1 Enhance quality of planning and engineering and develop "market-wise" products through prediction of changes in business environment and user needs				
Quality	1.1 Assess market trends accurately through improvement of market research	1.2 Ensure accurate manufacturing with new functions through improvement of preliminary evaluation at the R & D stage	1.3 Establish product objectives through improved market research and accurate identification of required quality	1.4 Achieve quality goals after establishing market-oriented quality objectives and applying engineering analysis techniques	1.5 Improve technical evaluation ability and execute accurate quality evaluation
			Quality #1 Improve quality assurance activities for new product development and ensure the quality of new products		
			Implement design review (DR) of suggested themes and identify feasibility for development plan	Improve DR at each step of the product development stage, and verify degree of performance in targeted quality	
Cost					

83

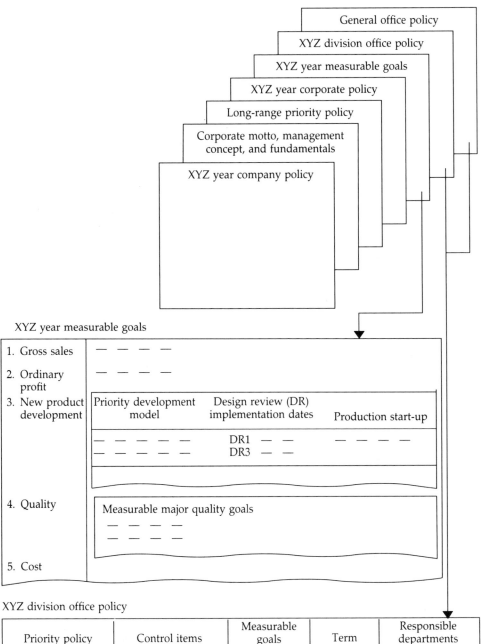

FIGURE 4.5
Structure of the annual policy statement

AN EXAMPLE OF NEW PRODUCT DEVELOPMENT (TOYOTA FORKLIFT X300)

The Relationship between New Product Development and Cross-Functional Management

Each division office is responsible for the development of new products. The process begins with input of the long-range business plan and annual policy of a division office. Departments of the division office responsible for new product development—from product planning through production preparation—assume development tasks based upon quality assurance activities utilizing the quality assurance system (see Figure 4.6). Management reviews of actual achievement are conducted in the manner shown below.

1. Reviews of each department are conducted by managers to check and follow up at predetermined intervals.
2. Quality/cost committee meetings with the division vice president are held monthly for each functional area, and subsequently are reviewed by the cross-functional management committee. (See Figure 4.2.)
3. Design review (DR) is conducted at each development step at a predetermined time by the division office president, to determine whether it is appropriate to advance to the next process. Important design reviews (e.g., DR 1, 3, 5, and 6 in Figure 4.6) are conducted by the board of the executive committee (see the development committee in Figure 4.2) in a presidential diagnosis format.

Quality Assurance Activity in the Development of New Products (Development of the X300)

Overview

A sample design review system may be clarified through discussion of the development of the super-quality X300 at Toyota Forklift, where the design review system was introduced and integration of quality at the early stages succeeded through interdepartmental cooperation.

Basic Ideas

The basic ideas behind the development of the X300 were "quality first" and the "market-in" concept. The goal was to provide excellent products

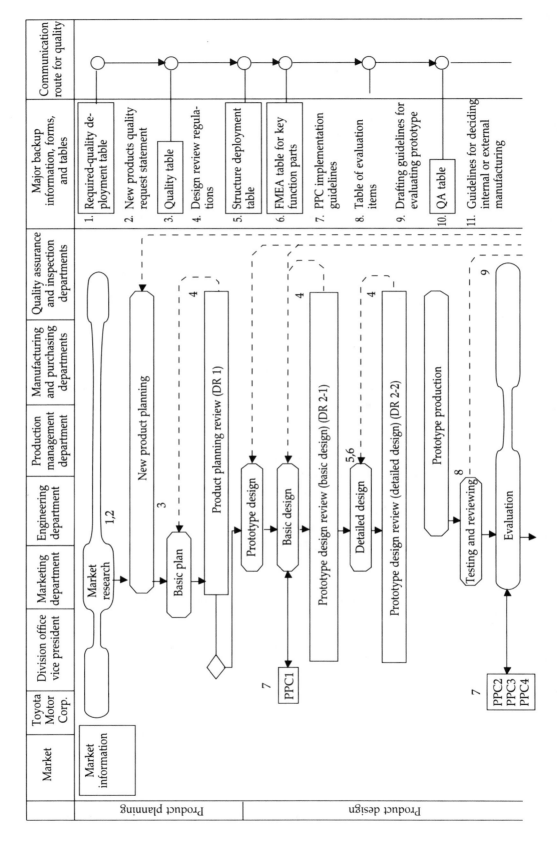

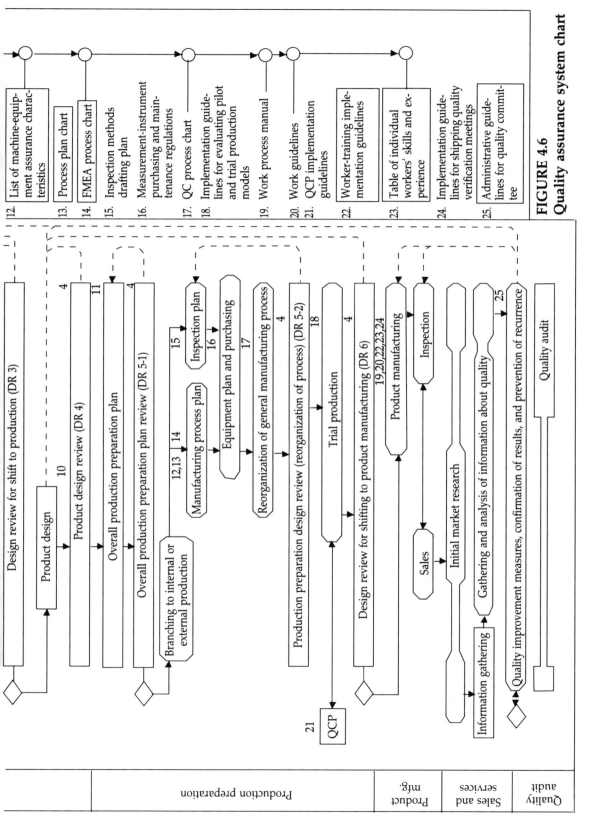

FIGURE 4.6
Quality assurance system chart

12. List of machine-equipment assurance characteristics
13. Process plan chart
14. FMEA process chart
15. Inspection methods drafting plan
16. Measurement-instrument purchasing and maintenance regulations
17. QC process chart
18. Implementation guidelines for evaluating pilot and trial production models
19. Work process manual
20. Work guidelines
21. QCP implementation guidelines
22. Worker-training implementation guidelines
23. Table of individual workers' skills and experience
24. Implementation guidelines for shipping quality verification meetings
25. Administrative guidelines for quality committee

87

through farsighted prediction of market trends and customer needs, and to win customer satisfaction and trust.

Key Activities

Quality assurance activities in new product development integrated quality at the product planning, product design, and production preparation steps through development system improvement, application of reliability techniques, and implementation of design reviews. The key activities of each step are listed below.

- Product Planning: Accurate assessment of customer needs through segmented market research. Establishment of dominant quality targets through application of a quality table.
- Product Design: Preliminary evaluation by new-function structure deployment, leading functions, and application of FMEA. Implementation of reliability evaluation based on surveys of actual usage situations.
- Production Preparation: Entry of equipment assurance characteristics in quality characteristics. Investigation through application of FMEA to process and optimum allocation of human resources. Securing process capability through routine work training program.

Vigorous implementation of design reviews and thorough follow-up from product planning to manufacturing of the new product ensured superior quality.

Quality Assurance in New Product Development

Quality Improvement in Product Planning. In order to address the diversified and sophisticated needs of customers and the market, product planning for the X300, which was done during the TQC promotion period, included surveys of the market environment and engineering trends. Surveys were conducted on all markets by districts and by industrial classification:

1. Visits to overseas dealers
2. Objective market research conducted by outside organizations
3. Direct information-gathering from users, focusing on actual conditions of use.

Through cooperation by the marketing and engineering departments, required quality functions were deployed, and sales points and quality objectives were established by making out a quality table.

Design review 1 (product planning review) was conducted by the departments concerned to determine the feasibility of the plan, which included study of "bottleneck engineering." Because of these activities, superquality sales points could be established, and sales leadership after market entry became predictable. Design reviews were continued after the product planning review, and evaluation of the planning quality objective was vigorously pursued. The product planning system is shown in Figures 4.7 and 4.8.

Quality Improvement in Product Design. Thorough advance reviews and verifications of evaluation were conducted during X300 product development to ensure superior quality. In the early stages, quality planning was systematically carried out by implementing design reviews with the full participation of all departments concerned. At the prototype design stage, structural deployment was carried out to establish engineering policy. Consequently, "bottleneck engineering" problems and leading function items were thoroughly analyzed. In order to ensure reliability, FMEA was implemented to improve design and to clarify evaluation items.

At the prototype evaluation stage, test conditions and evaluation criteria were established through surveys of actual usage conditions, and an accelerated endurance bench test was conducted. Life expectancy was estimated on the basis of the test results and survey data, further ensuring reliability.

Thanks to thorough implementation of these activities, the company could verify that the design quality of the X300 was on target, and successfully reduced the number of design modifications after completion of the drawings. Figure 4.8 shows quality deployment during the product design stage and its relationship to the design review system.

Quality Improvement in Production Preparation. For the X300, improvement measures included expansion of internal manufacturing for key components, introduction of new equipment and new engineering techniques required by automation, and various improvement activities to ensure process capabilities at each step of the entire process.

During the process planning stage, quality characteristics were translated into characteristics of machine-equipment assurance, using the engineering department's QA table. Application of the FMEA permitted early discovery of bottleneck engineering problems resulting from equipment and production method. Subsequently, purchase orders for equipment and equipment specifications were prepared simultaneously. Ultimately, production preparation time was reduced, and became predictable and verifiable through DR 5-1 (general plan review).

During the equipment purchasing stage, machine capability was ensured. During the process reorganization stage, optimum allocation of

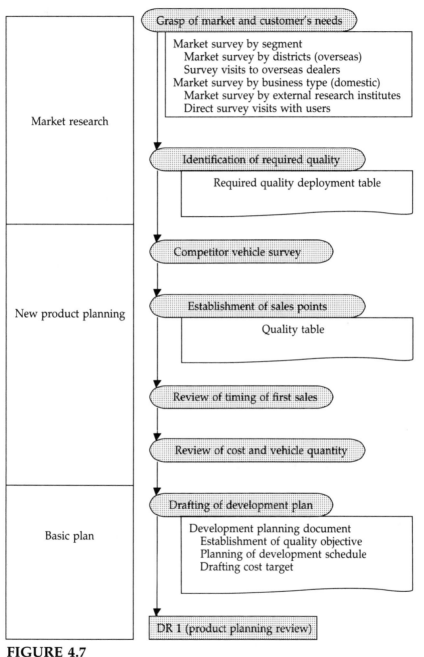

FIGURE 4.7
Product planning system

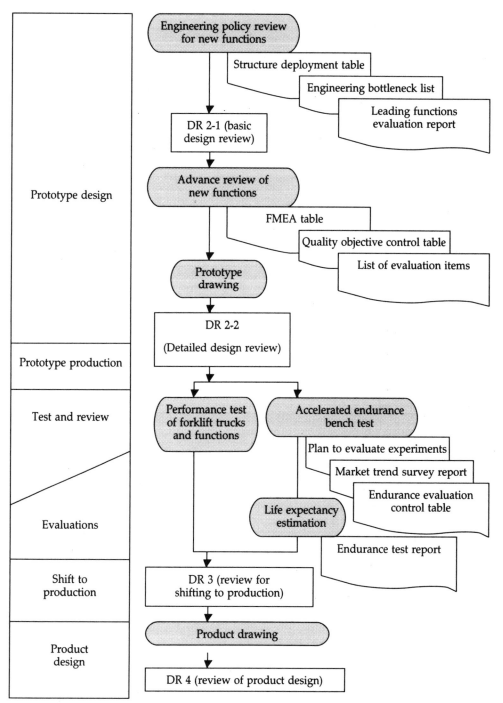

FIGURE 4.8
Product design system

human resources was pursued by improving worker skills through routine training programs. After these activities, the process for ensuring machine capability was accelerated, worker training time was adequately allocated, and process capacity was ensured within the prescribed margin.

During the last stage of production preparation, integration of quality was verified through implementation of DR 6 (review for shift to product manufacturing) with full participation of all departments concerned. Figure 4.9 shows quality deployment in production preparation and its relationship to the design review system.

Improvement in Design Review.   The company's design review is governed by the design review regulation, which is based on quality assurance regulations and the division office design review operation guidelines. Major contents include objectives, definitions, classification (names), persons responsible for decision making, and operation guidelines (e.g., review items, reviewers, implementation plans, backup data, and meeting minutes). Table 4.5 lists the major design reviews, their objectives, and persons responsible for decision making. Thus, vigorous execution of the design review at each step of the entire process precludes the passage of unsolved problems to subsequent steps of the process, thereby facilitating development of new products as planned.

In the development of the X300, the importance of systematic design reviews during the early stages was recognized through evaluation of previous models. "Project T" was designed to involve the concerned departments in a development promotion system in which comprehensive design review was implemented beginning with the product planning stage. Subsequently, a system was established to discover problems in the early stages and to follow up all activities closely in every design review stage. Figure 4.10 shows the general outline of design reviews.

Design review 1 (product planning review) is implemented during the product planning stage primarily to ensure that "super sales points" can be achieved. DR 1 also reviews overall aspects of quality, cost, and delivery, and verifies that the planning is justifiable. At the same time, dominance in the market and duration of dominance after the product's entry into the market are verified, based on prediction of competitors' development time frames and engineering capabilities.

Design reviews 2, 3, and 4 (prototype design review, review for shifting to production, and product design review) are conducted primarily to assess the achievement status of the quality objectives at the product design stage. Appropriate directions are given at that time to correct underachievement. It should be pointed out that an earlier method of evaluating prototype forklift trucks in relation to a specific user group was inadequate. Therefore, a new monitoring evaluation system was established to include

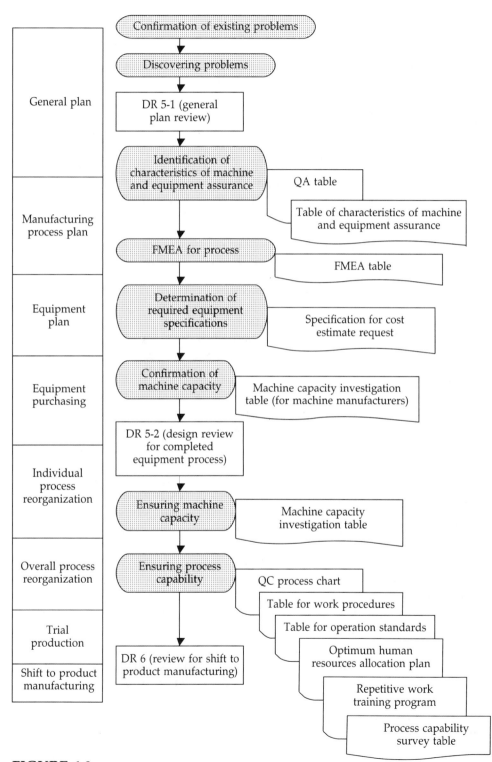

FIGURE 4.9
Production preparation system

TABLE 4.5
Design reviews, objectives, and persons responsible for
decision making

Code numbers of major design review classifications	Major design reviews	Objectives of design reviews	Person responsible for decision making
DR 1	Product planning review	Pass or fail decision for shifting to trial production	Division office vice president
DR 2	Prototype design review	Conformance of design quality to basic plan	Engineering department senior manager
DR 3	Review for shifting to production	Pass or fail decision for shifting to trial production	Division office vice president
DR 4	Product design review	Conformance of design quality to overall quality targets	Engineering department manager
DR 5	Production preparation review	Pass or fail decision on conformance of overall production preparation plan	Division office vice president
DR 6	Review for shifting to product manufacturing	Pass-or-fail decision for shifting to product manufacturing	Division office vice president

evaluation by our competitors as well as our own users. Consequently, confidence of market dominance was gained. (See Figure 4.11.)

Design review 5 (production preparation review) was implemented during the production preparation stage to review the feasibility of the overall production preparation plan. Active participation of the production engineering department from DR 1 onward made early review of the production preparation plan possible and helped to speed up production preparation.

Design review 6 (review for shifting to product manufacturing) was implemented to review the achievement status of key quality targets, such as the degree of process capability achievement, job training level, and production preparedness. Confirmation of achievement of planned targets through development activity verified that the X300 was a superior product.

These activities helped to achieve interdepartmental cooperation, to plan key quality targets and production preparation within a fixed period, and to expedite smooth "landing" of the product.

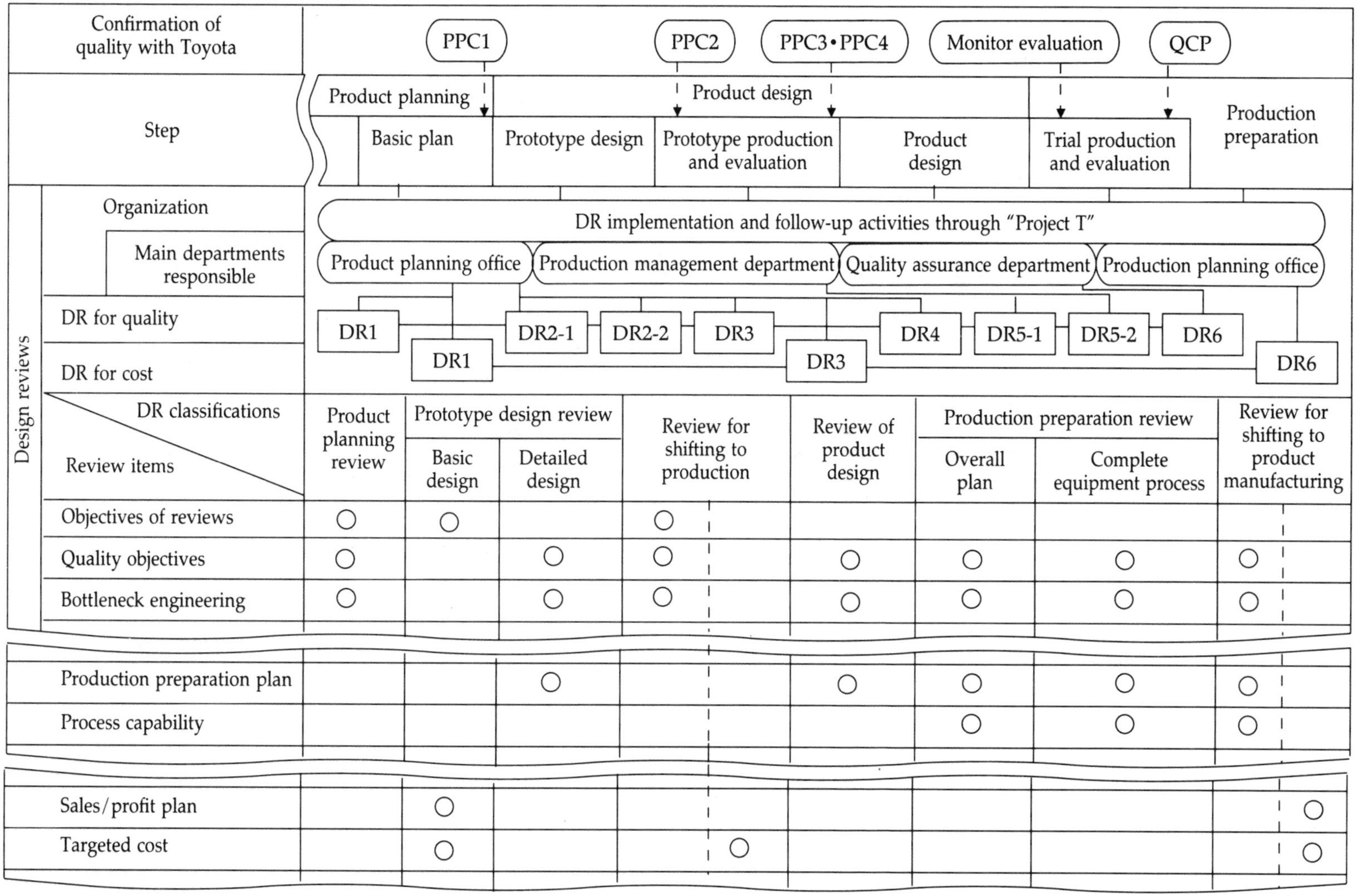

FIGURE 4.10
Overview of design review (product X300)

Confirmation of quality with Toyota

Step						
Product planning (PPC1)	Prototype design (PPC2)	Prototype production and evaluation	Product design (PPC3·PPC4)	Monitor evaluation	Trial production and evaluation	Production preparation (QCP)
Basic plan	Prototype design	Prototype production and evaluation	Product design			

Organization / Main departments responsible

Product planning office — DR1, DR1
Production management department — DR2-1, DR2-2, DR3
Quality assurance department — DR3, DR4, DR5-1, DR5-2, DR6
Production planning office — DR6

DR implementation and follow-up activities through "Project T"

Design reviews

DR classifications / Review items	Product planning review	Prototype design review — Basic design	Prototype design review — Detailed design	Review for shifting to production	Review of product design	Production preparation review — Overall plan	Production preparation review — Complete equipment process	Review for shifting to product manufacturing
Objectives of reviews	○	○		○				
Quality objectives	○		○	○	○	○	○	○
Bottleneck engineering	○		○	○	○	○	○	○
Production preparation plan					○	○	○	○
Process capability						○	○	○
Sales / profit plan	○							○
Targeted cost	○			○				○

95

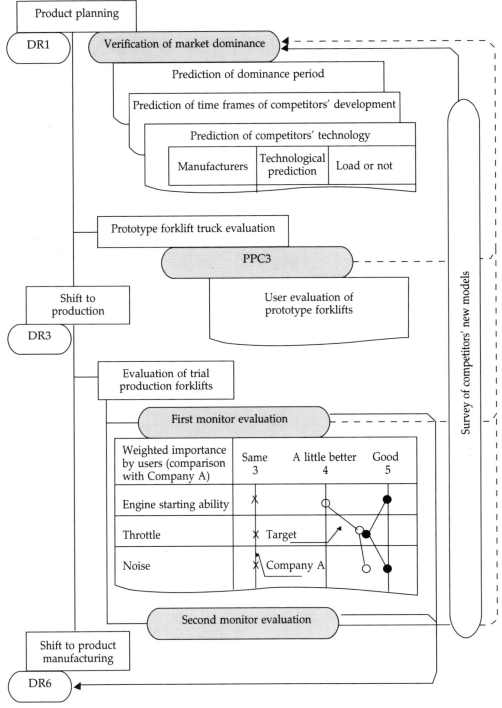

FIGURE 4.11
Verification of market dominance (product X300)

CONCLUDING REMARKS

From the inception of TQC activity, top management of the company attempted to link functions of the management committee with those of division offices in order to establish a cross-functional management system and to upgrade the system and its activities annually. As a result, the company successfully solved many problems, promoted standardization of systems, and achieved efficient management. It is our intention to practice policy management and cross-functional management simultaneously so as to achieve continuous improvement of corporate quality and management efficiency in the future.

Development of New Products at Yukuhashi Plant, Yaskawa Electric Manufacturing Company, Ltd.
Takeji Uchida

INTRODUCTION

Since its founding, Yaskawa Electric has been developing, producing, and selling electric motors and control instruments, and has prospered because of the confidence and trust of its customers.

Yukuhashi plant, which employs approximately 860 persons, manufactures control instruments critical to automation. The plant has developed and accumulated considerable electromation application technology and systems engineering expertise. With solid engineering backup, the plant has been developing, designing, and manufacturing electrical machinery systems used for power distribution in the steel, chemical, and machinery industries; variable-speed control instruments; and the SF6 gas switch.

Customers in a slow economy always demand optimum equipment and systems. Their needs for electromation application systems and their components—variable-speed control instruments—have become increasingly diversified and sophisticated. Therefore, strengthening the development system for new products to meet changing customer needs is the principal issue in plant management.

In an effort to establish "durable corporate quality to meet changes in the business environment"—the motto at the time TQC was introduced in 1981—the plant implemented a quality improvement program based on an active "quality-first" philosophy. With an emphasis on new product development, the advanced development and design system at Yukuhashi

(ADDS-Y)—a quality assurance program—was implemented to incorporate quality from the initial developmental stage through the final production stage. (See Figure 4.12.)

The variable-speed drive with AC motor and a transistor inverter has been rapidly developed in recent years. As a result of its expanding availability and applicability, the market has increasingly been asking for more multifunctions, high capacity, greater system development, greater reliability, further miniaturization, and cost reduction. Because of the reduction of the product's life cycle, competition with other manufacturers has become increasingly keen, especially with rapid technological advancement, unfavorable foreign exchange rates, and market discrimination problems.

OVERVIEW OF CROSS-FUNCTIONAL MANAGEMENT

Companywide Cross-Functional Management

The concept of cross-functional management was introduced at the same time that TQC was introduced. The company changed its existing organizational structure, established generic key management items, appointed general coordinating executives, established a general staff support department, and organized its cross-functional management system. (See Chapter 5.)

Cross-Functional Management at the Plant

As stated before, three major plant products are system electrical machinery products, variable-speed control instruments, and the SF6 gas switch. Because these products differ in basic technology, configuration, and production systems, management by product and by department (development and design—manufacturing—inspection) and cross-functional management have been exercised simultaneously. To manage cross-functionally, generic key functions—new product development, quality assurance, cost management, and delivery control—are identified. (See Figure 4.13.)

The management committee and the TQC promotion committee were established to upgrade plant management and operational structure. In order to promote the key generic functions, cross-functional committees were established, and the committees interfaced with line departments through initiation and evaluation of improvement plans. (See Table 4.6.)

In order to satisfy the midterm and annual business plans, four generic key functions are coordinated by the staff support department and fed

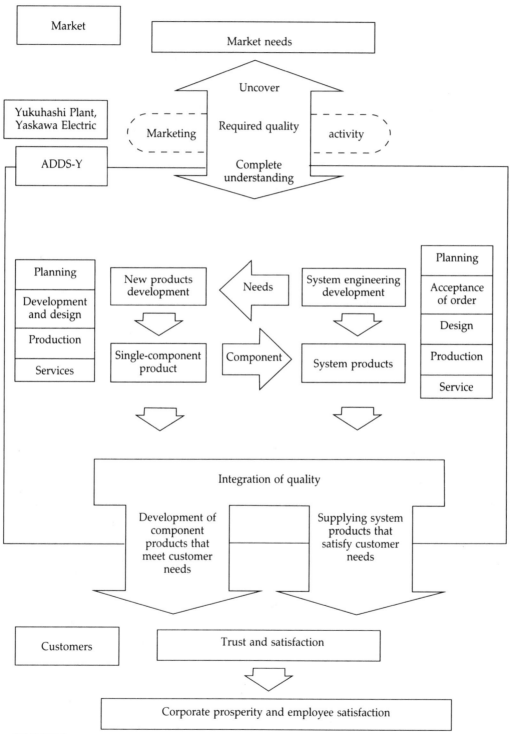

FIGURE 4.12
Conceptual chart of ADDS-Y total quality assurance program

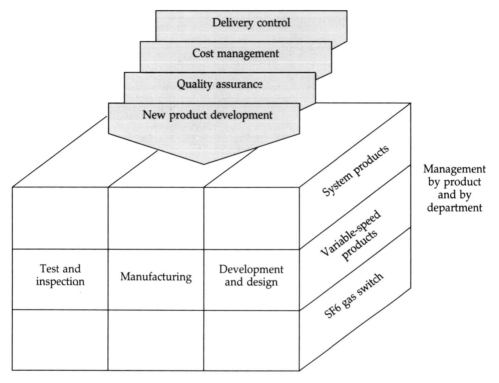

Cross-functional management

FIGURE 4.13
Cross-functional management at Yukuhashi plant

back to the plant manager to assist him in formulating his annual policy and policy deployment. Plantwide activities, "plan-do-check-act" (PDCA), are carried out for organizational improvement. Cross-functional management is implemented in all departments and subdepartments through a policy management system. The status of its implementation is assessed by the department responsible on a monthly basis, and it is evaluated by the cross-functional committee and adjusted with implementing departments. PDCA is deployed for cross-functional management to analyze the improvement status of the key functions biannually, to reidentify results and problems, to resolve policy problems, and to take the business environment into consideration. Figure 4.14 shows the policy management system.

In cross-functional management for new product development, quality, cost, and development scheduling are managed from the planning stage through the initial production stage.

TABLE 4.6
Cross-functional committees at Yukuhashi plant

	Name	Objectives and functions	Meeting frequency	Chairperson	Responsible department
General management	Management committee	Review and coordination of management plan (medium- and short-term plans) Review and coordination of monthly work	Once a month	Plant manager	Accounting department
	TQC promotion committee	Review and coordination of key TQC promotion items (policy management)	As necessary (averaging twice a month)	Plant manager	TQC office
Cross-functional committees	Product development committee	Review and coordination of policy and plan in development of new products Review and coordination of product planning Quality evaluation and coordination during development stage	As necessary (averaging once a month)	Plant manager	Engineering department
	Quality committee	Review and coordination of quality assurance program Evaluation and coordination of key quality problems	Twice a month	Plant manager	Quality assurance office
	Cost committee	Review and coordination of policy concerning medium- and short-term cost management Review and coordination of cost management problems	As necessary (averaging once a month)	Plant manager	Engineering department
	Production committee	Review and coordination of manufacturing methods for ordered products Review and coordination of manufacturing schedule for ordered products	As necessary (averaging once every two months)	Production planning department manager	Production planning department

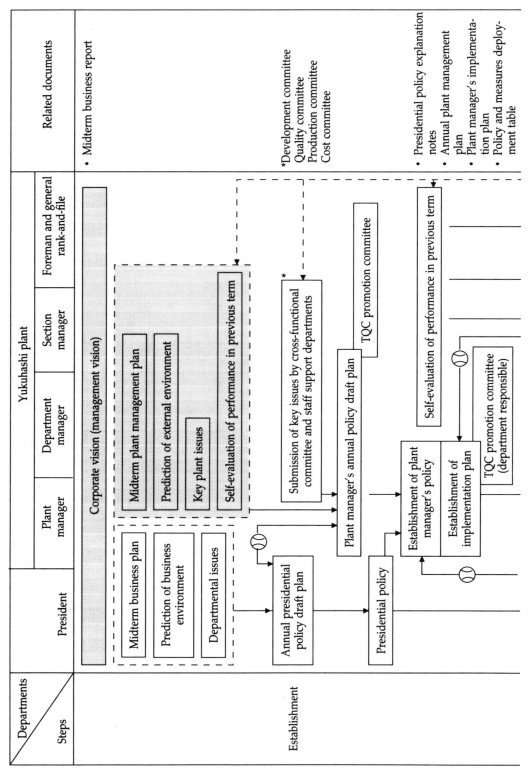

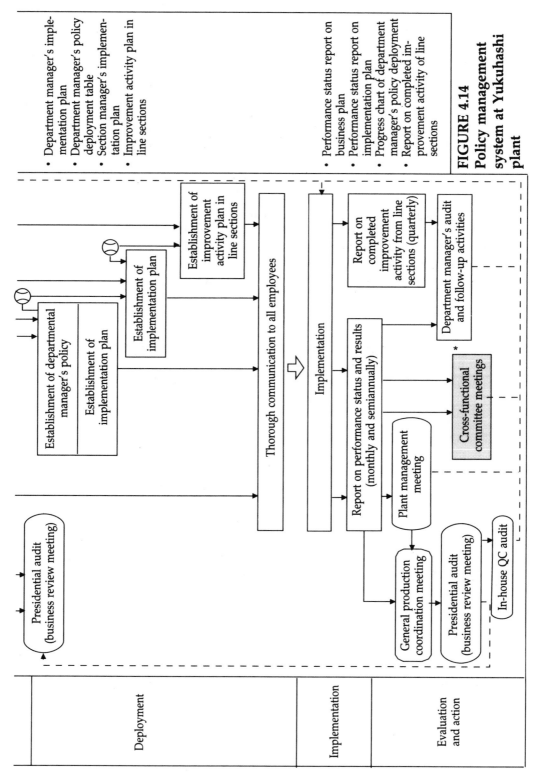

FIGURE 4.14 Policy management system at Yukuhashi plant

- Department manager's implementation plan
- Department manager's policy deployment table
- Section manager's implementation plan
- Improvement activity plan in line sections

- Performance status report on business plan
- Performance status report on implementation plan
- Progress chart of department manager's policy deployment
- Report on completed improvement activity of line sections

Establishment of departmental manager's policy

Establishment of implementation plan

Establishment of implementation plan

Establishment of improvement activity plan in line sections

Thorough communication to all employees

Implementation

Report on completed improvement activity from line sections (quarterly)

Department manager's audit and follow-up activities

Report on performance status and results (monthly and semiannually)

*Cross-functional committee meetings

Plant management meeting

Presidential audit (business review meeting)

General production coordination meeting

Presidential audit (business review meeting)

In-house QC audit

Deployment

Implementation

Evaluation and action

NEW PRODUCT DEVELOPMENT

History

The company's system of new product development is tripartite and responds to short-, medium-, and long-term development time frames. (See Table 4.7.)

The company's activities for new product development are grouped into three categories: short-range, medium-range, and long-range. The short-range development activity for new products, undertaken independently by the Yukuhashi plant, is discussed below. The basic idea was "to assess accurately the needs of the market and customer . . . and to develop visionary new products that are competitive." Five priority activities were implemented, aiming at the creation of attractive quality and the integra-

TABLE 4.7
Grouping of new product development at Yaskawa Electric Manufacturing Company, Ltd.

Grouping of new product development	*Development contents*	*Engineering*	*Unit responsible*
Short-range new products	Development responds to customers' direct and specific demands in a timely manner	It is based on engineering that is established and verified through research, development, experimentation, and experience	Engineers at each plant
Medium-range new products	Development aims at expansion of existing products through technological innovations; it encompasses development of consolidated technologies from every plant over a period of one to two years	It requires innovative technology development	Engineering development center
Long-range new products	New product development, a new line of business to be included in the midterm business plan, involves advanced and independent technology applied to development of new products	It requires development of advanced, creative, and independent technology	Research center Tokyo development center

tion of quality into every step of the development stage. (See Figure 4.15.) They are:

1. Support the sales department, identify customer needs accurately, and plan for competitive products

2. Uncover and solve bottleneck engineering problems in order to meet changes in the market and customer needs

3. Consolidate existing engineering capacity and integrate quality at the development and design stages

4. Improve production preparation and ensure quality at the earliest manufacturing stage

5. Gather quality-related information from the market and feed the information back to the initial process of development in order to facilitate integration of quality through "upstream control."

The new product development system, operational methods for development, and standardization of forms and tables were upgraded. (See Figure 4.16.)

Commercialization Planning

The commercialization planning is implemented in two steps. The first step is to review specific product plans for a given market segment, including timing requirements. The review is implemented through the application of market analysis to the electronic motor application market in the context of overall engineering trend analysis. Taking the midterm development plan into consideration, a development theme is selected. (See Figures 4.17 and 4.18.)

Specific required quality in the targeted market was analyzed by the sales department as a core group during the second step. Specific targeted quality objectives were analyzed and organized into a quality-function deployment table; this was followed by the establishment of a prototype concept, featured sales points, and key quality requirements. (See Figure 4.19.) In establishing the prototype concept, verbal description of the concept was important, as were correlation analysis of required quality and identification of specific requirements. Analysis of quality requirements demands in-depth thinking. The analytical method for the development of the inverter series was implemented by linking it to objectives of the product. (See Table 4.8.)

The prototype concept, sales points, key quality requirements, cost target, development schedule, and prediction of purchase orders are identified in commercialization planning step 2.

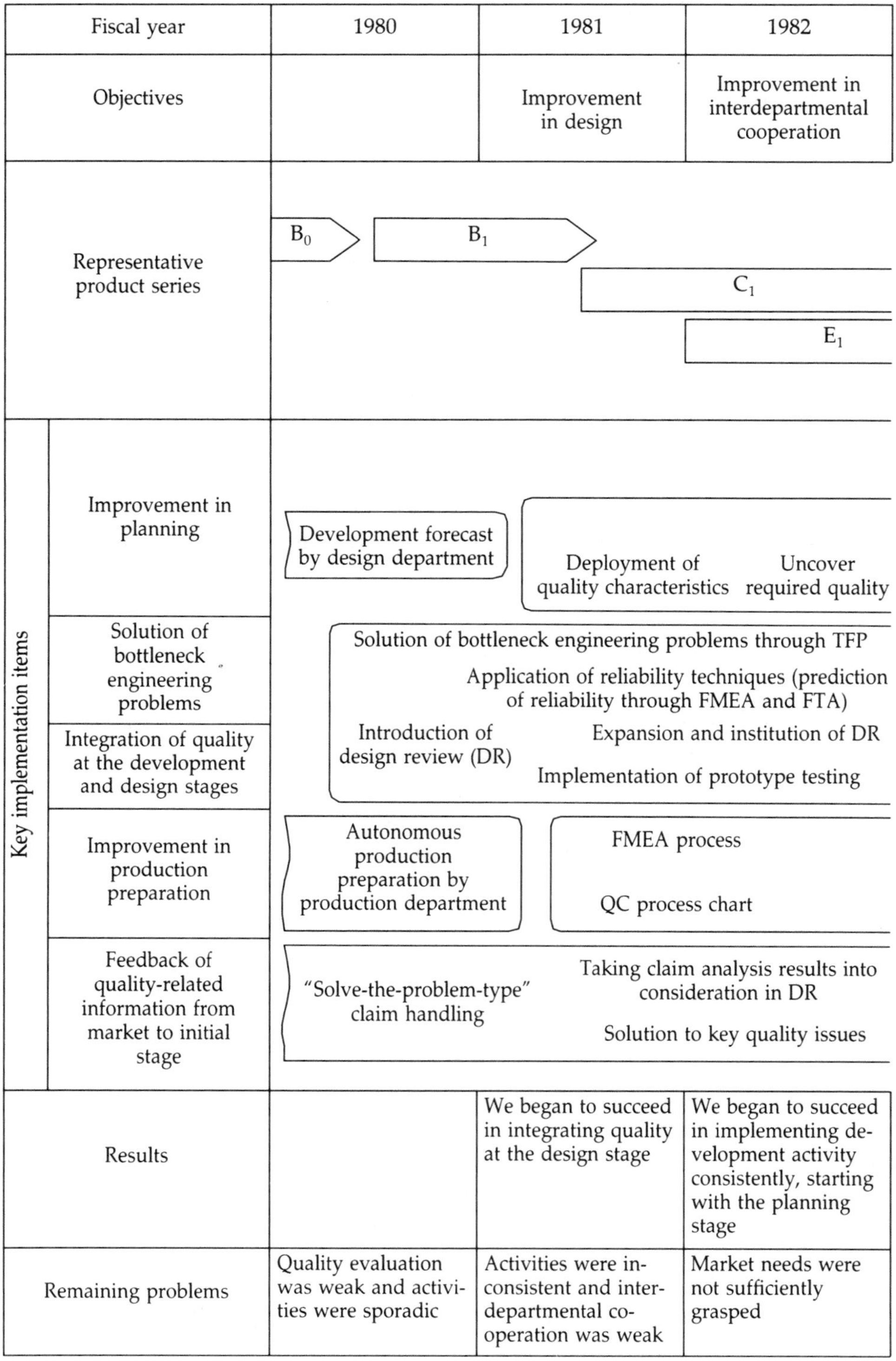

Fiscal year	1980	1981	1982
Objectives		Improvement in design	Improvement in interdepartmental cooperation

Representative product series	B_0 → B_1 →		
		C_1	
			E_1

Key implementation items

| Improvement in planning | Development forecast by design department | Deployment of quality characteristics   Uncover required quality | |

| Solution of bottleneck engineering problems | Solution of bottleneck engineering problems through TFP | | |
| | Application of reliability techniques (prediction of reliability through FMEA and FTA) | | |

| Integration of quality at the development and design stages | Introduction of design review (DR) | Expansion and institution of DR | |
| | | Implementation of prototype testing | |

| Improvement in production preparation | Autonomous production preparation by production department | FMEA process | |
| | | QC process chart | |

| Feedback of quality-related information from market to initial stage | "Solve-the-problem-type" claim handling | Taking claim analysis results into consideration in DR | |
| | | Solution to key quality issues | |

| Results | | We began to succeed in integrating quality at the design stage | We began to succeed in implementing development activity consistently, starting with the planning stage |
| Remaining problems | Quality evaluation was weak and activities were sporadic | Activities were inconsistent and interdepartmental co-operation was weak | Market needs were not sufficiently grasped |

FIGURE 4.15
History of new product development

1983	1984	1985	1986	1987
Product planning through improved cooperation with sales department	"Upstream quality control" in bottleneck engineering	Improvement in quality target setting	Realization of competitive cost	Advance activity at the germinal stage

A_1

A_2

B_2

B_3

C_2

C_3

D_1

F

G

Commercialization planning tied to sales department   Commercialization planning linked to business strategy

Three-dimensional management of QCR at planning stage   Improvement in cost planning

Quality application deployment   Quality characteristic level — Application deployment

Three-dimensional management of QCR   Codevelopment with parts manufacturers   Preparation for "leading technology"

Application of statistical methods (design of experiments and parameters)   Improvement in parts reliability evaluation

Improvement of prototype testing   "Abusing test"

Development from QA table to QC process chart and work standards   Preliminary preparation by RE and reversed RE

Early warning system

Taking failure analysis results into consideration for design evaluation test

"Early trouble" management   Failure analysis for electronic parts

We succeeded in developing new products with sales points	Delay in development was reduced	Targeted quality came into clear focus	Development activity began to produce competitive new products	
Solutions to bottleneck engineering problems were weak	Quality target setting was inadequate	Quality of cost management was weak	Development seeds for the subsequent development period were lacking	

Departments / Steps

Steps: Commercialization planning

Departments:
- Market and customers — Sales
- Presidential cross-functional management
- General office — Departments
- Yukuhashi plant — Plant manager | Product planning | System development | Development and design | Manufacturing engineering | Administrative work and manufacturing | Quality control (test)
- Committees
- Major standards, tables, and forms

Flowchart elements:

- Engineering trend analysis
- Sales strategy by market segment
- Policy for products and technique
- Midrange business plan
- In-house information collection (system products)
- In-house information collection (individual components)
- Product development meeting
- Request for development
- Uncovering bottleneck engineering problems
- Submission of development theme(s)
- Review of development themes
- Product development committee
- Commercialization planning (I)
- General meeting for development
- Decision-making on development themes
- Commercialization planning (II and III)
- Review of commercialization planning
- Approval

Committees:
- Cost estimate review committee
- Product development committee
- General development committee

Major standards, tables, and forms:
- Administrative regulations for product development
- Administrative regulations for product development committee
- Product development requirements documentation
- General table of R & D plans submitted
- Bottleneck engineering deployment table
- Commercialization planning documentation
- Required-quality function deployment table
- Administrative regulations for DR
- Product planning document

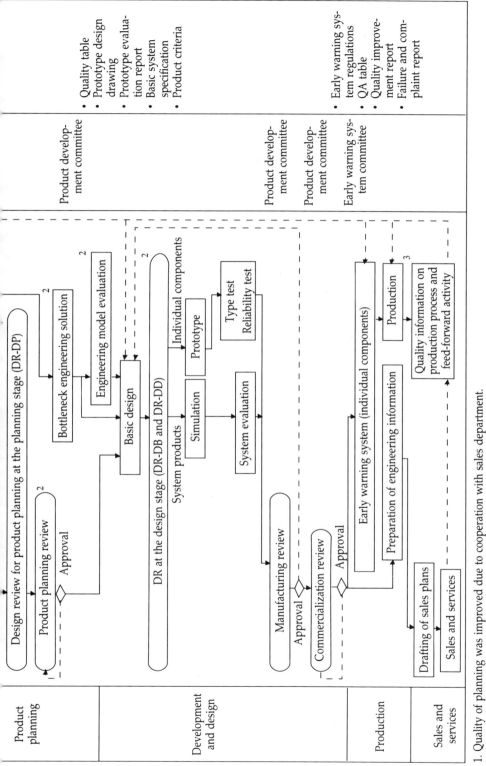

FIGURE 4.16
Development system

1. Quality of planning was improved due to cooperation with sales department.
2. Quality integration began to be successful during the early stages of planning and development.
3. Information feedback system for quality began to be successful, and quality of recipient departments in the initial process began to be upgraded.

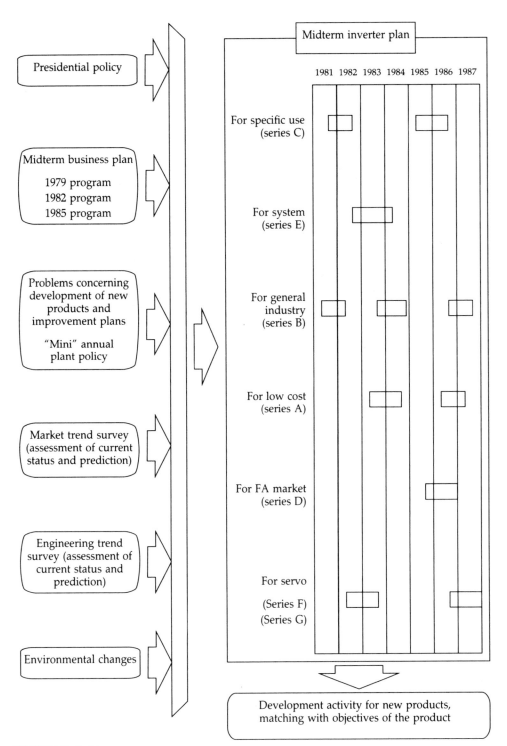

FIGURE 4.17
Inverter development strategy

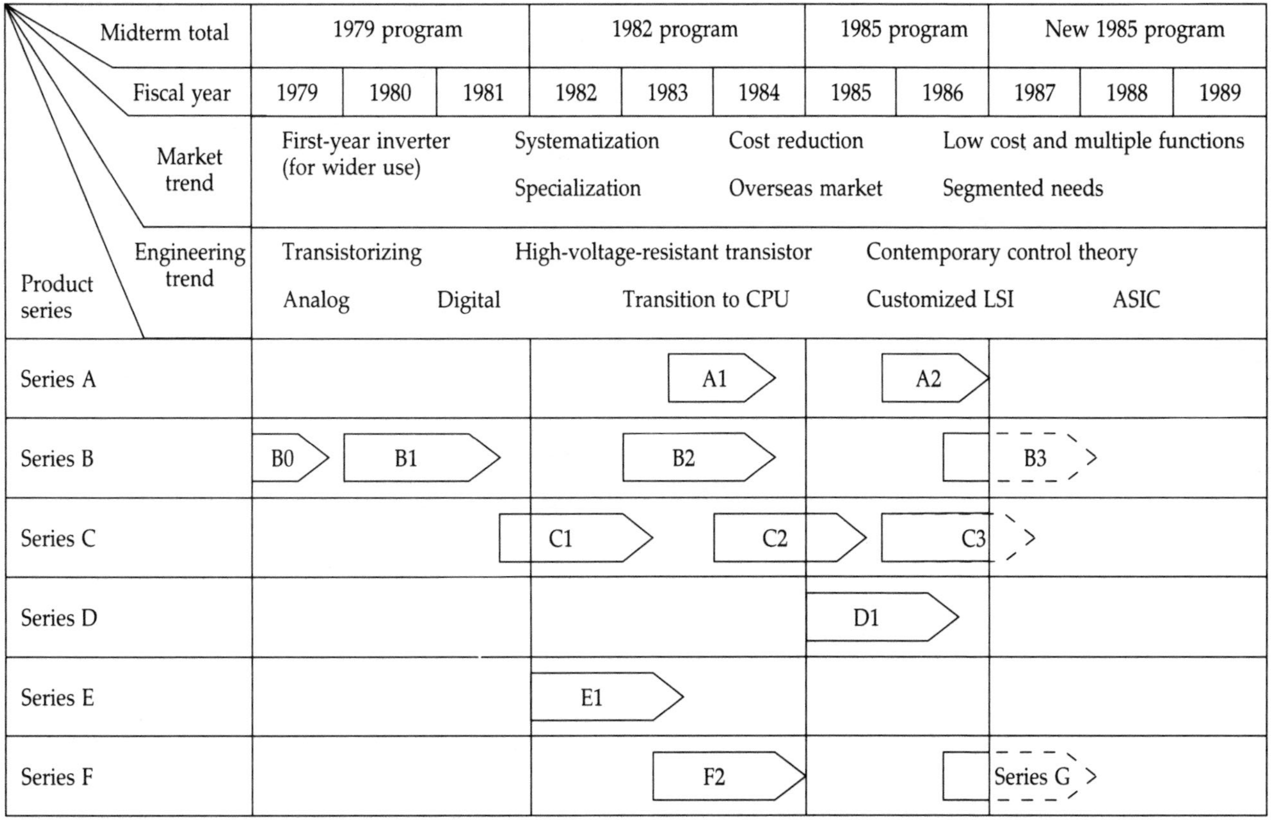

Midterm total	1979 program			1982 program			1985 program		New 1985 program		
Fiscal year	1979	1980	1981	1982	1983	1984	1985	1986	1987	1988	1989
Market trend	First-year inverter (for wider use)			Systematization Specialization			Cost reduction Overseas market		Low cost and multiple functions Segmented needs		
Engineering trend	Transistorizing Analog		Digital	High-voltage-resistant transistor Transition to CPU			Contemporary control theory Customized LSI		ASIC		
Series A						A1		A2			
Series B	B0	B1			B2				B3		
Series C			C1			C2		C3			
Series D							D1				
Series E				E1							
Series F						F2			Series G		

FIGURE 4.18
Midterm inverter development plan

FIGURE 4.19 Required-quality deployment table for series B

Required quality (Primary / Secondary / Tertiary)			01 Electrical characteristics — 011 Rating				Degree of importance	Evaluation — Company's current products	Company M	Company F	Company S	Company's new products	Featured sales points	Concept
			0111 Rated voltage	0112 Rated amperage	0113 Input capacity	0114 Efficiency								
01 Ease of plan	011 Availability of wide variety of models	Match capacity with motor model	○	○	◎		B	△	○	◎	○	◎		
		Greater capacity for 200-volt series	○	○	○		A	○	◎	◎	○	◎		
		Greater capacity for 400-volt series	○	○	○		A	○	◎	○	○	◎		
		Availability of designated series				○	A	△	○	◎	◎	◎	○	Multifunction
	012 Availability of wide variety of operation modes	Availability of reverse operation mode	○				A	△	○	○	○	◎		
		Availability of direct inching			◎		A	△	○	○	○	◎		
		Exchangeable with old products					A	△	○	△	○	◎	◎	Multifunction
02 Accurate rotation (Functions / Capacity)	021 Accuracy in start-up	High starter torque					A	△	△	△	△	◎	◎	Durable inverter
		Automatic compensation					B	△	△	△	△		◎	Durable inverter
		Greater DG² tolerance					A	△	△	△			◎	
	022 Availability of various loads	Automatic compensation					A	△	△			◎		
		Greater DG² tolerance					A	◎						

Degree of importance: A, B, B', C

Evaluation: ◎, ○, △, ×   Correlation: ◎, ○, △

Stratified degree of importance in required quality

Ranking	A	B	B'	C	Total
Numbers	86	22	40	7	155
Percent	56	14	25	5	100

112

TABLE 4.8
Analysis method for required quality

Marketing objectives	Name of series	Analysis method for required quality
To beat the competition in the low-cost market segment	Series A	• Specification analysis of competing products • Analysis and prediction of market price
To meet varied needs in the general industrial machine market	Series B	• Grasp of quality requirements by industrial group • Understanding of capacity distribution by industrial group
	Series D	• Assessment of price by industrial group • Purchase order prediction by industrial group
To beat the competition in a specific market segment	Series C	• Trend assessment of major competitors • Grasp of quality required by major customers • Grasp of specific needs
To beat the competition in specific systems	Series E	• Reorganization of system engineering, cultivated by the company over a long period of time • Discovery of actual needs through technical proposal
	Series F Series G	• Grasp of quality required by the "championship class customers" • Discovery of actual needs through technical proposal (joint development)

Product Planning

The prototype concept, quality target, and cost target established in the commercialization planning process are further reviewed in the product planning process to determine feasibility in terms of engineering, manufacturing, and delivery time. After the introduction of TQC, planning quality has been improved through the application of quality-function deployment techniques and three-dimensional management for quality, cost, and reliability (QCR). Efforts are focused on implementation of competitive product planning. (See Figure 4.20.) Three major improvements are:

1. Application of the quality application deployment table in order to enhance attractive quality

2. Use of "engineering-application" and "quality characteristic levels" deployment tables in order to establish optimum quality targets

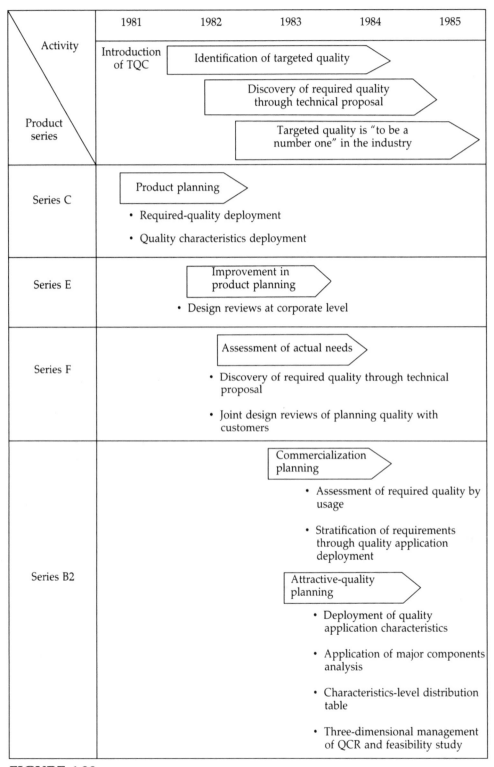

FIGURE 4.20
Improvement of product planning

3. Preliminary feasibility review of QCR targets and implementation of three-dimensional QCR management to uncover bottleneck engineering problems.

Quality Application Deployment

The specific correlation between required quality objectives and inverter applications was identified by applying a deployment table relating quality to application. Major quality characteristics were extracted in correlation with the targeted market segment. Then, quality targets were established at a higher level than those of competitors and "attractive quality" (sales points) was upgraded. (See Figure 4.21.)

Establishment of an Optimum Quality Target

In the past, characteristic values for quality targets were based on the experience and knowledge of planning personnel and on a comparative analysis of competitors' products. However, this practice emphasized conformance to special practices relevant to past problems, adjustability for various uses and types of machines, and market dominance over the competitors' products. Therefore, there was a tendency to set all characteristic values to the highest level. In order to avoid an excessively high quality level for B^2 products, matrices (engineering-to-application deployment tables) were drafted for variable-speed-drive engineering and application areas. In these matrices, several criteria were established for major drive functions, and functional level requirements for each application area were identified. (See Figure 4.22.)

Based on this matrix table, three levels for major inverter quality characteristics were established, and the required numerical quality level for each application was reviewed. Subsequently, a quality characteristic/applications deployment table was created. (See Figure 4.23.) Application of this table helped establish generic quality targets in various applicable fields. In the case of quality targets in special application fields where the quality requirements were highly functional and sophisticated, optional application methods were utilized.

Creation and application of this type of quality deployment table prevented omissions of required quality from various applications, added attractive quality that met high-grade and variable needs, and facilitated establishment of balanced target values in terms of quality, cost, and reliability.

Three-Dimensional Management of QCR at the Planning Stage

Key points for efficient development and design include a preliminary review of simultaneous realization of QCR at the planning stage, discovery

Quality characteristic/application deployment table

| Required quality | | | Alternative quality | | | Quality characteristic deployment — Electrical characteristics — 012 rating | | | | | | Quality application deployment — Application | | | | | |
Basic	Primary	Secondary	Tertiary			0121 rated voltage	0122 rated amperage	0123 electrical source capacity	0124 efficiency	0125 overload stress capacity (continuous)	0126 overload stress capacity (1 minute)	011 simple variable-speed Pump	Reciprocating pump	Fan blower	Compressor	012 multidrive Tread conveyor	Rotary
I. Functions	01 Easy to design	011 wide variety of models available	Capacity variable according to motor model			○	○	◎			○	○	○	○	○	○	○
			Greater capacity for 200 V series			○	○	○			○	○	○	○			○
			Greater capacity for 400 V series			○	○	○				○	○	○			○
			Specialized series available						◎								○
Capacity		021 wide variety of driving modes available	Reverse operation possible														
			Direct inching possible							○	○	○			○	○	○
			Interchangeable with old products							◎	◎	○	○		○	○	◎
IV service	11 after-sales service	021 accurate starting	Scope of guarantee clear														
			In-service guidance available														
			Spare parts readily available									○	○	○		○	○
		Specification values	Planning characteristics			x x x	○○○ ○○○	○○○ ○○○									
			Company M			• • •	• • •	x x x x x x	x x x x x x	• • •	• • •						
			Company F			○○○	• • •	• • •	• • •	x x x	x x x						

FIGURE 4.21
Quality characteristic/application deployment table

			Simple variable-speed drive						Actuator			
Application engineering / Alternative characteristics		Application	Pump	Reciprocating pump	Fan blower	Compressor	Scrambler	Gear pump	Bogey	Hoist run	Crane horizontal run	Crane (vertical) hoisting
Basic control system	Single drive	Speed control	◯	◯	◯	◯	◯	◯	◯	◯	◯	◯
		Electric current torque control										
	Sectional motor drive	Draw control										
		Electric current (tension) control										
		Tension control										
		Dancing roll control										
		Rated output control										
	Servo drive	Location control							◯	◯	◯	◯
		Tracking control										
Control	Speed control parameter	1:1.5 or less										
		1:3 or less	◯									
		1:10 or less	◯	◯	◯	◯	◯	◯				
		1:50 or less					△	△				
Driving	Related driving	Driving by controller	△	△	△	△	△	△				
		Helper drive										
		Interchangeable with old models	◯		◯		◯				◯	
		Prediction of purchase orders										
		Targeted market	◎	◯	◎	◯	◎		◎	◯	◯	◯

FIGURE 4.22
Engineering-to-application deployment table

FIGURE 4.23 Quality characteristic levels/applications deployment table

Quality characteristics		Items	Specification	Single variable-speed drive						Multimotor drive				Actuator		
				Pump	Reciprocating pump	Fan blower	Compressor	Scrambler	Gear pump	Tread conveyor	Rotary	Calender	Rotary cutter	Bogey	Hoist run	Crane horizontal run
		Degree of importance		A	B	A	B	A	C	B	A	B	B	A	A	A
Basic part	Electrical characteristics	Source voltage	180 256V	○	○	○	○	○	○	○	○	○	○	○	○	○
		Input power factor	Greater than 95%	○	○	○	○	○	○	○	○	○	○	○	○	○
		Inverter efficiency	Greater than 95%	○	○	○	○	○	○	○	○	○	○	○	○	○
		Output frequency accuracy	1%	○	○	○	△	△	△		○	△	△		○	
			0.1%	△	△	△	○	○	○	○	△	○	○	○		○
			0.01%										△			
		Maximum frequency	120Hz	○	○	○	○	○	○	○	○	○	○	○	○	○
			240Hz		△							△				
			360Hz						○							
		Frequency analyzer capacity	1/256	○	○	○	○	△	○	△	○	△		○	○	△
			1/1024	○	△	○	○	○	○	○	△	○	○	△	○	○
Option	Added XYZ	Interfering with instrumentation signals		○				○								
		AVR functions							○							

of problems and bottleneck engineering, and identification of specific solutions.

Design reviews are conducted to discover problems and to evaluate improvement measures through the consolidated knowledge and experience of professionals. Plans to adopt new technology and new parts were reviewed to predict reliability problems through FMEA and FTA. Figure 4.24 shows a three-dimensional management system of quality, cost, and reliability.

Solutions to Bottleneck Engineering Problems

Application of Statistical Methods

Improvement activities begin in the development stage of bottleneck engineering problems discovered during the planning stage. It is important to establish feasible techniques and engineering during this stage not only in terms of functions and characteristics but also in terms of reliability.

Many of the bottleneck engineering problems are difficult to solve by theoretical analysis alone, and development activities are often administered with verification of functions and capacities through partial electromagnetic experiments. It is important that the circuit constant is identified through contributing factors: dispersion of a given component's characteristics, deterioration by aging, power-source fluctuations, impact of temperature changes, and product reliability. Therefore, the company has not only been applying specific techniques of theoretical analysis and experiments but also statistical methods, such as design of experiments and parameter design, so that bottleneck engineering problems can be solved efficiently. Table 4.9 and Figure 4.25 show a sample application of statistical methods, applied to Product B.

Three-Dimensional Management of QCR during the Development and Design Stages

A three-dimensional management system for quality, cost, and reliability was constructed for the accurate and efficient application of techniques during the development and design stages to realize QCR targets that were established during the planning stage. Consistent application of the system from the conceptual design stage to the manufacturing review stage has proven to be effective. (See Figure 4.26.)

Inverter functions were divided into basic groups, and QCR targets that were identified in the product planning stage were assigned to each group. Assignment of quality targets was used to satisfy required functions and capabilities for each basic functional group through which requirements of

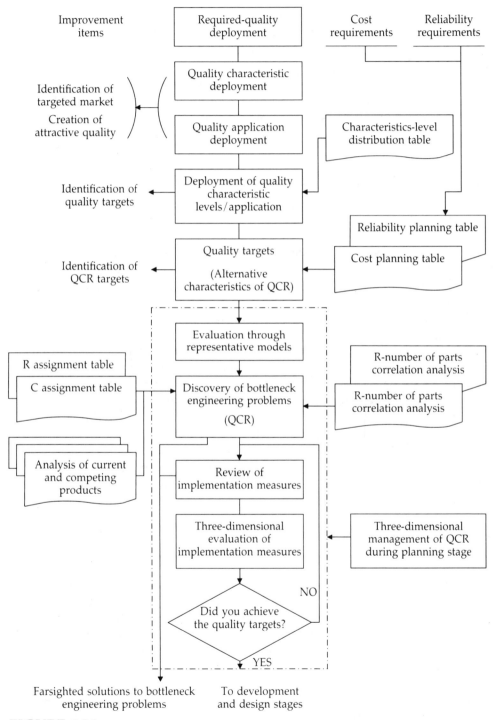

FIGURE 4.24
Three-dimensional management of quality, cost, and reliability (QCR) during the planning stage

TABLE 4.9
Sample application of statistical methods

No.	Themes	Techniques
1	Preventive measures against racing condition	Experiments by orthogonal arrays (L_{32})
2	Establishment of parallel connection engineering for transistors	Experiments by orthogonal arrays (L_{32} and L_{27})
3	Optimum design for impedance unit	Experiments by orthogonal arrays (L_{32})
4	Confirmation of DCCT selection criteria	*t*-test and estimation
5	Determination of constant for DC-DC converter	Experiments by orthogonal arrays (L_{16})
6	Reduction of dispersion for analog detection circuit	Parameter design and tolerance design

the inverter's functions and capabilities were also satisfied. Cost target assignment took place through cost analysis of similar products and application of the cost planning table. Reliability target assignment was possible through the application of correlation analysis of the number of parts and the failure rate, and use of fault tree diagrams.

Information relating to current standard and alternative circuits, such as functions, capabilities, cost, and reliability, was recorded in an evaluation table for QCR according to basic function group. After comparative analysis and reviews, simultaneous pursuits and trade-offs of QCR were made. Through this process, an optimum circuit was selected for each cross-functional group, and whether the inverter's QCR target could be achieved was evaluated by reconciliation. This overall evaluation process helped to clarify bottleneck engineering problems concerning function, capabilities, cost, and reliability, and provided incentives for problem-solving activities.

Due to miniaturization and cost reduction, joint efforts to address bottleneck engineering problems with parts manufacturers have become very popular in recent years. In the event of joint development, establishment of clear targets and implementation of evaluation for QCR is very important.

Integration of Quality during the Development and Design Stages

A detailed product design is made after completion of the bottleneck engineering evaluation and establishment of the QCR planning target. During this stage, it is necessary to prevent any omissions in quality (function and characteristics) and to integrate complex reliability; success or

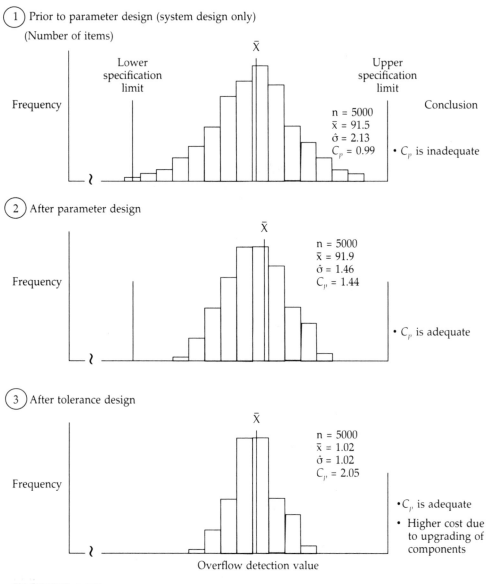

FIGURE 4.25
Sample implementation of parameter design

failure at this stage predicts initial quality and reliability for the entire life of the product.

The company vigorously applied all available reliability techniques and engineering know-how, utilizing trouble-shooting experience accumulated over a number of years. It ensured that every possible effort was made to prevent omissions and errors. (See Figure 4.27.)

This type of test included not only quality targets (function and characteristics) but also reliability, using prototype models. The reliability test included an "abusing" test—a test to make sure that no operational errors, no abnormal action, and no equipment damage would result under any combination of the worst possible conditions throughout the life of the product. Also included was a test to verify the inverter's "robustness," that is, to check for operational errors triggered by noise and by component degradation due to the repetition of operations. (See Figure 4.28.)

Improvement in Production Preparation

In order to ensure integration of conformance quality and design quality in the manufacturing process without any failures, premanufacturing preparation is required. Manufacturing drawings and a supplementary QA table are drafted in advance so that information on quality is accurately communicated without any omissions. Based on this information, the design, manufacturing engineering, manufacturing, and inspection departments cooperatively undertake the following key activities (see Figure 4.29):

1. Preparation of QC process chart and work standards from the manufacturing QA table, and preparation of tools for foolproofing
2. Development of test standards, manufacturing test equipment, and test procedures from the test QA table.

An early trouble management system involving all departments has been incorporated into the initial stage of the production of new products to ensure early discovery of quality, cost, and delivery problems so that they may be corrected.

Feedback of Quality-Related Information to an Early Process

The early warning system is in place for all new products over a period of one year after market entry. The purpose of this system is to assess all information concerning failures and customer complaints in the market during the early stage and to stabilize quality promptly through vigorous quality improvement activities. If critical quality problems are uncovered,

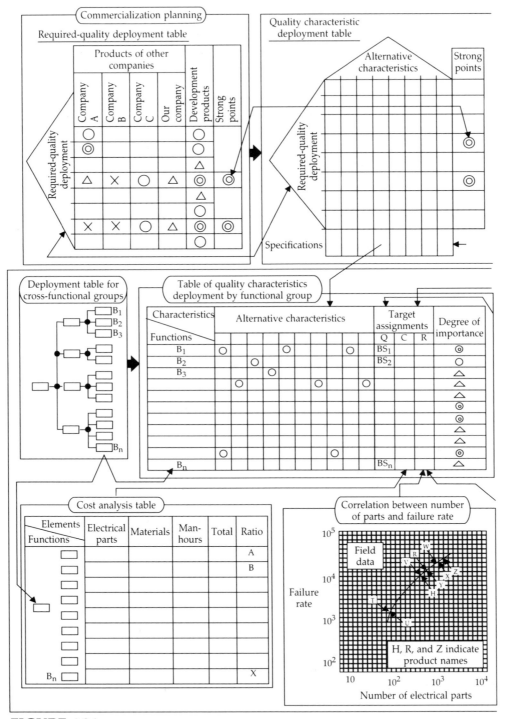

FIGURE 4.26
Three-dimensional QCR management system

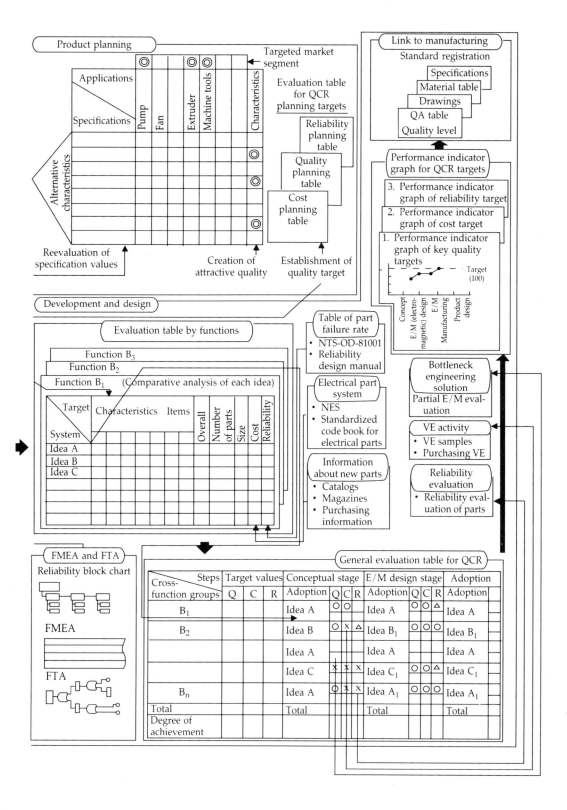

Product names	Development year	Reliability prediction	Reliability block diagram	FMEA	FTA	Design review	Reliability test (test evaluation of new parts)	Redundancy system	Deleting	Foolproof system	Fail-safe system	Trade-off	Maintainability
Series B₁	1981	○		○			○		○				
Series C₁	1981	○		○	○	○	○		○				
Series F₂	1983	○				○	○		○		○		○
Series E₁	1983	○	○	○	○	○	○		○	○	○		○
Series B₂	1984	○	○	○	○	○	○		○	○		○	○
Series D₁	1985	○	○	○	○	○	○	○	○	○	○	○	○
Series C₃	1985	○	○	○	○	○	○		○	○	○	○	○

(Reliability design columns: Reliability prediction through Trade-off)

FIGURE 4.27
Implementation status of reliability design

Stress No.	Temperature			Noise				Electrical source voltage			Load factor		Operation mode		
	0°C	25°C	45°C	None	Pulse	Relay	Wave distortions	+10%	0%	−10%	0%	100%	100%	10%	Acceleration
30			●			●		●				●	●		

FIGURE 4.28
Sample "abusing test"

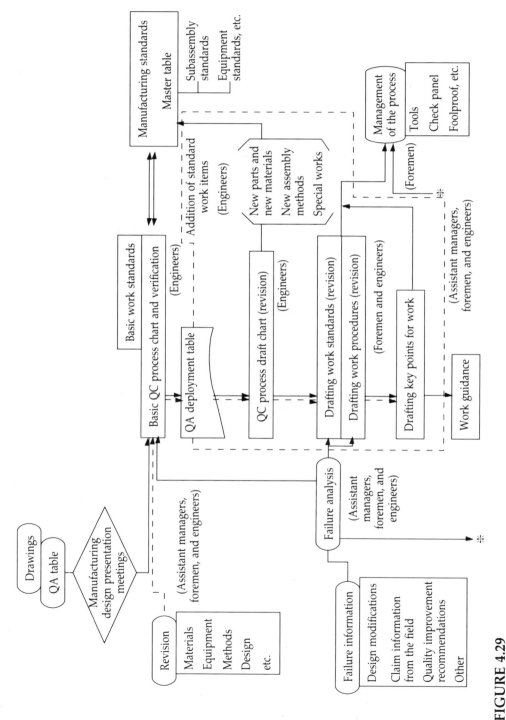

FIGURE 4.29
Production preparation through QA table deployment

not only is recurrence prevented but system improvements for development and daily work are pursued on the basis of identification of problem areas during the development. (See Figure 4.30.)

RESULTS OF CROSS-FUNCTIONAL MANAGEMENT

It is clear that corporate quality improvement and sustained capabilities in developing winning products are not accomplished overnight in a competitive and mature business. Problems concerning the process for each development theme must be uncovered and improvement measures applied to the subsequent process. Also, practice of PDCA (plan-do-check-act) must be repeated for continued improvement in development activity.

Development of new products through cross-functional plant management is continuously carried out to improve the system of development activity, to improve development work, and to replicate improvements. Consequently, a consistent system to ensure quality from the development stage through the final product has been established and the following results achieved.

1. Development themes were prioritized, linking to the midterm management plan.
2. Quality of planning, attractive quality, and quality conformance were improved.
3. Early solution of bottleneck engineering problems became possible, and delays in development delivery dates were reduced.
4. Quality was consistently integrated from the early stages of development and design, and early problems in new products were significantly reduced.
5. Development of new products with a good balance of quality, cost, and reliability became possible.

CONCLUSION

As stated earlier, the ability to develop new products at the plant improved thanks to cross-functional management. However, the business environment has been changing rapidly, with unfavorable foreign exchange rates against the yen, trade frictions, and the restructuring of the manufacturing industry. Engineering in electronics, control technology, and new material development have been advancing by leaps and bounds.

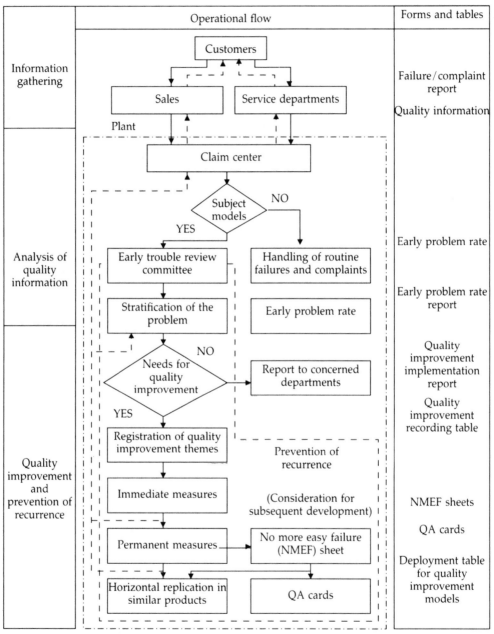

FIGURE 4.30
Early problem management system

The market for variable-speed drives has matured and customers have been constantly seeking new values. Corporate survival and growth depend on the creation of these new values and sustaining competition in the marketplace. We must be committed to creating an effective system for new product development through the practice of PDCA and continuous improvement.

5

Quality Assurance and Cross-Functional Management

Quality Assurance Activity at Yaskawa Electric Manufacturing Company, Ltd.
Kiyoshi Yokoyama

COMPANY OVERVIEW

Yaskawa Electric Company was founded in 1915 by Daigoro Yaskawa and has been a thriving manufacturer and distributor of industrial electrical motors and control instruments ever since. From the time of its founding, the company has provided heavy electrical machinery to the steel, chemical, and machine industries through the application of a unique electric motor technology. The company's "mechatronics" products, which meet factory automation needs in the domestic and overseas markets, have been provided in recent years through high utilization of electronics technology. A key product, the super-efficient motion control, combines a high-capacity servo motor with microelectronics. It is highly regarded as one of the pioneering products in the engineering world; it made mechatronics products possible, paving the way for robotics. In 1984 the company held capital amounting to some ¥10.6 billion, employed approximately 4,500 people, and grossed some ¥112.3 billion.

CROSS-FUNCTIONAL MANAGEMENT AND QUALITY ASSURANCE

Cross-functional management at Yaskawa began with the introduction of TQC, the reorganization of its existing structure, and the establishment of important generic management activities and a staff support office for the general promotion of cross-functional management. Since then, the cross-functional management system has been reorganized to identify departmental responsibilities. (See Figure 5.1.)

The company's cross-functional management addresses two characteristic areas: (1) generic functions, including quality assurance and cost control, and (2) basic line functions of sales departments and plants, such as manufacturing and sales. (See Figure 5.2.)

In addition, the concept of "management by individual product" is closely linked with efficient management of specialty merchandise. (See Figure 5.3.)

Corporate vision and policy with regard to the quality assurance function are clarified under the leadership of a coordinator. Prioritized problems are acted upon with companywide cooperation, and a quality assurance system by product is upgraded.

QUALITY ASSURANCE ACTIVITY

Currently, quality assurance activities are of two major types: creating "attractive quality" and manufacturing only products of the highest quality. I wish to discuss how the company, a custom-order manufacturer, ensures the attractive quality of its products in every department from the earliest stages of product development.

Fundamentals of Quality Assurance

It is the practice of the company to develop basic quality assurance policy, midterm policy, and short-term policy in accordance with management's perception of the corporate charter, and to commit itself to customer service through steady quality improvement. (See Figure 5.4.)

Quality Assurance in the Developmental Stage: Targeting for "Attractive Quality"

With "Quality Engineering at Yaskawa" as its motto, the company has been responding to specific customer needs through the application of a unique quality of engineering. It has developed many products before its competitors and has gained customer confidence and market share by producing world-class quality products. However, there was room for improvement by systematically identifying needs in the overall marketplace and providing appropriate products. The economy slowed down as a consequence of the oil crisis, and the market began to change by leaps and

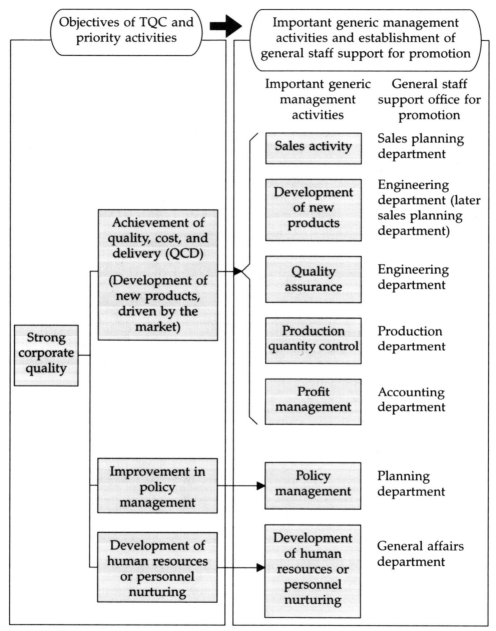

FIGURE 5.1
Important generic management activities

Departments

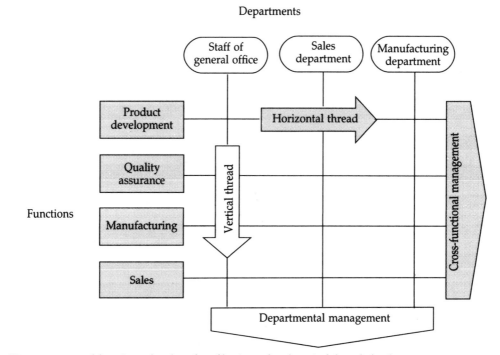

*Departments and functions play the roles of horizontal and vertical threads for the company.

Purposes of cross-functional management: to review interdepartmental issues that require companywide cooperation and coordination; to identify problems of each department, taking into account correlation with the company as a whole; to promote implementation; to follow up; and to act.

Purpose of departmental management: to implement assigned cross-functional management activities in a specific manner and to bring about results based on a thorough understanding of cross-functional management.

FIGURE 5.2
Conceptual chart of departmental management and cross-functional management

bounds because of growth in the microelectronics industry. Changes in the economy have occurred so fast that the existence and growth of manufacturing have depended heavily on the success or failure of new product development.

Reorganization of the business structure was planned to expand the mechatronics business through the establishment of durable corporate quality that would respond to any changes in business environment, as stated at the time TQC was introduced. Consequently, expansion objectives were targeted in developing new products for the growing mechatronics market.

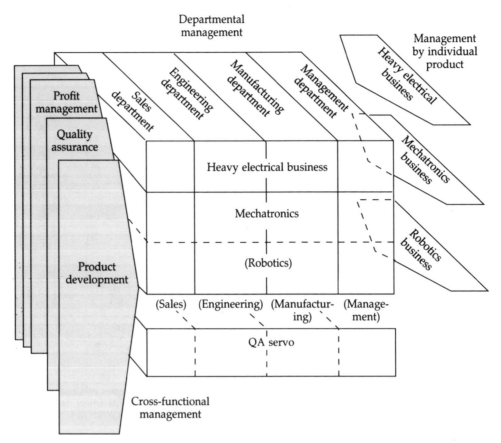

FIGURE 5.3
Cross-functional management and management by individual products

Management vision	Basic quality assurance policy
The mission of this company is to contribute to the development of the community and to human welfare through its business activities. It commits itself to the realization of this mission as follows. 1. It is committed to the development and improvement of world-class engineering with a quality orientation. 2. It strives to improve management efficiency and to secure the necessary profits for corporate survival and growth. 3. It responds to customer needs in accordance with market forces and promotes total customer service.	The company practices quality-oriented management vigorously and provides products that lead to its customers' trust and satisfaction.

FIGURE 5.4
Management vision and basic quality assurance policy

Objectives included the development of new products in a timely manner through the "market-in" (customer oriented) concept and development of new products to ensure a dominant market share well in advance of the competition.

Therefore, developmental problems relating to new products were analyzed, and market trends and needs were quickly and accurately predicted through quality analysis in the marketplace, which is considered a priority activity. Commercialization planning was strengthened by searching for new technology, engineering trend analysis, and improvement of "head start" activities. (See Figure 5.5.) Specific priority activities are discussed below. (See Table 5.1.)

Improvement in Information Gathering, Accumulation, Analysis, and Application of Results

Traditionally, most market information has been gathered through customer contacts and contract negotiations, then utilized as needed. However, this method lacks continuity and makes it difficult to accumulate meaningful data.

After the introduction of TQC, the sales department developed new ways to gather information by market, by customer, and by product instead of using biased information gathered from special-interest customers. Subsequently, a new system was put into place to assess market trends by market subsegments through customer surveys of product trends. (See Figure 5.6.)

General information was gathered from marketing cards (see Figure 5.7) and customer files (see Figure 5.8), then fed into an ongoing data-gathering system. It was then filed, and analyzed by the commercialization planning and product planning departments of the plant responsible for the application of commercialization planning.

Quality Improvement in Commercialization Planning

Traditionally, planning for new products was carried out by plant engineering departments and tailored to the needs of a limited customer group. It was, therefore, inadequate in assessing the actual needs of a more general customer group. As a result, sales tended to be weak and improvement in products was constantly needed. To address such problems, a commercialization planning system was introduced that included a commercialization planning section incorporated into the sales department, with the department head concurrently head of the section. In addition, the system promoted improvement by structural reorganization through improved cooperation between the sales department and the plant.

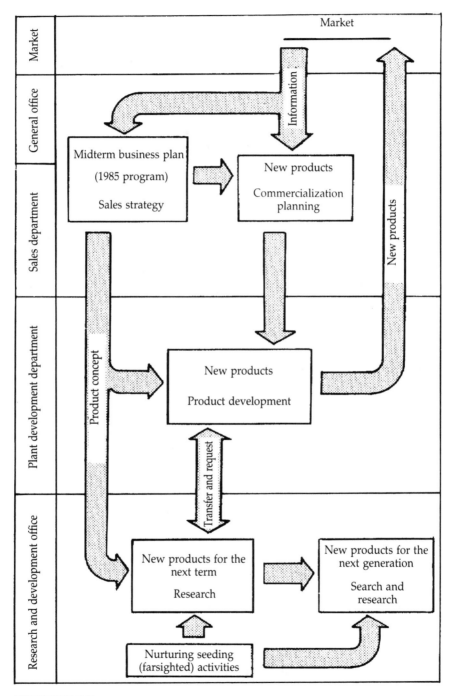

FIGURE 5.5
Basic system chart for product development

TABLE 5.1
Development of new products

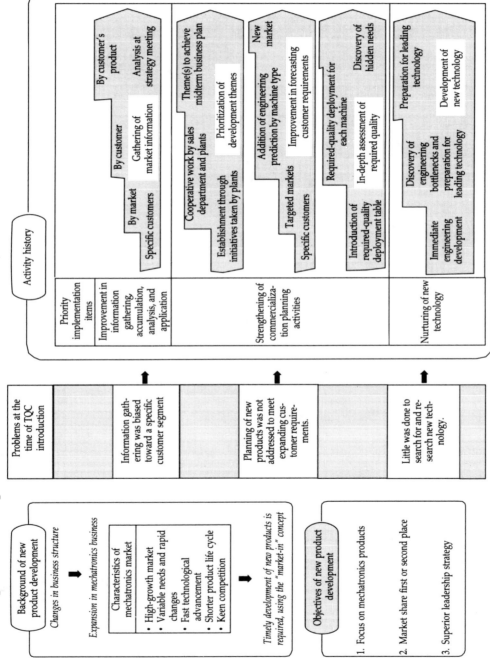

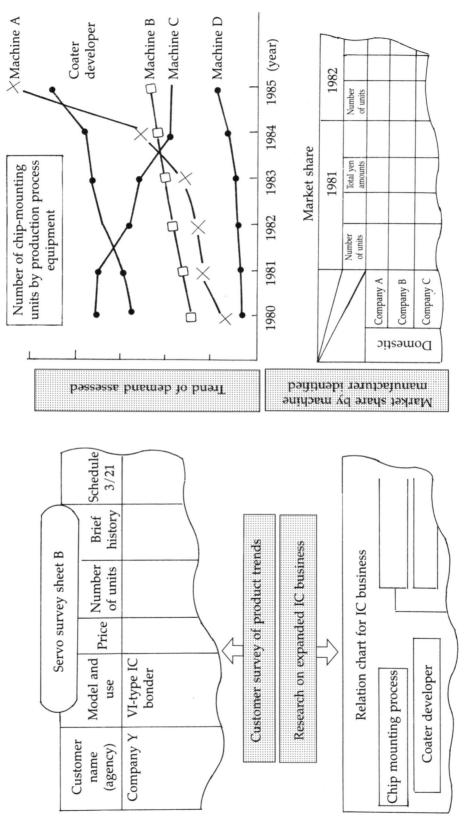

FIGURE 5.6
Market trend analysis: IC products manufactured by semiconductor machine manufacturers

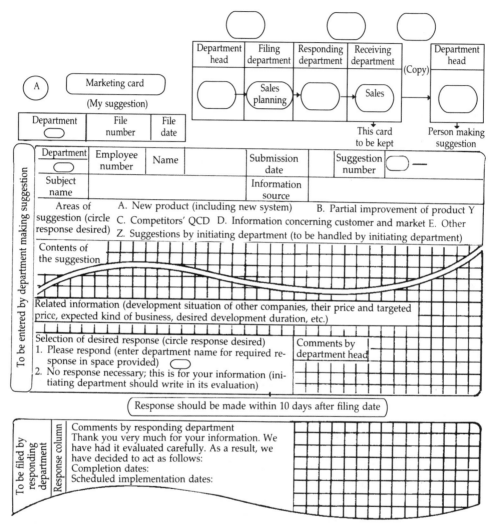

FIGURE 5.7
Marketing card

Understanding of required quality was improved by increasing the number of items in the required-quality deployment table (see Figure 5.9) and by in-depth analysis of those items by market segment and by usage. In addition, information concerning latent customer needs was vigorously sought by making repeated suggestions to customers. Comparative analysis of competitors' products and reidentification of sales points were completed. These activities have made it possible to establish targeted quality with balanced quality, cost, and delivery. Targeted quality was

```
                    ┌──────────────────────────┐
────────────────────│    Customer file index   │──────────────────────────
                    └──────────────────────────┘
```

(Items)	(Forms)
1. Customer summary (1)	CC-1
Customer summary (2)	2
Customer summary (3)	3
② Product survey by customer	4
3. Machine used for product Y	5
4. Delivery performance for product Y	6
5. Purchase order prediction sheet	7
6. Share table	8
7. In-depth analysis of one sample case	9
⑧ Development of new products through customer participation	10
9. Claims situations	11
10. Record of information about product Y quality	12
11. Customer-required items	13
12. "Information sheet" file	
13. Miscellaneous information file	

FIGURE 5.8
Sample customer file
Information about each product was gathered through customer participation.

catalogued in advance and the results were verified through solicitation of customer feedback, using the periodic customer monitoring report. (See Figure 5.10.)

Development of New Technology

Development efforts at the time TQC was introduced were focused on existing products competing in the market over the short term. Therefore, activities for medium-to-long-range research and engineering development lacked continuity, and leading technology was eroding. The development of new technology was carried out through development of such component engineering as microcomputer, servo, and detection engineering. The results were replicated in development departments at the various plants. In addition, efforts to discover engineering bottlenecks and to solve head-start problems were made by the plant development departments at the same time. (See Figure 5.11.)

The need for long-range prediction of engineering trends and development of new technology became increasingly important as development activity for commercialization progressed. Companywide engineering subcommittees were formed to review every major engineering area, to attempt long-range prediction of engineering trends, to search for long-range new technology, and to solidify research activities. In addition to internal efforts to develop new technology, external and cooperative ef-

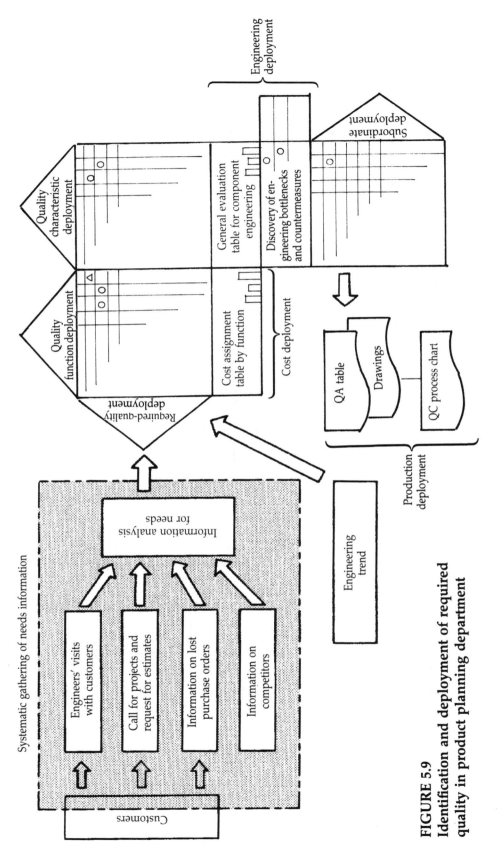

FIGURE 5.9
Identification and deployment of required quality in product planning department

Periodic customer monitor report (for technological trend prediction)

Items	Contents			
	Periodic customer monitoring report			Draft date
	(For industry trend prediction)			
	Customer name	Kind of business	Survey date and time	
	Subject model name	Name	Investigator	
	Survey purposes	Related products we make	Related sales departments in our company	
Needs trend — 1. Customer needs; 2. Overseas needs	Business changes on demand side	Overseas	Domestic	
Future trends — 1. Domestic trendsetting; 2. Overseas trendsetting				
Product development trend — 1. Trendsetting based on existing needs; 2. Trendsetting based on predicted needs; 3. Trendsetting based on existing and predicted needs	Overseas and exports	Domestic industry and other companies	Customer	

FIGURE 5.10
Periodic customer monitor report

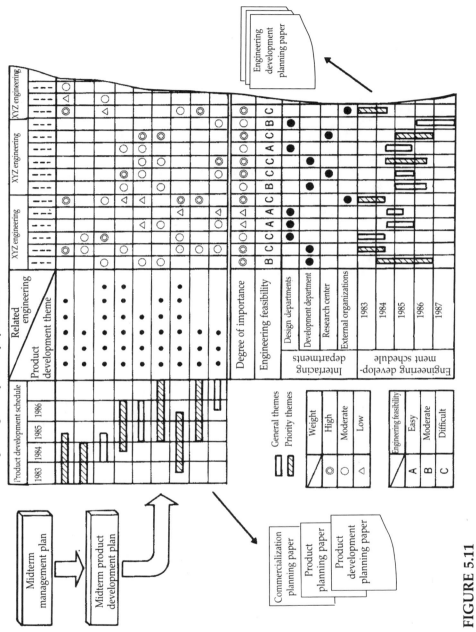

FIGURE 5.11
Midterm product development plan and engineering development plan

TABLE 5.2
Companywide quality assurance system chart (mechatronics products)

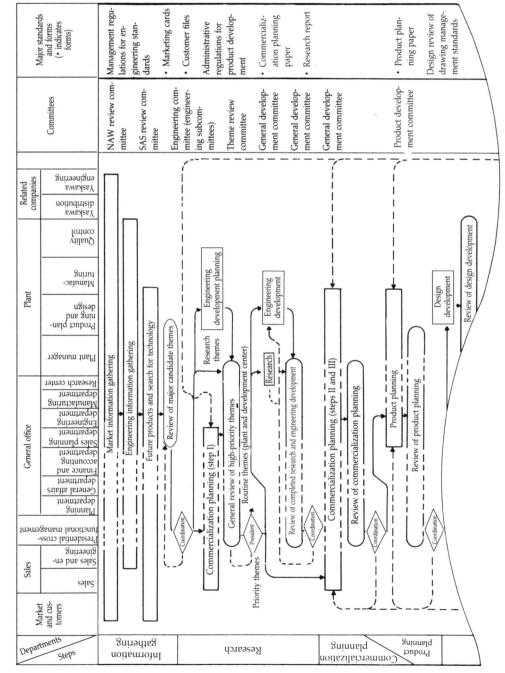

Steps / Departments	Market and customers	Sales		Presidential cross-functional management	General office						Research center	Plant manager	Plant				Quality control	Related companies		Committees	Major standards and forms (• indicates forms)
		Sales	Sales and engineering		Planning department	General affairs department	Finance and accounting department	Sales planning department	Engineering department	Manufacturing department	Research center	Plant manager	Product planning and design	Manufacturing			Yaskawa distribution	Yaskawa engineering		
Information gathering													Market information gathering							NAW review committee	Management regulations for engineering standards
													Engineering information gathering							SAS review committee	
													Future products and search for technology							Engineering committee (engineering subcommittees)	• Marketing cards
											Review of major candidate themes										• Customer files
Research													Research themes	Engineering development planning						Theme review committee	Administrative regulations for product development
				Coordination	Commercialization planning (step I)															General development committee	
					General review of high-priority themes															General development committee	• Commercialization planning paper
	Priority themes			President	Routine themes (plant and development center)						Research	Engineering development								General development committee	• Research report
					Review of completed research and engineering development																
Commercialization / Product planning				Coordination	Commercialization planning (steps II and III)																
					Review of commercialization planning															Product development committee	• Product planning paper
				Coordination	Product planning																
					Review of product planning								Design development								Design review of drawing management standards
				Coordination									Review of design development								

forts were made with domestic research institutes and domestic and overseas branches of various engineering firms so that information about new technology could be collected and research on the most advanced technology maintained.

Example: Development of New Servo Product

With the objective of developing attractive quality, a quality assurance system was reorganized and improved at the development stage. (See Table 5.2.) By utilizing the system, new servo products were developed through the teamwork of the sales department, plant, and general office. (See Figure 5.12.)

Quality Assurance for Individually Subcontracted Products in the Sales Department: Discovery of Required Quality in the New Market

"Accurate Prediction and Aggressive Sales" was used in the sales department as a motto to identify changes in customer needs. Customers and market needs were analyzed in advance, and new products and new markets were aggressively cultivated with the close cooperation of the engineering and manufacturing departments. (See Figure 5.13.)

One of the key quality assurance activities of the sales department is to collect and transmit information concerning customer requirements quickly and accurately to the plants. The majority of customer complaints originate in an incorrect response to customer requirements. In practice, the sales department, which interfaces with customers if and when such problems are encountered, is not proactive. Consequently, information on quality in the files was not being utilized to the fullest extent and quality was not built into products in the early stages. A required-quality table was created in recognition of the importance of required-quality deployment from the time customer complaints are first received. Furthermore, the estimation check sheet (see Figure 5.14) was reorganized to respond accurately to customer inquiries about products for which assignable quality is generally available at the time of estimation. However, specification changes frequently occurred after acceptance of the order due to the lack of recognition of exact customer wants. To discover these customer wants, the system suggestion program was implemented and true customer needs were earnestly sought. (See Figure 5.15.)

In addition, engineering system presentation meetings were held in order to make the system suggestion program attractive; the results of the meetings were evaluated using check sheets. Meetings with customers were also held, leading to improved results, and a communication system

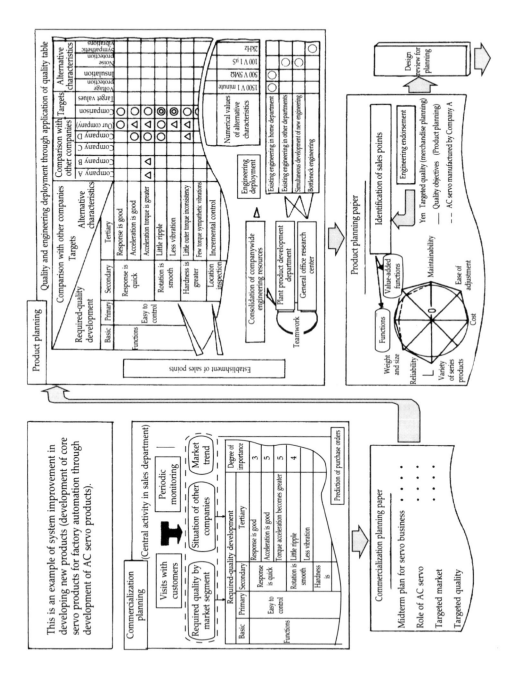

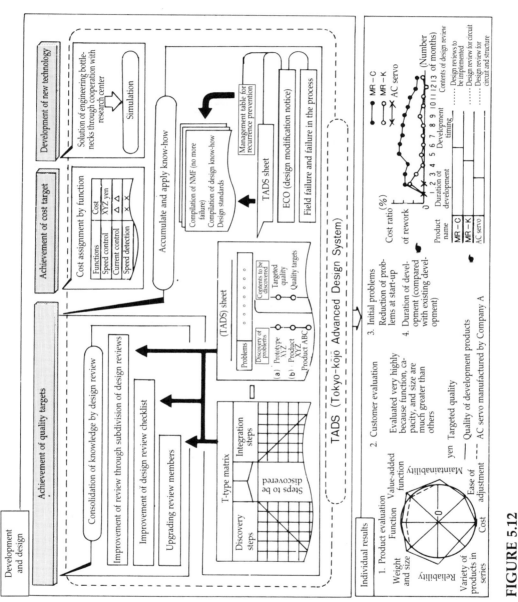

FIGURE 5.12
Development of new servo product (AC servo)

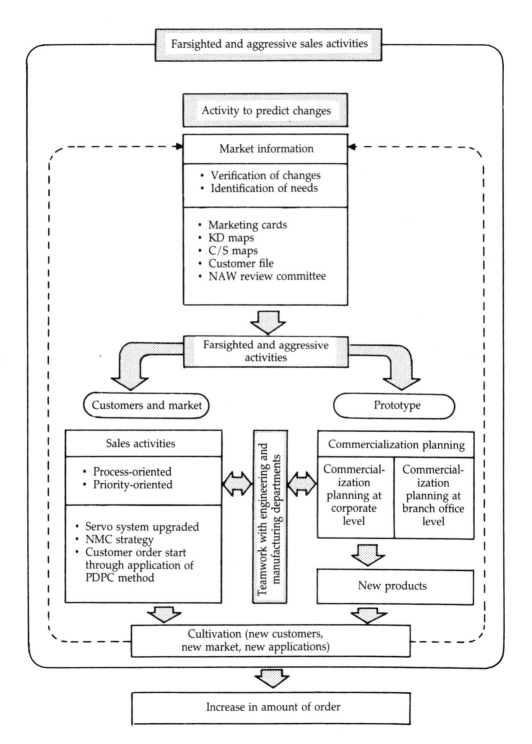

FIGURE 5.13
Farsighted and aggressive sales activities

		Machine specifications
Type	1. Fourdrinier	
	2. Cylinder	
	3. Other	SYM. FORM
Width	Wire width	5300 mm
	Paper width	4780 mm
Paper	Paper	NEWSPAPER
	Weight	45 ~ 70g/m^2

FIGURE 5.14
Estimation check sheet

was established using a QA sheet so that accurate requirements of the initial processing departments could be transmitted to subsequent processing departments. (See Figure 5.16.)

The correlation chart–PDPC sheet (see Figure 5.17) was utilized to solve engineering problems, while the engineering diagram (see Figure 5.18)—intended to be used as a deployment diagram for the control system—was established for practical application by every employee.

Standardization Activities

Diversified customer needs require flexible response in the form of unique ideas, high reliability, and quality service. The company's basic

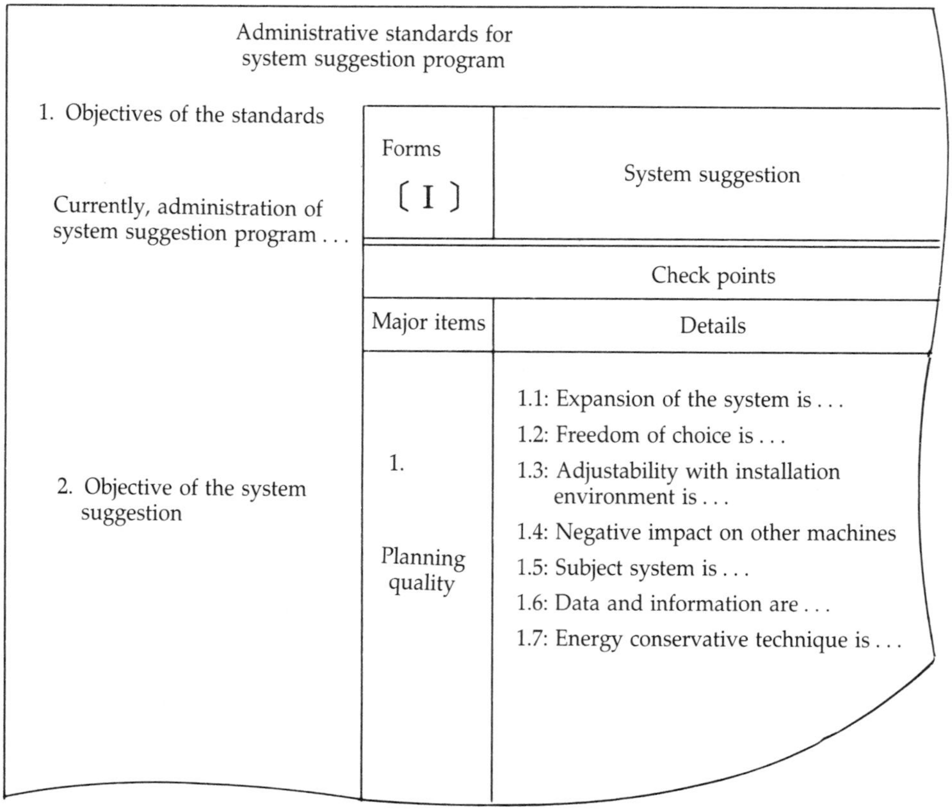

Administrative standards for system suggestion program		
1. Objectives of the standards	Forms [I]	System suggestion
Currently, administration of system suggestion program . . .		
		Check points
	Major items	Details
2. Objective of the system suggestion	1. Planning quality	1.1: Expansion of the system is . . . 1.2: Freedom of choice is . . . 1.3: Adjustability with installation environment is . . . 1.4: Negative impact on other machines 1.5: Subject system is . . . 1.6: Data and information are . . . 1.7: Energy conservative technique is . . .

FIGURE 5.15
Format for system suggestion program

policy has been to respond to diversified customer needs with standardization and high reliability. In order to make this a reality in the company's products—from individual components to system products—efforts have been made to establish a system to provide a stable supply of high-reliability products, including establishment of the appropriate quality levels for components, standardization of hardware, and promotion of commonality in hardware through software improvements.

Sample standardization activity is discussed below. (See Figure 5.19.) Our company's system products are used for all sorts of industrial machines, and requirements vary greatly. The requirements are stratified by usages and by customer segments. These requirements are further stratified by fixed parts and variable parts. Commonality in hardware has been promoted through software improvements, and standardization to meet the diversified requirements has been implemented. Consequently, quality and reliability have been upgraded through reduction in the number of components.

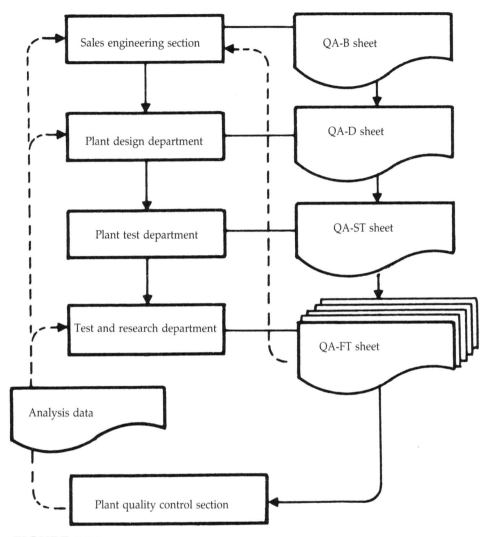

FIGURE 5.16
Communication system for required-quality information

SUMMARY

Diverse customer needs and accelerated technological advancement are making development cycles for new products shorter and competition for quality keener. In response to these changes, a quality assurance system, management system, and standardization have been constantly improved by all departments. It is our intention to put this system into practice, to learn from failures, and to provide quality products through long-range planning of quality management.

Sales activities were systematically and concurrently implemented with process control, applying the correlation chart and PDPC sheets.

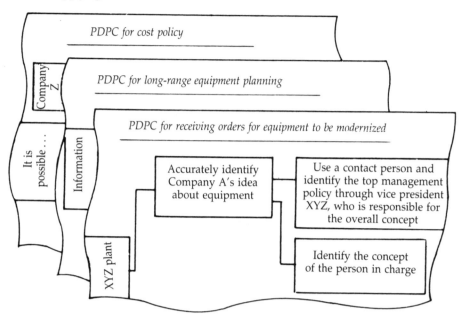

A sample PDPC is shown in receiving orders for equipment to be modernized.

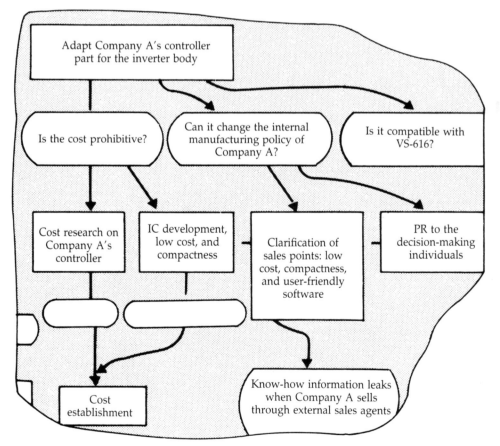

FIGURE 5.17
Correlation chart–PDPC sheet

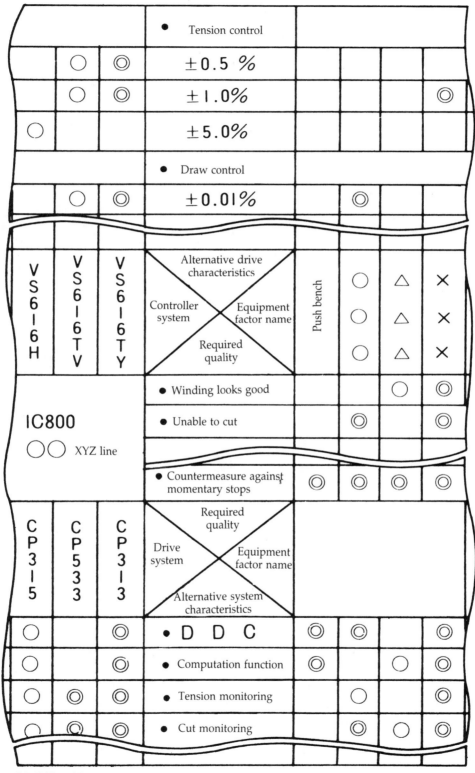

FIGURE 5.18
Engineering diagram

Problems	Standardization		
	First step ⟹	Second step ⟹	Third step
1. All-purpose system products have been re-organized; however, response to diversified needs is weak, and orders for products cannot be increased because of limited usability and customer interest	Identify by functional system (construction) elements of individually ordered products. Stratify and standardize them (e.g., parts, module units, intermediary products)	Standardization of system products and intermediary products to promote cost effectiveness and optimal functioning	Standardization aimed at flexible responses to diversified needs
2. More orders for non-standardized products are being received; consequently, product quality depends largely on the engineering skill of the designers	• Improvement of manufacturing efficiency • Consideration of hardware development through application engineering • Shift to multifunctions in a single model • Response to diversified needs through maximum combinations and minimum models	• Cost minimization • Separation of configurations according to fixed or variable parts and response to diversified needs through variable parts and options • Reduction of number of parts through expanded use of fixed parts	• Partial substitution of software for fixed and variable parts, and flexible responses to diversified customer requirements by software • Reliability upgrade through reduction of number of parts
	Number of components for variable-speed drive system, a configuration factor of system products (Example) Number of components 1,400 items	Number of components for variable-speed drive system Number of components 900 items	Number of components for variable-speed drive system Number of components 400 items

FIGURE 5.19
Example of standardization

Quality Assurance Activity and Cross-Functional Management at Aisin A.W. Company, Ltd.
Haruki Sugihara

INTRODUCTION

The company was established as a joint venture by Aisin Seiki (formerly Aichi Kogyo) and Borg Warner Corporation in May 1969, and is a specialized manufacturer of automatic transmissions for automobiles.

Due to the rapid growth of the demand for cars in the domestic market, safe and comfortable automobiles were required. Aichi Kogyo started to produce automatic transmissions in 1961—the first manufactured in Japan. The need to develop competitive products for the overseas automobile market came at a later time to meet the increased export of automobiles. Aisin Seiki and Borg Warner, which had enjoyed friendly relations for over ten years, entered into a joint venture to manufacture automatic transmissions to meet the needs of the growing automobile industry. The respective needs of the two companies—introduction of advanced technology from overseas and entry into the Japanese market—were thus both satisfied.

At its inception, the company faced many difficult challenges because of the rapidly changing business environment. TQC was introduced in 1973 with the management philosophy "quality first" to upgrade quality and strengthen the company. Coping with difficulties, the company made efforts to meet the market requirement goals of management by utilizing the participation of all employees.

However, the company's business environment deteriorated further in the 1980s because of global compact car "wars" and the transition to front-wheel-drive vehicles. The V85 program, a management strategy, was introduced to deal with this crisis. Total productive maintenance was introduced in 1983 to supersede the V85 program and to provide a strategy for corporate survival. To date, the company has vigorously engaged in quality assurance through three core programs: "Automatics" (the company's own management information system), reliability management, and productive maintenance.

These activities led to the development and manufacture of entirely new products, and success in selling products to new customers in both domestic and overseas markets. The company was awarded the Deming Application Prize in 1977—the first time the prize was ever awarded to a joint venture. The Japan Quality Control Medal followed in 1982, and the Productive Maintenance Award for Plant Excellence in 1985.

The company has since established the V90 program, aiming at its success and survival in the twenty-first century, and is doing its best to reach the goals of the V90 through the collective creativity and talent of its employees.

The equity rate between Aisin Seiki and Borg Warner was changed to 90% for Aisin Seiki and 10% for Borg Warner in June 1981. In November 1987, Aisin Seiki purchased all shares from Borg Warner and ended the joint venture relationship.

The new company's name was also changed to Aisin A.W. Company, Ltd. in order to start afresh with new hope for future success. A.W., the abbreviation of Aisin Warner, was retained because it was well known in domestic and overseas markets, and Aisin was retained for corporate identity, to show membership in the Aisin group of companies. The company holds ¥3.24 billion in capital stock and employs 3,000 persons. Its annual gross sales amount to ¥170 billion.

CHARACTERISTICS OF COMPANY MANAGEMENT

With the "quality first" management philosophy, the company considers thorough quality assurance to be a necessary backbone for serving the community and sustaining company prosperity. In addition, the company sets its policies for five-year periods and tries to attain the highest possible goal with a sense of commitment and mission. Management strategy is based on this philosophy; details are discussed in the following sections. The company's "quality first" concept is explained in Figures 5.20 and 5.21.

THE HISTORY OF TQC PROMOTION

Since the introduction of TQC in 1973, the company has actively promoted it with the following objectives.

1. Respect humanity, develop creative and vital human beings, and utilize human resources effectively.
2. Promote "spiral-up" management quality improvement through total employee participation in QC activities, and create strong corporate quality that is adaptable to changes in the business environment.
3. Implement quality assurance thoroughly through cooperation with customers and vendors, and contribute to the community through attractive quality based on the long-range prediction of market and customer needs.

Because of successful results obtained by TQC implementation, the company was referred to as the "quality company." The history of the company's TQC is divided into three periods, as described in Table 5.3. (See Table 5.3.)

QUALITY ASSURANCE AND CROSS-FUNCTIONAL MANAGEMENT

The Quality Assurance System at the Company

The basic thought has been to predict the needs of the market and customers; to provide attractive-quality products in a timely manner, thus contributing to the community; and to gain the trust of the market and customers. Based on this, the quality assurance system is supported by

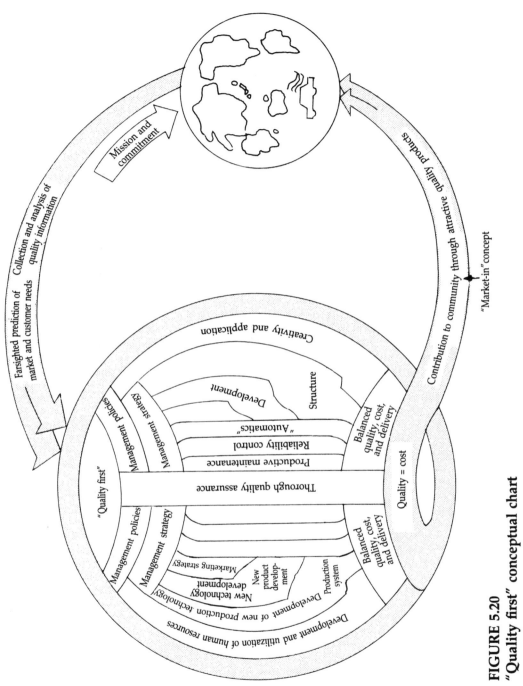

FIGURE 5.20
"Quality first" conceptual chart

159

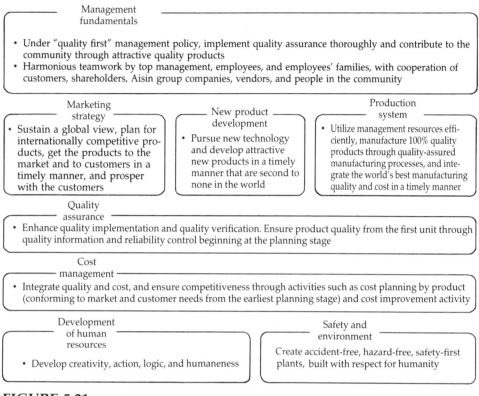

FIGURE 5.21
"Quality first" principles

three core programs: "automatics," reliability management, and productive maintenance. The system has been improved throughout the entire process, from long-range planning to services. A conceptual chart of quality assurance is shown in Figure 5.22.

Quality Assurance and Cross-Functional Management

Accelerated turnaround time for new product development and manufacturing preparation became a critical issue in the 1980s. Integration of quality and quality verification through total employee participation were urgently needed in the stages from commercialization planning to sales and services. In order to complete this chain of activities and to link marketing strategy and subsequent processes (such as new product development, production systems, and cost management) with successful management strategy, the quality assurance system involving total employee participation had to be fine-tuned.

TABLE 5.3
History of TQC promotion

		1969–79	1980–85	1986–present
Social environment		High growth/uncertain low growth; Motorization	Continuation of low growth; Global preference for compact cars	Acceleration of trade friction; Stronger yen in foreign exchange market
Management strategy		Adjustment to global marketing and diversification through winning a "war" in fuel economy and quality	Victory in compact-car "wars," and adjustments to changing conditions	Victory in overall car "wars" and adjustments to rapid changes in the market
Objectives of TQC promotion		Creation of corporate quality through "quality first" and improvement in development ability	Creation of corporate quality through creativity and vitality	Creation of flexible and strong corporation
Key activities Personnel		• Implementation of QC training by employees at the managerial level • Introduction of QC circle activity • Promotion of program for creative ideas and suggestions	• Stimulation of creative work environment through an effective use of *Kibo-no-Oka* (Hope Hill incentive program) • Employee training to ensure quality orientation and skill in equipment operation	• Training and development for midlevel managers and development of human resources • Creation of experts in one subject who have talent for many other subjects
Management	Executive audits	• Implementation of companywide audit system (internal audit) • Departmental inspection (for managers) and management improvement	• Implementation of on-site inspection system (for assistant managers and foremen) and management improvement • Implementation of executive audits for individual areas of responsibility	• Discovery of issues through implementation of presidential audits • Implementation of cross-functional audits
	Information	• Establishment of 1-year and 5-year plans • Establishment of "Automatics" program and applications	• Quality improvement in prediction and analysis through simulation	• Construction of "Q-LAN" and "C-LAN"
Quality assurance		• Improvement of evaluation of design quality involving customers and vendors • Improvement of reliability control	• Use of design reviews by reliability planning and other committees • Stronger quality assurance through use of improved and well-maintained equipment	• Development of consistent evaluation systems for everything from vehicles to individual parts • Implementation of cross-functional quality inspection and discovery of hidden opportunities
Self-evaluation		Improvement of coordination of activities	Discovery of opportunities and development of human resources	

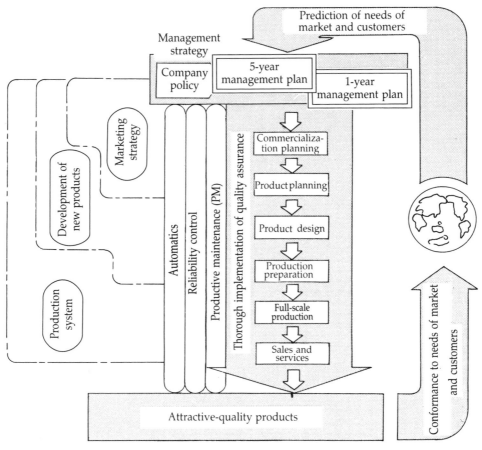

FIGURE 5.22
Conceptual chart for quality assurance

The administrative system for quality-assurance activities is shown in Figure 5.23. Characteristics of the system are listed below.

1. Targets are identified at each step of the process for thorough implementation of quality assurance through coordination by the reliability planning committee. Design reviews are conducted at each step of the process to evaluate and confirm the integration of quality and quality verification. These reviews verify planning letters that support deployment of management strategy. Quality assurance activities facilitated the timely development of attractive quality products superior to those of other companies and led to the achievement of a 100% quality-assured production line, ensuring the quality of the very first unit in full-scale production.

2. At the planning and design stages, required quality for market and customers is identified for purposes of thorough quality assurance. Market-

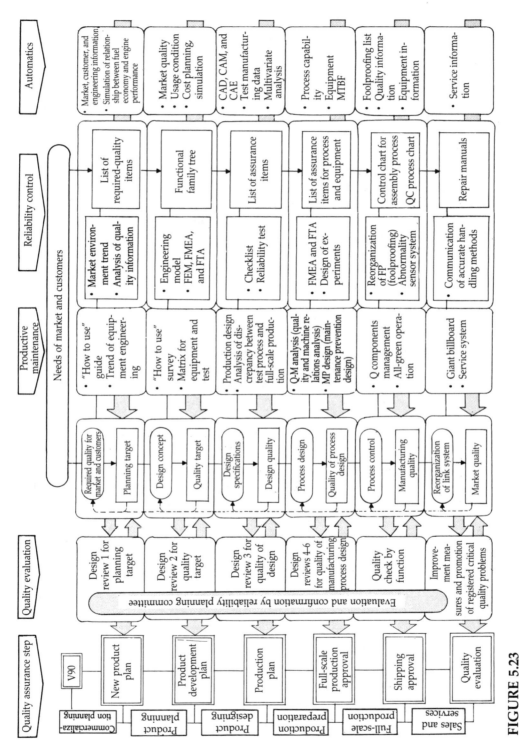

FIGURE 5.23
Administrative system for quality assurance activities

ing and engineering trends are predicted, and research and development are conducted in a timely manner. Correlations between quality characteristics and structures are analyzed to uncover engineering problems, and a basic conceptual design is drawn that is attractive and includes engineering feasibility. Subsequently, planning targets are tied to management strategy.

3. At the design stage, designs and test methods are linked with quality function deployment and reliability assurance through application of CAD, CAM, and CAE. Early reliability design is done on the basis of quality prediction from engineering models and FEM. In addition, engineering problems are uncovered by application of reliability techniques such as FMEA and FTA, and deployment of quality functions. Solutions to the problems are addressed by all the combined groups of individuals and teams.

4. At the production preparation stage, a viable conceptual blueprint for basic design addressing production engineering problems is drawn up, based on analysis of design quality at the production engineering stage. The blueprint is drawn to integrate and check quality and to upgrade process design for equipment maintenance. These quality assurance activities not only help evaluate and verify quality of process design but also clarify quality assurance items for each process. In addition, production preparation is broken down into production framework, process design, and equipment design. The reliability planning committee conducts design reviews for each of these subordinate steps to ensure a 100% quality assured production line (QAL).

5. At the full-scale production stage, the quality of work up to production preparation, which deals with equipment and human factors, is built into the standards. Total employee participation in maintenance and vigorous implementation of management and maintenance through the "All-Green Operation" program ensure the quality of every unit produced. The quality of key functions of the product is upgraded by means of thorough inspection of blueprints, equipment, standards, and operators for each key function. Engineering results gained through the activities conducted at this stage are evaluated and standardized with a view to their future product potential. A conceptual chart for cross-functional quality verification is shown in Figure 5.24.

6. Targets for quality, cost, and production quantity, and identification of the departments responsible for reaching these targets, are clarified to achieve closer interdepartmental cooperation. Quality assurance by total employee participation is promoted by companywide reconciliation of balanced quality, cost, and delivery, and by specifying documenting departments for planning (including scheduling of management strategy deployment), designing, and evaluation. Interdepartmental cooperation is represented in Figure 5.25.

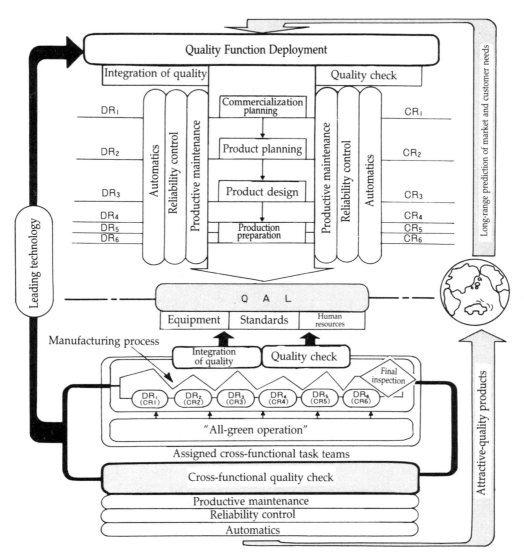

FIGURE 5.24
Conceptual chart for cross-functional quality check

ACHIEVEMENTS

The company, committed to its "quality first" management philosophy, upgraded TQC and aggressively developed new products. Thorough implementation of quality assurance helped gain the trust of the market and customers. The popularity of passenger vehicles equipped with automatic transmissions and the superior quality of our company's transmissions have placed them among the most strategically important consumer pro-

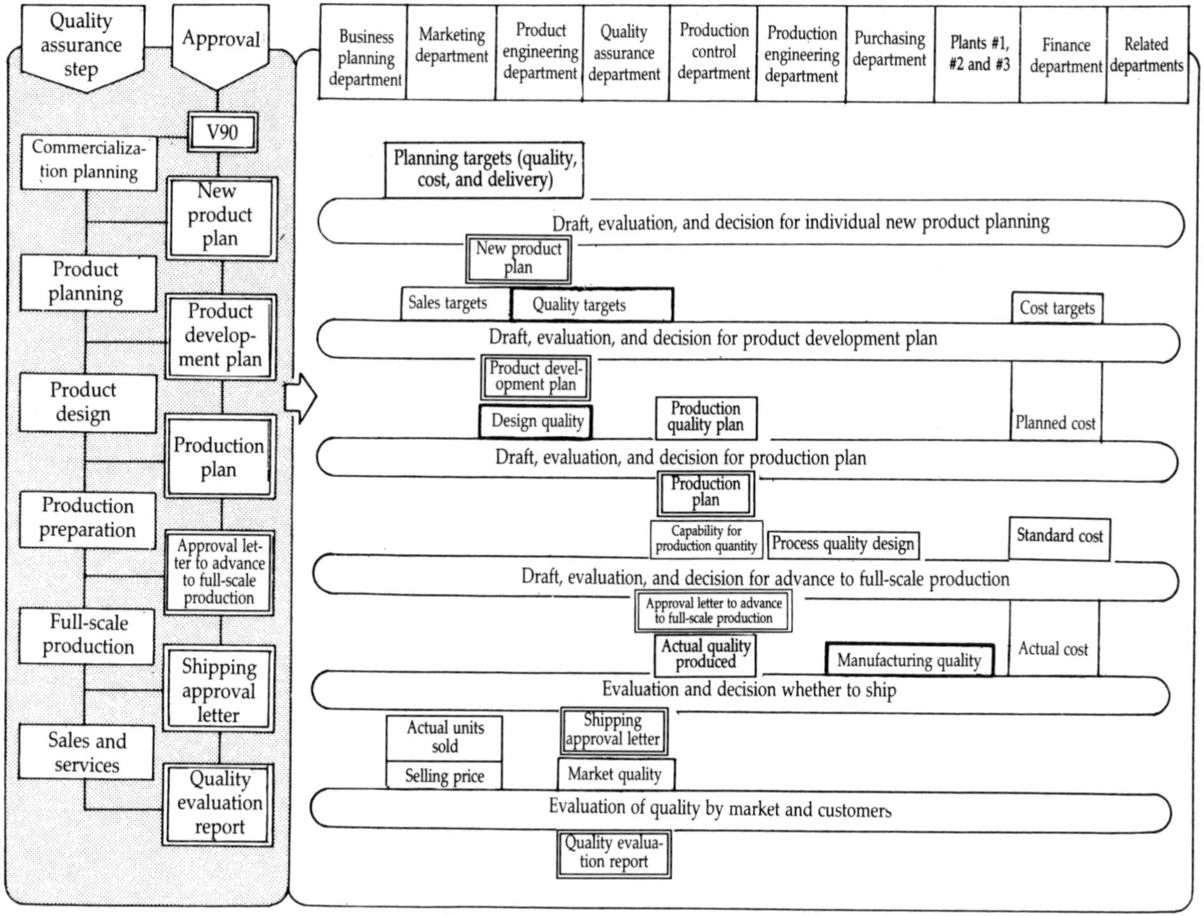

FIGURE 5.25
Interdepartmental cooperation

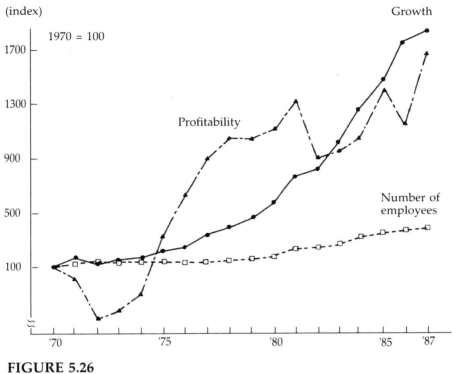

FIGURE 5.26
Profitability and growth

ducts. The company has overcome a number of challenges and difficulties from the day of its founding. It has succeeded in building a sound basis for marketing strategy, new product development, and an effective production system, and has proved to be a "survival company."

The results are summarized below.

1. Market shares of automatic transmissions grew thanks to top-flight development and production in the areas of fuel economy, reliability, and compactness of design.

2. Profitability and growth increased.

3. Company products characterized by outstanding quality, functional superiority, and competitive cost gained the trust of the market and customers, and consequently the corporate image as a specialized manufacturer of automatic transmissions was significantly enhanced. (See Figure 5.26.)

6

Cost Management and Cross-Functional Management

Cost Management at Toyota Auto Body Company, Ltd.
Kenichi Sato

CROSS-FUNCTIONAL MANAGEMENT AT TOYOTA AUTO BODY COMPANY, LTD.

Cross-Functional and Step-by-Step Management

Cross-functional management at the company must be discussed before cost management because the latter is considered as an example or aspect of cross-functional management in this chapter. As shown in Figure 6.1, cross-functional management has been divided into the areas of quality, cost, production, delivery, personnel/safety, and general management. General management addresses inseparable subfunctions stemming from long-range management issues. (See Figure 6.1.)

Cross-functional and step-by-step management are introduced and developed according to a concept illustrated in Figure 6.1. The concept is to combine units or departments into groups of a certain size and function and to identify each group as a step.

Because of their total involvement in processes from development to production, individual departments of our company are always working on the development of several models simultaneously. In this business environment, step-by-step management is introduced to implement "upstream management" and to ensure quality assurance at each step of the development process. The upstream management system was already in place for individual development projects at the time TQC was introduced.

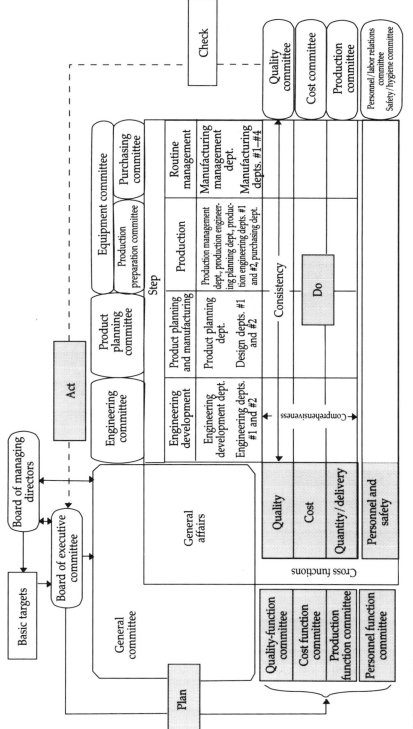

FIGURE 6.1
Cross-functional and step-by-step management

169

To enhance the implementation of TQC and quality assurance, step-by-step management has been adopted on a permanent basis.

The steps are arranged in order of developmental flow: engineering development; product planning and manufacturing (planning, designing, testing, and evaluating); production (production preparation); and routine management (full-scale production). At each step, coordination for cross-functional management and verification of quality assurance play major roles in step-by-step management.

Policy Management

Policy is developed and managed within the framework shown in Figure 6.2. In the policy development process, a long-range management

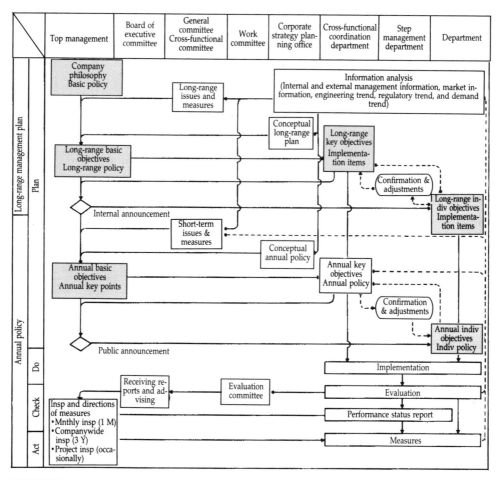

FIGURE 6.2
Company policy system

plan (five-year plan) is linked with a one-year plan as an annual policy. Targets and implementation items to achieve these targets are identified, and targets are concurrently developed for functions, for steps, and for each departmental action. Details of target development are shown in Figure 6.2.

Figure 6.3 shows how the cost function targets are developed. In developing these targets, consideration is given to the search for methods of implementation to achieve high-level targets and to verify that achievement of low-level targets would ensure achievement of high-level targets. This type of target matrix chart is prepared for each function.

As shown in Figure 6.1, committees are set up to facilitate effective deployment of cross-functional and step-by-step management. The general committee, the quality function committee, and other cross-functional committees are listed on the left side of the chart. These committees are composed of executives from related areas. Although their primary responsibility is planning, the committees also review important issues that may arise during the implementation phase.

During the steps phase, those committees are composed of executives and senior managers from relevant areas. They are responsible for coordinating target and implementation activities and subsequently for checking the target assurance status of the development process.

The quality committee and other committees on the right side of Figure 6.1 are referred to collectively as the work committee. Committee meetings for senior managers are initiated by a coordinating executive who is responsible for a particular area of each cross function. The work committee is responsible for the development of company policy related to functions, and for checking and coordination during the policy development process.

SUMMARY OF COST MANAGEMENT

Development of Targets

A specific method of cross-functional management using cost management is discussed in this section.

An executive coordinating cost function is responsible for the achievement of corporate objectives—a cost function target; achievement status of the cost function target becomes a control point. Concurrently, the achievement status of step targets and departmental targets in a target tree diagram (see Figure 6.3) becomes a checkpoint.

Achievement of these cost function targets will ultimately lead to a profit target—a fundamental corporate objective. These cost function targets are expressed as a gross sales target and a gross cost target that

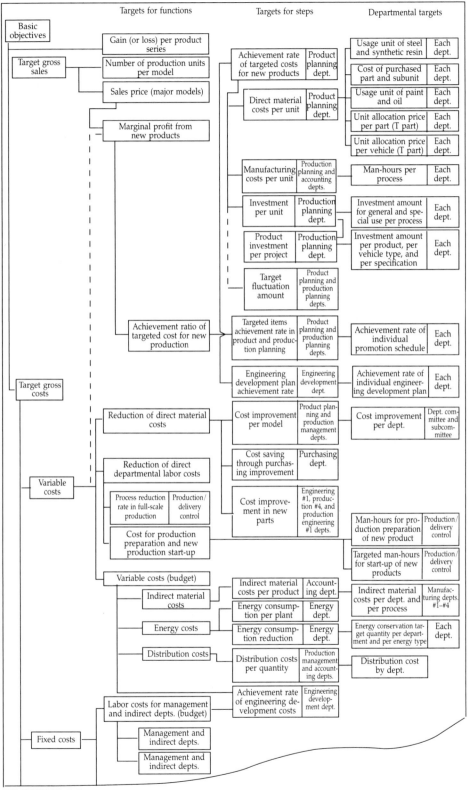

FIGURE 6.3
Cost function target tree diagram

together create a profit target. Also expressed are functions, steps, and departmental targets to achieve cost function targets. Taking the previous year's performance and environmental changes into consideration, the cost-function committee establishes these targets while readdressing the remaining issues. The logical flow of profit target and cost control is shown in Figure 6.4.

After targeted items and target values have been established in the form of a target tree diagram, the targets for different functions are reconciled by executives who are assigned to each function. Two functions may be described in different ways and yet may be addressing the same event from different angles; some confusion among the implementing departments cannot be avoided if different aspects of the targets are presented. Therefore, agreement must be reached on target items and target levels between functional groups. These target items and specific implementation activities to achieve the targets should be expressed clearly. Thus, corporate attitudes are clearly defined, their jurisdiction is understood by the implementing departments, and control is easily maintained. For this reason, an item may be presented as a cost function target and also be used as a checkpoint in the quality function, or vice versa.

Administrative Aspects of Cost Management

Primary cost control activities for assurance of targeted profits are the following:

1. Increased marginal profit through new product cost-planning activities:

    • Increased number of units sold through development of attractive products

    • Increased marginal profit per unit during the new product development stage

2. Reduction of total cost through cost improvement activities:

    • Reduction of variable costs, such as improvement of original unit for calculating cost (weight of raw materials, unit cost of parts, man-hours, etc.) and elimination of losses

    • Cost containment and reduction of fixed cost (equipment costs, management, labor costs) on a long-term basis.

The relationship between assurance of profit targets and cost control is explained in Figure 6.4.

Let us examine the relationship between cost control activity and the profit plan shown in Figure 6.5. The objective of the profit plan is to achieve

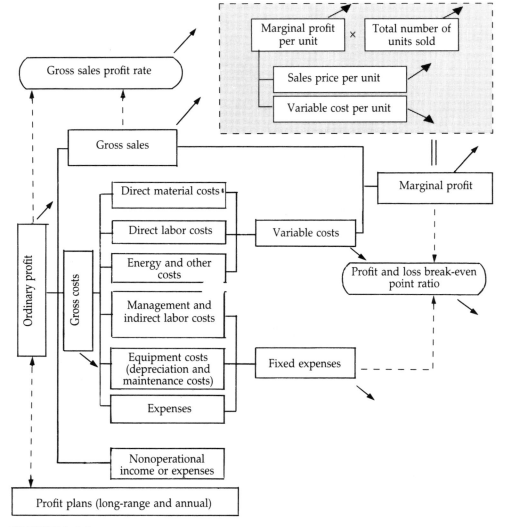

FIGURE 6.4
Assurance of target profit and cost management

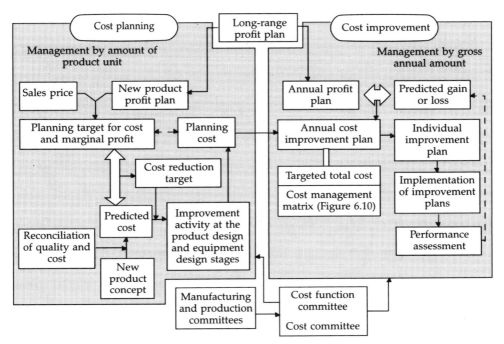

FIGURE 6.5
Cost management administration diagram

the annual ordinary profit target through coordinated activities in cost planning and cost improvement. Profit plans are established for short-range (annual) and long-range (five-year) plans.

The long-range profit plan is a rolling plan that is reviewed annually for the five subsequent years. The first-year plan of the long-range plan becomes an annual profit plan after the annual review.

Some cost control activities are aimed at tangible short-range results while others are aimed at expected long-range results. The conceptual relationship to the profit plan is shown in Figure 6.6.

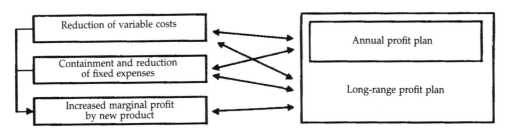

FIGURE 6.6
Relationship of cost management to profit plans

Role of the Cross-Functional Coordination Department

To promote cross-functional management, some key points relevant to the coordinating office must be discussed.

The first key point is the creation of a total system. This needs no further explanation, since one of the cross-functional management objectives is achievement of company objectives through interdepartmental cooperation. There are two pitfalls to avoid during implementation. The first is a situation in which the system is hastily created and overmanaged. The system may also be the intellectual creation of the professional staff and turn out to be unrealistic for the line departments. It must be borne in mind that management costs money, and therefore the effectiveness of management must be discussed. The system must be securely based on the merit of the constant rotation of management cycles PDCA. This means that the total system includes in-depth review of the plan (P) at the corporate level. The second pitfall is lack of a priority mind-set based upon a total assessment of the system, since all control items may not be fully assessed.

The second key point is credibility. The cross-functional coordination department may superficially be regarded as a department with power. Yet it is really powerless, since the actual work is done, and results contributed, by other departments. Therefore, the department must gain understanding and credibility in the implementation departments. It must be supported by a clear-cut objective that is related to successful results and gives the implementation departments a certain degree of freedom. These departments must be made aware of, and be given, information and incentives to establish self-motivated plans. For the departments to understand the objectives of the functions, those departments concerned with the target-setting process must be involved.

Review processes conducted by the cost function committee and cost committee to establish a long-range management plan and to further develop the plan into an annual plan have proven effective and are indispensable. Cost information, such as the relationship between departmental assigned cost and cost improvement targets and individual cost data at a lower organizational level, must be analyzed and made known to all departments. This information is gathered and compiled as consolidated cost data, and distributed to all managers in the company twice a year. Those staff members who are assigned this work in the coordination department must constantly be in touch with all departments of the company. Fair evaluation and successful coordination by these persons are possible only if they keep abreast of departmental activities and a meeting of minds takes place.

The third key point is that problem-solving initiatives are the responsibility of the coordination department. A problem in this case is a gap between objectives and actual performance. If there is a problem area that needs to be identified and addressed, the department must offer appropriate help and support in arriving at a solution. Merely evaluating the results and using pressure tactics will inevitably encourage "fire fighting" management, and success cannot be expected. In short, the role of the coordination department should be the facilitation of problem-free departmental operation in the company. The next two sections will discuss the practical application of cost management, using cost planning and cost improvement in light of the above three points.

COST PLANNING

Cost Planning System

The cost planning system is shown on the left side of Figure 6.5. There are several development types at the company. The most basic type, based on Toyota's fundamental concept, begins with product planning for body components.

In this case, the cost function begins with a reconciliation between the sales price to the Toyota Motor Corporation and the company's needs based on the profit plan. During this phase, cost planning geared to profit planning is developed, taking into account conformance to quality, the target number of units, and the target marginal profit per unit. An approach to establishing a targeted marginal profit is explained in Figure 6.7. Quality and cost issues are weighed and reconciled in order to achieve target quality within the parameters of complex market needs. Target cost, determined at this stage, will be implemented by departments such as design, product planning, and production engineering planning. The quality function and cost function departments must take an active role in supporting the implementation departments.

During the implementation stage of the target cost, the quality function deployment table is utilized. (See Figure 6.8.) In the table, information concerning required quality in the market is translated into measurable quality characteristics (primary quality items) to make it manageable. The target level is identified for each quality characteristic, and the characteristics are prioritized. Quality targets are then correlated with cost targets. This stage determines what cost will be assigned to each quality characteristic. At this stage, the cost of the vehicle is distributed for each function, by component or part, and for each combination of location and part. Concurrent with this distribution, optimum balance of quality and cost per vehicle is established to achieve the total target cost.

The role of the coordination department during the planning stage includes being a cross-functional coordinator in target setting, assisting in

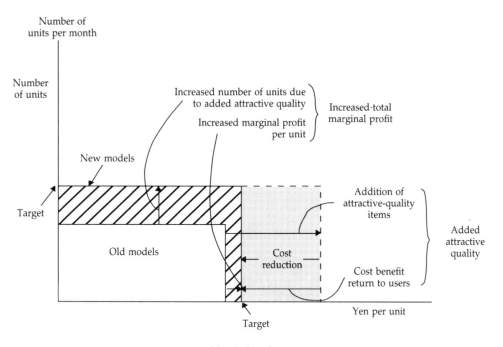

FIGURE 6.7
Establishment of marginal profit target

target assignment, and being a cross-functional adjuster during the implementation of the targeted objectives. In carrying out responsibilities, correct evaluation plays a significant role. The evaluation and reconciliation process is diagrammed at the bottom of Figure 6.8.

Implementation Status of Cost Planning

Since the effects of cost reduction at the new product planning, design, and production preparation stages are greater than those of cost reduction at the production stage, cost reduction programs are enforced on a project-by-project basis.

Concerning cost planning for newly developed vehicles, "creative cost reduction"—a companywide cost reduction program—is implemented to improve review activities during the earliest development stage (conceptual planning and conceptual design) and to upgrade interdepartmental cooperation. Focal points are shown in the shaded area of Figure 6.9.

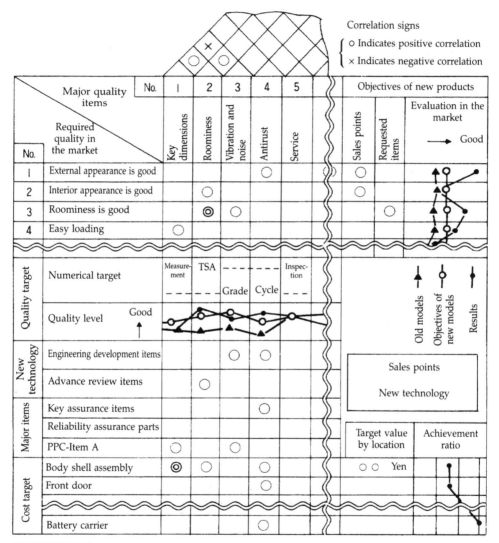

FIGURE 6.8
Quality deployment table

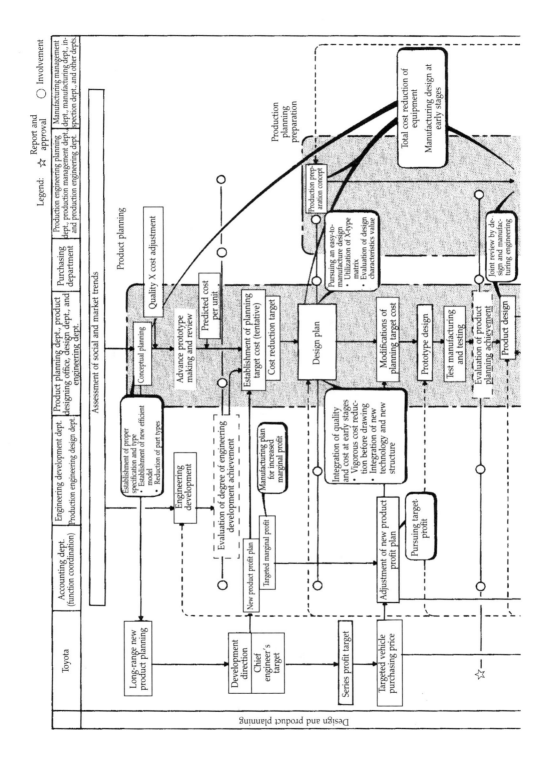

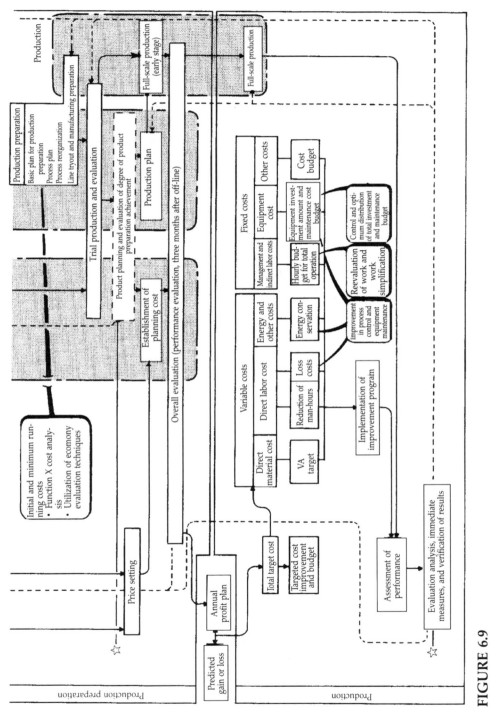

FIGURE 6.9
Cost management system chart

COST IMPROVEMENT

Cost Improvement System

The cost improvement system is illustrated on the right side of Figure 6.5. Since this system is not too different from those of other companies, detailed discussion is unnecessary. However, key points are discussed in the cost management matrix chart. Details are expanded in Figure 6.10.

The left side of Figure 6.10 illustrates that all manageable cost items are correlated with financial cost items; the latter are separated into variable and fixed costs. It is necessary for the cost function department to consider the relation between the results of cost management and period income (or loss) planning. The logical links are explained in Figure 6.4.

Detailed cost items, such as "fixed" and "variable" in this format, are correlated with departmental improvement activity. They are further broken down to the most detailed, or "raw cost," level. The upper part of Figure 6.10 exhibits departmental assigned cost and departmental cost improvement targets by category. These cost management activities are managed by individual department and by individual cost item.

This sample corresponds to the budget control and/or cost management methods in many companies. The company's cost management includes departmental contributions to overall management as well as to given cost improvement targets. One characteristic of this cost management is the identification of quantitative departmental contribution to overall management through logical correlation, as shown in Figure 6.4. The chart is designed in an easy-to-understand manner to show what departmental priorities are, how to implement policies autonomously, and how a department can make decisions on the balance of quality and delivery. Motivation and initiative, stemming from understanding and commitment, are required for successful results.

Success of the annual cost improvement plan can be ensured through assignment of total target cost by department and by cost item at the most detailed level. Success of the annual profit plan can be ensured similarly.

The contents of these plans may be tied to overall management policies as specific management targets, and will require further action. These plans stimulate focused actions through identification of departmental cost share and cost improvement targets for selected issues identified by top management in a given situation and at a given time.

Implementation Status of Cost Improvement

Cost Improvement through Reduction of Variable Costs

Reduction of variable costs at the full-scale production stage includes material cost reduction, reduction of the number of direct processes, elim-

FIGURE 6.10 Cost management matrix

Management division / Identification of target value by management activity

Accounting list of manageable cost items — Breakdown of costs

Management activities:
- ① Cost planning activities for new products
- ② Cost maintenance and cost improvement activities by department and by cost item
  - VA activity: Key vehicle models; Parts or other vehicles
  - Rework cost reduction activity
  - Activities for man-hour reduction in production departments: Switch to new products; Routine work activities
  - Reduction of gross labor hours (budget)
  - OPM activity
  - Cost reduction (budget)
  - Equipment investment reduction (budget)
- ③ Cost improvement activity for specific cost items
  - TPM activity
  - Routine production-loss reduction
  - Maintenance cost reduction
  - Energy conservation
  - Cost reduction for development and production preparation
  - Start-up loss and manufacturing preparation cost reduction
- ④ Profit management for particular items
  - Marginal profit management by product
  - Gain (or loss) management by plant

Column legend:
1 = ① Cost planning activities for new products;
2 = VA Key vehicle models; 3 = VA Parts or other vehicles;
4 = Rework cost reduction activity; 5 = Switch to new products;
6 = Routine work activities; 7 = Reduction of gross labor hours (budget);
8 = OPM activity; 9 = Cost reduction (budget);
10 = Equipment investment reduction (budget); 11 = TPM activity;
12 = Routine production-loss reduction; 13 = Maintenance cost reduction;
14 = Energy conservation; 15 = Cost reduction for development and production preparation;
16 = Start-up loss and manufacturing preparation cost reduction;
17 = Marginal profit management by product; 18 = Gain (or loss) management by plant

Cost item	1	2	3	4	5	6	7	8	9	10	11	12	13	14	15	16	17	18
Variable costs — Direct material costs	○	○	○	○													○	○
Labor costs (Fixed) — Direct production department: Total full-scale prod					○	○					○	○				○		○
Labor costs (Fixed) — Direct production department: Specific task					○	○										○		○
Labor costs (Fixed) — Management and non-manufacturing depts: Admin & eng personnel							○	○							○			○
Labor costs (Fixed) — Management and non-manufacturing depts: Indirect workers							○	○							○			○
Costs (Variable) — Variable expenses		○	○						○		○		○	○			○	○
Costs (Fixed) — Ordinary expenses	○								○		○		○					○
Fixed costs — Depreciation cost: Special equipment										○	○							○
Fixed costs — Depreciation cost: General equipment										○	○							○
Major department responsible																		

Notes on left column: "Direct volume production"; "Separate investment plan"

Right-side annotations:
- Responsible major department
- Establish a responsible department for each cost item → Identification of responsible management department
- Establish a responsible department for each management activity

ination of loss in the production process, and an energy conservation program. In the interest of eliminating loss in the production process, several improvement programs are analyzed and implemented. Results have been successful in improving changeover costs stemming from model changes, line-stop loss, and modification loss.

The idea that quality assurance means cost reduction is institutionalized in the company and has been supported by company experience in the past. The expanded concept of quality assurance in the production process, which included "upstream" assurance activities in early processes, brought successful cost reduction as a natural consequence.

Cost Improvement through Containment and Reduction of Fixed Costs

A long-range cost reduction program has been implemented to contain and to reduce ever-increasing fixed costs. The program ranges from reduction of fixed labor cost and fixed equipment cost (primarily capital investment and maintenance cost of equipment) through work improvement activities (office productivity maximum, OPM activity) by management and nonmanufacturing departments.

Rapidly increasing fixed labor costs, due to the increased number of employees and increasing annual salaries in the management and nonmanufacturing departments, triggered a cost reduction program called OPM, in 1983. At the same time, a permanent unit for companywide promotion of OPM was established.

Reduction of employees in the management and nonmanufacturing departments was promoted through the review and simplification of work, expanded application of computers, and demonstration of top management's leadership through work improvement presentation meetings.

In drafting an annual equipment investment plan, emphasis is placed on reduction of the investment ceiling and containment of the depreciation cost level by a complete investigation of investment needs and prioritized investment distributions.

In establishing an individual equipment plan, consideration is given to both initial and total cost reduction. Considerations include ease of manufacturing (reduced manufacturing processes) and running cost (e.g., operation and maintenance costs). Investment improvement has been implemented through the application of the "function X cost analysis" and economy evaluation techniques. "Function X cost analysis" is a technique used to formulate an improvement plan by eliminating the over-cost portion of the investment cost and the running cost of each equipment function.

Major cost improvement activities through reduction of variable costs and containment and reduction of fixed costs are shown in the shaded section at the bottom of Figure 6.9.

CONCLUSION

Cross-functional management at the company has been discussed. The role of the cross-functional coordinating office is significant because it addresses companywide issues in order to make cross-functional management effective. All employees must be involved in these activities and must have clear understanding and strong commitment. Furthermore, targets must be presented to them and the rationale behind the actions must be understood.

Another important point, of course, is the firm establishment of a system to prevent recurrence of failures. Cost planning and cost improvement activities have likewise been discussed. All these activities are supported by firmly established sustaining activities. Keeping up a system is always a challenge for any cross-functional coordinating office.

Cross-Functional Cost Management at TAKENAKA Corporation
Mitsuhiro Ozaki

MANAGEMENT PHILOSOPHY AND TQC ACTIVITY AT THE COMPANY

Since its founding, TAKENAKA Corporation has been managed by the "quality first" concept and with the corporate motto—"Contribute to the community by always providing the very best construction"—in mind.

As a result of our products' success, a reputation for quality and customer confidence has been established within the community of builders and the public. The company introduced TQC in 1976 to solidify further customer confidence, to improve corporate quality and quality of construction, and to upgrade performance. In 1979, the company was awarded the Deming Application Prize, the first time that honor was accorded to a construction company.

BACKGROUND AND ENHANCEMENT OF CROSS-FUNCTIONAL MANAGEMENT

Because of the unique nature of the construction business, our corporate structure was organized according to individual projects. The organization was divided into local districts, with a management structure defined by job skill or professional job type. Teamwork by departments of the main office and division offices had become weaker because of the diversification of projects, expansion of professional specialization, and increased growth of the organization. Issues such as so-called "sectionalism" and "sectional optimization" surfaced within the organization. The existing committee system and project team system attempted to intervene and to solve problems. However, room for improvement remained because responsibility and authority were unclear and problems were solved individually. Therefore, a breakthrough from existing conditions and improvement in policy management were due. To revise policy management thoroughly, a better structure and a system for cross-functional management that would encompass all division offices and departments of the main office were necessary. (See Figure 6.11.)

OBJECTIVES FOR REORGANIZATION OF THE CROSS-FUNCTIONAL MANAGEMENT SYSTEM

The objective of cross-functional management at the company is to strengthen the management system by using horizontal corporate threads. More precisely, it is to enhance quality assurance and corporate performance by addressing cross-functional problems that cannot be solved by a single department. Those problems are identified by function (e.g., quality, profit, and other areas important to the achievement of corporate objectives), and improvement measures are assigned and implemented by existing units. The objective is also to upgrade quality assurance and corporate performance through improved interdivisional and interdepartmental teamwork and improved interstep management.

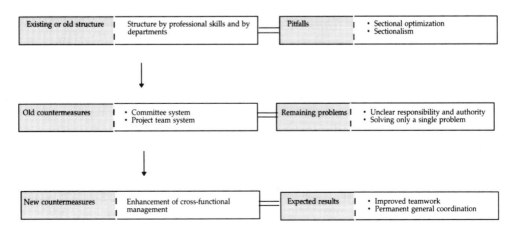

FIGURE 6.11
Objectives for promotion of cross-functional management

DEFINITION OF THE FUNCTIONS

There was a need to clarify in-house definitions of the functions before introducing cross-functional management. The definitions were discussed by the cross-functional management committee. Subject areas of management functions were narrowed down for easy comprehension by employees. There are four objective functions and nine supporting functions for the objective functions. Taking corporate vision into account, quality assurance is the most important of the four objective functions. High-quality products must be provided to the community through the continued existence of the company and expanded performance to realize the corporate vision. Therefore, profit management becomes an important objective function. Although both process schedule management and safety control are regarded as important objective functions, quality assurance and profit management were determined to be the major objective functions for cross-functional management at the company.

CONCEPTUAL FUNCTION CHART

Complex relationships exist among the functions, and two-dimensional explanation is difficult. The conceptual function chart shown in Figure 6.12 focuses mainly on quality assurance and profit management. This figure attempts to describe the correlation between the four steps (planning, design, construction, and after-sales service) and two key functions (quality and cost).

CROSS-FUNCTIONAL MANAGEMENT METHODOLOGY (CORPORATE LEVEL)

The cross-functional management facilitator committee was established as a unit specifically for cross-functional management at the corporate level. It is divided into two subcommittees, one in charge of quality assurance and the other in charge of profit management. Both subcommittees report directly to top executive management. Objectives and responsibilities of these cross-functional committees include (1) review of specific measures for cross-functional management—primarily those concerning quality assurance and profit management—and presentation of necessary recommendations to the president; (2) vigorous promotion of a meeting of minds between departments of the main office and division offices, and overall coordination for those departments; (3) promotion of quality management. The committee is regarded as the highest authority for the promotion of cross-functional management. It has been said that "the most important consideration for cross-functional management is that the cross-functional target needs to be determined before departmental target/policy."

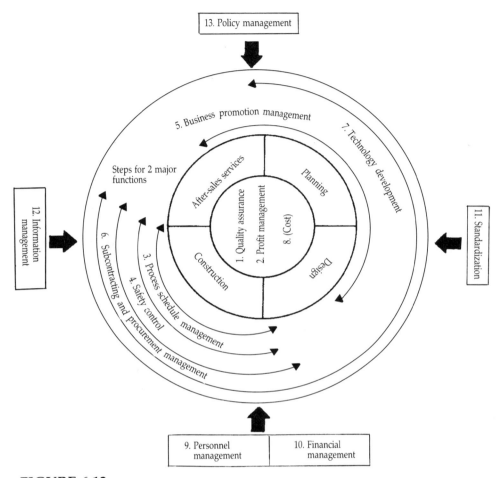

FIGURE 6.12
Conceptual function chart

Under the company's basic plan, management targets and functional targets of the main and division offices are established on the basis of two key functions: quality assurance and profit management. Cross-functional management is further developed for individual functions through the working of specific company policies, and through general managers' policies at the main office and division levels. (See Figure 6.13.)

DEPLOYMENT OF CROSS-FUNCTIONAL MANAGEMENT (MAIN AND DIVISION OFFICE LEVELS)

The cross-functional management facilitator committee is the highest body responsible for cross-functional management at the corporate level

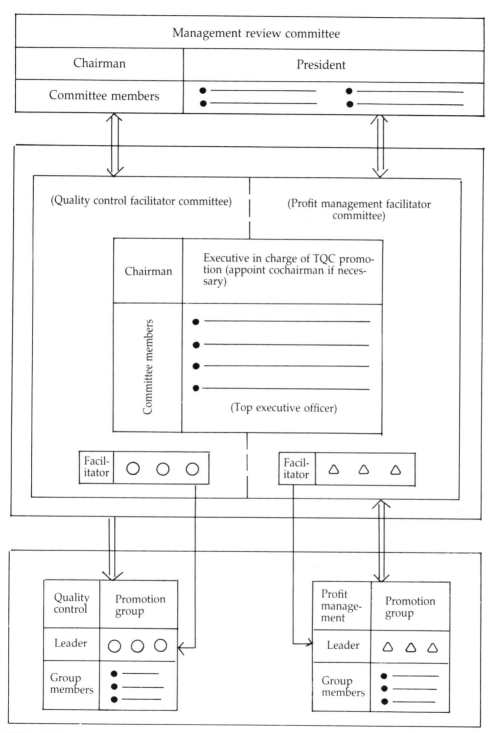

FIGURE 6.13
Simplified administrative chart for cross-functional facilitator committees

and coordinates interdepartmental teamwork. Similar organizations, such as the quality assurance and profit management subcommittees, are established at the main and division office levels to coordinate interdepartmental teamwork and policy deployment. Responsibilities of the profit management subcommittee include (1) drafting and coordinating the main and division offices' plans concerning profit management; (2) development, implementation, direction, guidance, and making of recommendations concerning the main and division offices' policies; (3) assessment of the main and division offices' activities for profit management; and (4) evaluation of the main and division offices' performance concerning profit management. The subcommittee is also responsible for interdepartmental communications and overall coordination concerning the profit management function.

TOTAL PROFIT MANAGEMENT SYSTEM

Based on corporate policies, a comprehensive profit management system is designed to implement the policies of general managers in main and division offices. The system includes profit management functional steps, flow charts, and control forms. Applying the system, interdepartmental coordination is implemented between management and manufacturing departments or among other departments.

The system is a useful vehicle for a cycle of activities: (1) establishing a plan, implementing it, carrying out an assessment, and zeroing in on the root cause of the gap between the plan and actual performance; (2) taking countermeasures; and (3) conducting a result analysis and self-evaluation for the remaining problems. The comprehensive profit management system involves and correlates all relevant departmental activities concerning the profit function. It includes contract acquisition activity and construction, personnel, financing, purchasing, and profit-related functions. (See Figure 6.14.)

The cost management system for an individual project is the most important system in the implementation stage. It is a comprehensive system that includes steps for planning suggestions, a basic plan, basic design, construction, and after-sales service. It describes specifically who does what, when, where, how, and why. A detailed discussion is provided in a later section of this chapter.

COST MANAGEMENT SYSTEM FOR
AN INDIVIDUAL PROJECT

Notes to the reader: Quality and profit have been treated as two key functions in the context of total management through the section "Total

Profit Management System." In the present section and hereinafter, the word *profit* is replaced by *cost* for discussion purposes because factors stemming from outside the company impact relatively insignificantly on processes from planning to production of individual projects.

Quality Management and Cross-Functional Management

It was stated earlier that cross-functional management is one of the specific methodologies of quality management. The company considers quality and cost as core functions. However, quality and cost are not managed separately: they are manifested as a result of mutual interactions. Therefore, they are inseparable, like the two sides of a coin, and are managed simultaneously.

There are two cross-functional systems—the quality assurance system and the cost management system—to manage quality and cost objectively according to a well-organized plan and with good overall balance. The cost management system chart for individual construction is shown in Figure 6.15.

Formulation and fine-tuning of quality assurance and cost management systems require time. Therefore, the importance of the process in the system is stressed to yield results. The results require evaluation by a standardized measurement method so that the existing system may be continuously improved.

Management Standardization and Feedback

The cost management system for individual construction projects can be divided roughly into two processes: the targeting process and the conforming process. Each is designed so that all steps can execute jobs under optimal, consistent, and well-coordinated conditions. These jobs require in-depth analysis of contents (or structure) and function. Generic elements should be extracted, applied widely, and authorized for routine work because the standardized way of management, with a certain set of rules but without arbitrary interpretation, is possible. (Figure 6.16 shows one step from the system chart.)

If the work is managed and checked by an individual employee, using this type of system chart, action will be taken in a timely and appropriate manner. This self-management minimizes the impact of varied individual skills and experiences. It reduces management dispersion to the greatest extent, and therefore furthers cooperation among the relevant departments.

On an individual construction project, individual know-how—the experience of a construction field manager, a construction contractor, an

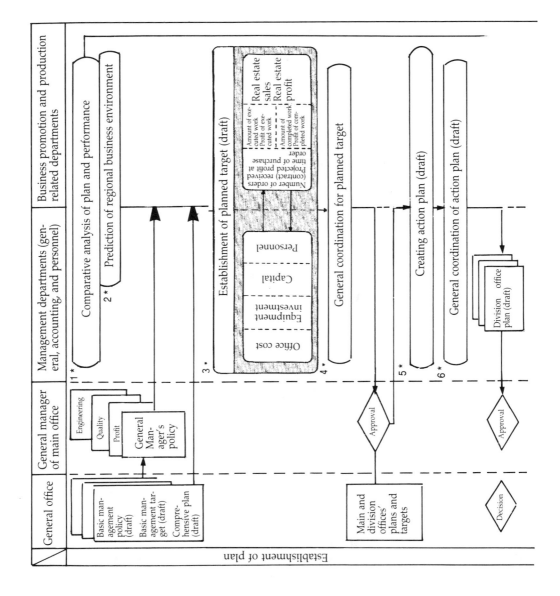

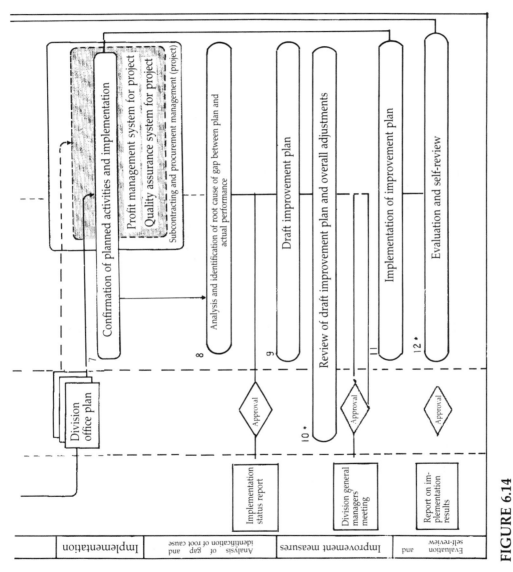

FIGURE 6.14
Total profit management system

193

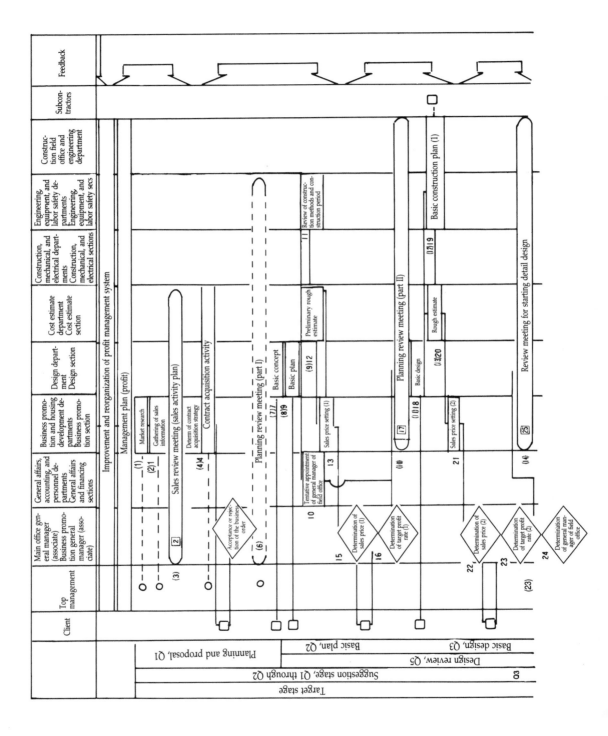

194

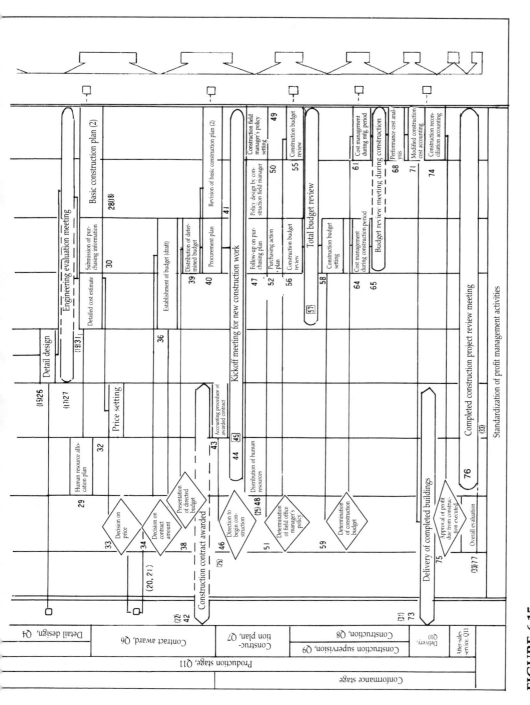

FIGURE 6.15
Individual construction cost management system chart, Osaka main office

195

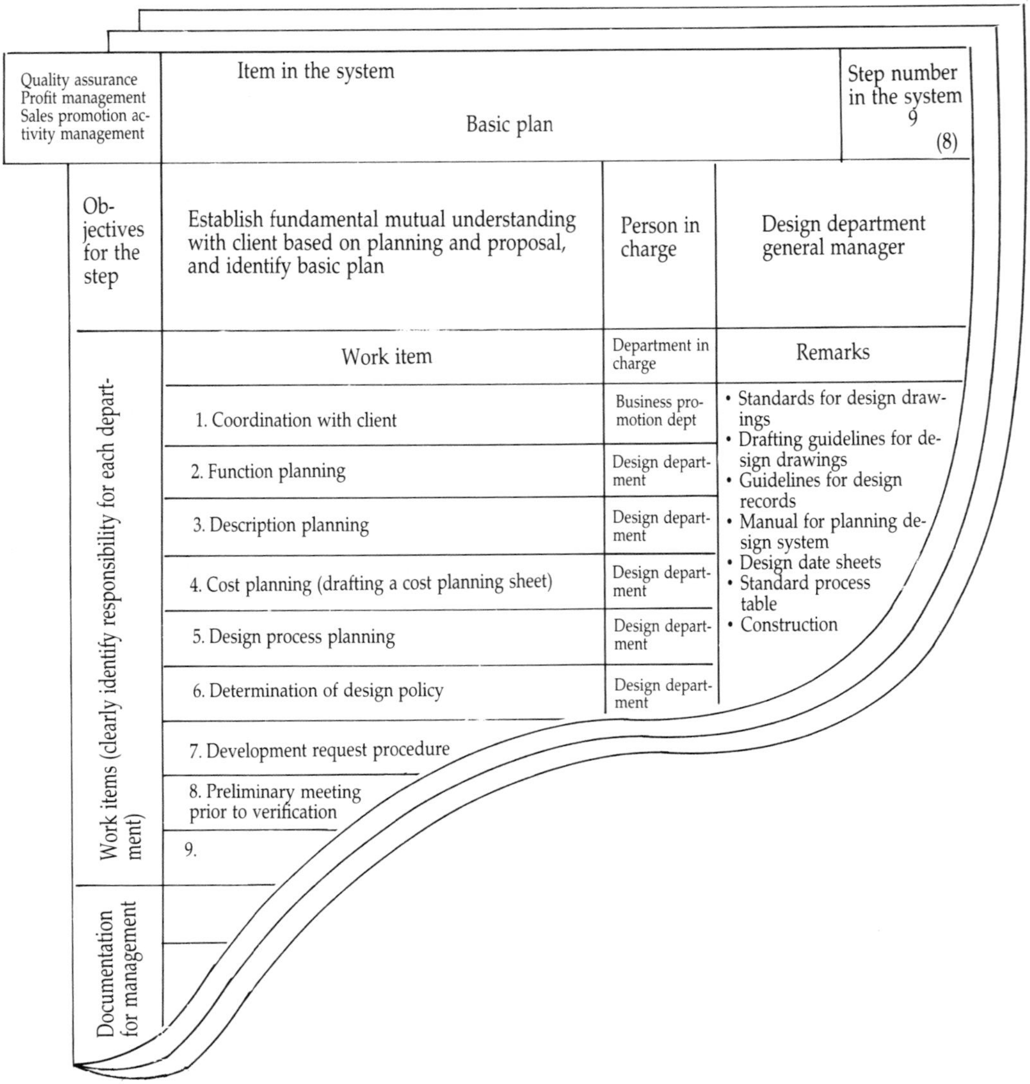

Quality assurance Profit management Sales promotion ac- tivity management	Item in the system Basic plan		Step number in the system 9 (8)
Ob- jectives for the step	Establish fundamental mutual understanding with client based on planning and proposal, and identify basic plan	Person in charge	Design department general manager
	Work item	Department in charge	Remarks
	1. Coordination with client	Business pro- motion dept	• Standards for design draw- ings • Drafting guidelines for de- sign drawings • Guidelines for design records • Manual for planning de- sign system • Design date sheets • Standard process table • Construction
	2. Function planning	Design depart- ment	
	3. Description planning	Design depart- ment	
	4. Cost planning (drafting a cost planning sheet)	Design depart- ment	
	5. Design process planning	Design depart- ment	
	6. Determination of design policy	Design depart- ment	
	7. Development request procedure		
	8. Preliminary meeting prior to verification		
	9.		

Work items (clearly identify responsibility for each depart-ment)

Documentation for management

FIGURE 6.16
Step 1 in system chart

administrator—impacts the project significantly. Individual knowledge and experience are valuable assets, and if such assets remain untapped, they cannot contribute to the company. Without widespread application by others, these assets remain individualistic, inflexible, and inapplicable. Therefore, they need to be reviewed from various angles so as to be flexible and to be accessible for application by all employees at all times.

Results of implementation conforming to the system chart are analyzed and reorganized systematically. The resulting information and know-how are shared with others through the completed construction project review meeting. (See Figure 6.15.) Continued promotion of these activities supports cross-functional management and revitalization of the company.

Activities based on the individual cost management system are not confined within the particular form of management of a specific construction cost. They are continuous activities to standardize acquired information, to replicate it for similar construction projects, and to upgrade companywide improvement activities.

In the following sections, major steps in the individual construction cost management system are explained according to the structure of the system chart, Figure 6.15.

COST MANAGEMENT IN THE TARGET STAGE

Cost management activity in the target stage involves both design and cost-estimate activities, with the two interacting.

After verification of the client's requests in the planning review meeting (6), any design conditions are added and the basic design conditions are adopted. (See Figure 6.15.)

Based on the conditions, the basic plan (9) is created. Its feasibility is verified by the preliminary rough estimate (12), calculated according to the basic plan. If the preliminary rough estimate does not conform to the clients' needs, it is returned to the basic plan stage for review; it is to prevent repeated occurrences of just such events that cross-functional management is used.

The basic plan is further developed in the next process (design review 1) by the planning review meeting (part II) (17). It evolves to *basic design* (18) as a specific plan, through cooperation from related departments so that the design comes closer to the developer's needs. Similarly, the basic plan is evaluated by the *rough estimate* (20), calculated according to the basic plan, so that the client's budgetary limitations can be satisfied. In the final consensus, the *basic design policy statement* becomes an integrated policy statement with a good balance of both the client's requests and designer's intentions.

The basic design policy statement goes through a final review process by the *review meeting for starting detailed design (design review 2)* (25), to draft the *detail design* (26) through the *detailed cost estimate* (31). This design review meeting includes the construction field manager as a committee member, in order to provide input from the design end. The expected outcome is a deeper understanding of the client's requests through a better understanding of design policy, an accurate linkage between the client's requests and the project policy, and a better understanding of construction control matters. (See Figure 6.17.)

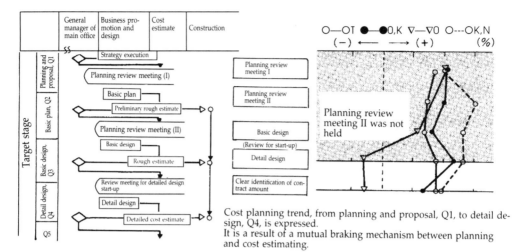

Cost planning trend, from planning and proposal, Q1, to detail design, Q4, is expressed.
It is a result of a mutual braking mechanism between planning and cost estimating.

FIGURE 6.17
Cost management activities in the target stage

In general, most clients' building plans are not solidified at the target stage. Their plans and concepts for the buildings become set when plans are broken down into details and reviewed in the specific context. (See Figure 6.18.) Therefore, prevention of future problems by accurate interfacing with the clients at every meeting becomes a key management point in the target stage.

The next subject to be discussed is cost reduction, primarily a construction method plan that is implemented concurrently with design planning. Cost reduction differs from design planning in that evaluation of the cost reduction plan takes place at the construction site. This means that a planner and an administrator are not the same person; therefore, the former must specify the plan as objectively and thoroughly as possible. The administrator, after having understood the intention of the planner, must add unique and creative ideas. For a better understanding of the planner's intentions, the construction start-up coordination meeting is held. (See Figure 6.19.)

COST REDUCTION ACTIVITY AT THE CONFORMANCE STAGE

The relationship between target and conformance in cost reduction is similar to that of the written script and actual performance of a play. A theatrical work is created in two domains: one is a faithful realization of the printed text and the other adds the personal creativity (interpretation) of the individual actors.

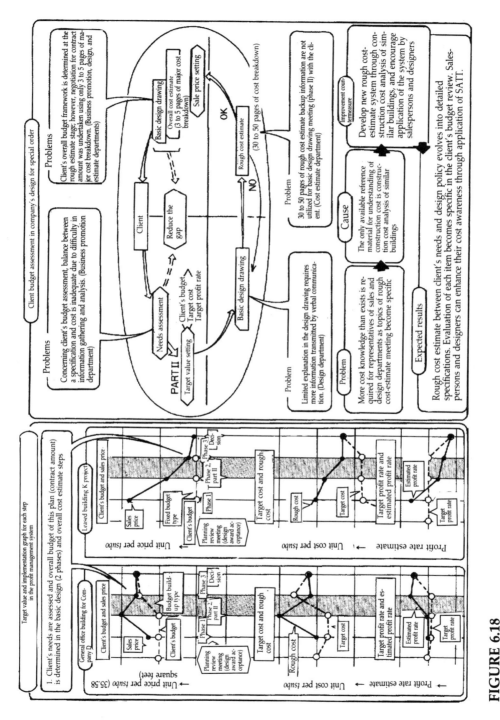

FIGURE 6.18
Sample design activity to integrate client's budget and profits

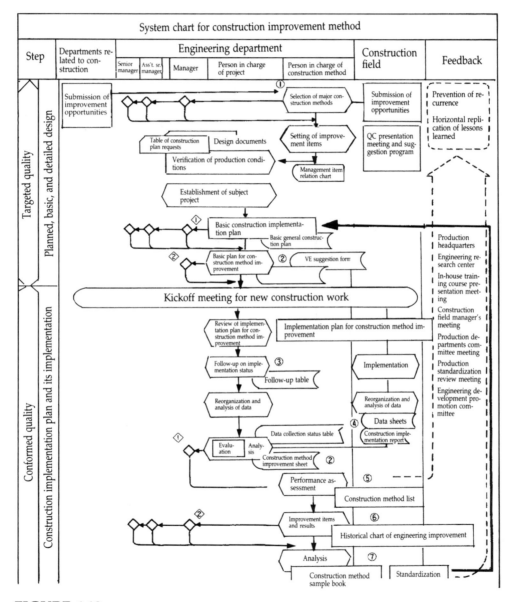

FIGURE 6.19
Construction method improvement system

Budget setting and budget control constitute two main segments of a cost management "scene." (See Figure 6.15.) The first segment is an opening scene that begins with the kickoff meeting for new construction work (44) and ends with the total budget review. The second segment is a concluding portion that includes the budget review meeting during construction (65) and the completed construction project review meeting (76).

In a budget setting, the distribution table by directed budget line item is equivalent to the printed script, and maintenance of the construction budget is equivalent to the actual performance.

Kickoff Meeting for New Construction Work

Accurate implementation of a plan, submitted in the target stage, requires accurate communication of the target. The kickoff meeting for new construction work involves an important committee that coordinates various types of reorganized information (conditions for production) in the target stage for the conformance stage.

The directed budget for individual construction projects, a calculation based on the company's management objectives, is submitted at the kickoff meeting for new construction work. Work procedures, work responsibilities, and processes to support the directed budget are also submitted at the meeting.

Therefore, administrative improvement of the committee involved is a key point in ensuring the prompt and accurate promotion of cross-functional management in subsequent activities. Even though the kickoff meeting for new construction work has already taken place, its importance is recognized as a major implementation item at the production stage within the system.

Construction Budget Setting

The conditions revealed at the kickoff meeting for new construction work are taken into account in the construction field manager's policy, a management policy for specific activities at the construction site. Simultaneously, the construction budget is drafted along with the construction field manager's policy setting (49).

The construction budget is an output from information provided by the kickoff meeting for new construction work, which includes a distribution of directed budget, a purchasing plan, a construction plan, a temporary construction plan, and a construction process chart.

In short, the prompt and speedy execution of an established plan in the previous process becomes critical. (See Figure 6.20.) In addition, the gap between the detailed budget and the directed budget must be accurately determined by closely checking the input information.

Total Review for Budget, Weekly Meeting, and the Feedback Function

The most focused construction budget that is submitted by the construction field office is reviewed by the total review for budget (57), and involves related departments. This review process also provides an opportunity to assess whether the cost estimate document from the previous process can assure quality for the next process. After the review, any recognized gaps are analyzed by cause, and the analysis results are fed

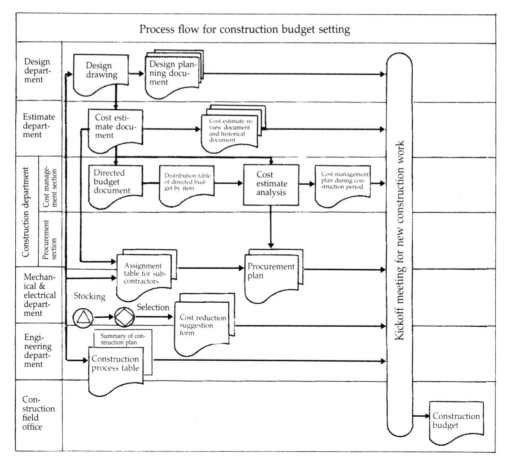

FIGURE 6.20
Construction budget-setting flow chart

back to the participating departments.

Cost Management Activity during the Construction Period

The construction field office's budget is submitted, reviewed along with the additional information from all departments, and approved by consensus. Once approved, cost management activity begins in accordance with the construction field office manager's policy.

Daily cost management activities during the construction period are grouped into procurement management (subcontracting and procurement management), engineering improvement activity (VE) in construction management, and daily cost reduction activities. All of these activities are included and implemented as control items and priority items in the construction field office manager's policy.

Procurement Management Activity

The main activity is procurement, according to the distribution table of directed budget by item specified by the kickoff meeting for new construction work. A consistent procurement technique has not always been applied in the construction business because of the unique character of the business. There is one-unit production for each individualized project, and varied conditions exist within each project. However, some experimental cost management activities—such as product cost analysis, assessment of work process, review of procurement order format, and quantity procurement—have proven to be successful.

In quantity procurement, characteristics of an individualized construction project and items to be purchased are cross-referenced. Four formats of the quantity procurement method have been devised and implemented. Absence of negative impact on construction quality is a precondition in this case. If multiple construction projects (frame construction and iron-frame construction, for example) can be subcontracted out, costs can be reduced. Also, simplification of construction management and reduction of construction time can be expected. In addition, some common and standardized items generic to individualized construction projects can be bought in quantity so as to receive discounts. (See Figure 6.21.)

Cost Reduction by Engineering Improvement

Cost reduction through construction method improvement, a part of construction field management, is the core of cost management at construction sites. It is a tangible activity based on the company's management

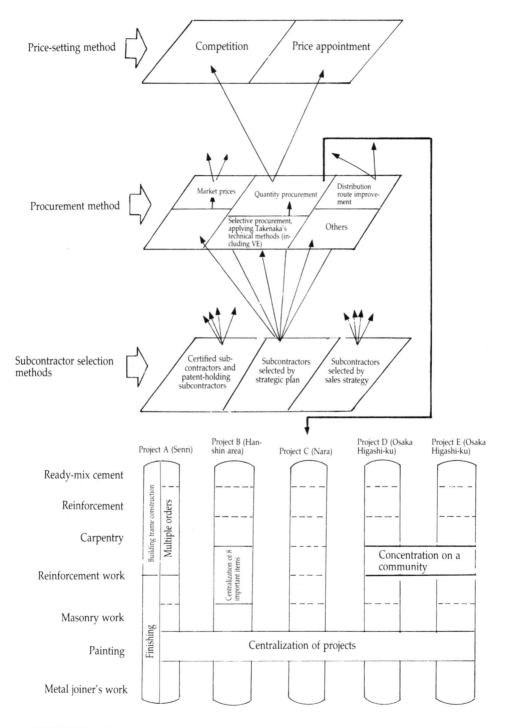

FIGURE 6.21
Procurement method and quantity procurement method (centralized procurement method)

policy of providing quality-conformed construction economically through the utilization of creative and imaginative ideas. The utilization of such ideas, however, should not be left to a single individual at a construction site. These ideas must be gathered from the existing specific engineering information, accumulated, and shared within the company. The cost reduction suggestion for construction field offices, submitted by internal departments to the kickoff meeting for new construction work, is one such tangible result. (See Figure 6.22.)

Other Daily Cost Reduction Activities

Costs as they appear in the construction budget documents are merely static quantities. When they are arranged on a time axis, however, they may reveal themselves as dynamic and variable. A steady budget maintenance activity (cost reduction activity) includes an arrangement of budget items according to the process time axis, monitoring and assessing varying costs as the process time proceeds, and planning and implementing countermeasures to readjust to the targeted budget. (See Figure 6.23.)

Cost Review Meeting during the Construction Period

As outlined above, maintenance and improvement activities in budget control are reviewed at the cost review meeting during the construction period. The gap between plan and performance is verified and reviewed, and accurate assessment for additional construction (the work not listed in the signed contract) is planned. One of the main reasons for this meeting is the early assessment of final loss or gain.

If any cause preventing the achievement of the targeted profit is identified at the meeting, all departments concerned will be notified promptly. A cooperative system is quickly established to ensure conformance to the directed budget.

The Completed Construction Project Review Meeting, Evaluation, and Standardization

Even though a particular cost control activity is discontinued upon completion of a construction project, the cost management system itself must be implemented continuously. To do so, all experience, information, and knowledge gained during the implementation of profit management

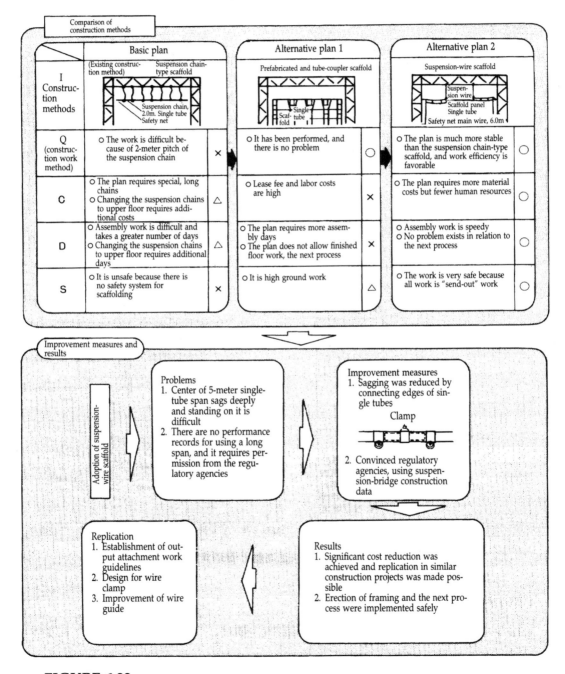

FIGURE 6.22
Example of cost reduction through on-site construction method improvement

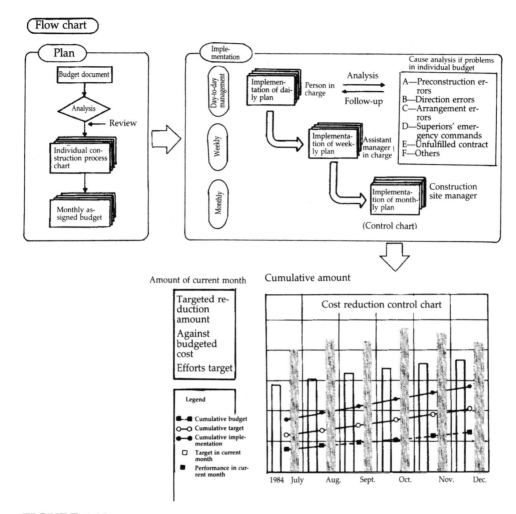

FIGURE 6.23
Daily cost reduction activity and maintenance data

for construction as part of the cross-functional management process must continue to be applied in the development of corporate management.

Much of the information, however, is not suitable for universal use as it stands, since it was gathered in a unique environment under unique conditions. This information must be evaluated by generic and predetermined measurement methods. It then needs to be categorized and reorganized according to the evaluation results, because information and know-how can contribute significantly to corporate growth only if they are standardized.

In addition, the nature of the activities at each step of the cost management system must conform to the targeted objectives. The evaluation must be objective and comprehensive. Successful cases must be replicated in similar construction. The system can be used as a guide for daily work, but must be constantly checked and revised through actual work experiences. (See Table 6.1.)

The individual construction cost management system chart (Figure 6.15) is by no means perfect. Therefore, we have to review it objectively and revise the system constantly by means of accurate data and experience. Quality improvement awareness, enhanced by open-mindedness to reality, provides the energy needed to develop and to advance a continuous quality improvement program.

RESULTS OF CROSS-FUNCTIONAL MANAGEMENT AND KEY POINTS TO REMEMBER

The most significant result of cross-functional management was the achievement of the initial objectives—the elimination of work duplication and enhancement of teamwork between departments. Some results through which employees' quality awareness is significantly enhanced are tangible, while others are intangible. Problems that could not be solved within a single department, and those that could be solved but yielded less spectacular results, began to be addressed through the cross-functional management approach. As a result, these interdepartmental problems were solved through improvement actions and interdepartmental reconciliation.

TABLE 6.1
Comprehensive cross-functional evaluation of an individual project

Comprehensive project management evaluation table										
Project name				Client						
Contract amount		Cost	Construction period	Safety		Departmental evaluation				
Business promotion	5·4·3·2·1	5·4·3·2·1	5·4·3·2·1	5·4·3·2·1		5·4·3·2·1				
	5·4·3·2·1	5·4·3·2·1	5·4·3·2·1				5·4·3·2·1		5·4·3·2·1	
	5·4·3·2·1		5·4·3·2·1	5·4·3·2·1		5·4·3·2·1				
	5·4·3·2·1	5·4·3·2·1					5·4·3·2·1		5·4·3·2·1	
Cross-functional evaluation	5·4·3·2·1	5·4·3·2·1	5·4·3·2·1	5·4·3·2·1		5·4·3·2·1			Compre-hensive evaluation	
	5·4·3·2·1	5·4·3·2·1		5·4·3·2·1			5·4·3·2·1			
	5·4·3·2·1	5·4·3·2·1	5·4·3·2·1	5·4·3·2·1		5·4·3·2·1				
Legend Evaluation of target / Evaluation of conformance	General manager	Personnel	Sales	Housing	Design	Estimate	Engineering	Equipment	Labor safety	Construction

Also, problem-solving became a permanent and comprehensive practice instead of an occasional and isolated one.

A key point in cross-functional management has always been involvement of top managers in organizing the promotion of cross-functional practices. Top managers must be involved in this process because actual problem-solving work depends on all the departments responsible for implementation. Significant results cannot be expected from cross-functional management without involvement by top managers.

Our challenge in the future will be how quickly we can analyze and implement each step on the way to solving cross-functional management problems, and how skillfully we will be able to improve the existing system to accelerate further the PDCA cycle activities.

7

Delivery Control and Cross-Functional Management

Delivery Control at JUKI Corporation: An Example of Cross-Functional Management Improvement
Takao Okayama

JUKI Corporation is a well-known manufacturer and distributor of JUKI brand products: industrial sewing machines, home sewing machines, and computer peripherals. TQC was introduced into the company in 1976, and the Deming Application Prize was awarded to the Industrial Sewing Machines Division in 1981. Cross-functional management was introduced in 1979, and is deployed by four cross-functional management committees: quality assurance, profit/cost management, delivery, and standardization.

The following sections discuss the concepts and promotion of cross-functional management by describing sample activities of the delivery control committee and related organizational units.

SUMMARY OF CROSS-FUNCTIONAL MANAGEMENT IN THE COMPANY

Cross-functional committees in the company play a pivotal role in companywide cross-functional management. Their role is shown in Figure 7.1.

After the introduction of TQC, key targets were set and promoted primarily in the context of the managerial problem-solving process. However, in spite of considerable effort, interdepartmental problems remained unsolved or were resolved slowly, overall teamwork of the company remained less than optimal, and measures to address the remaining problems

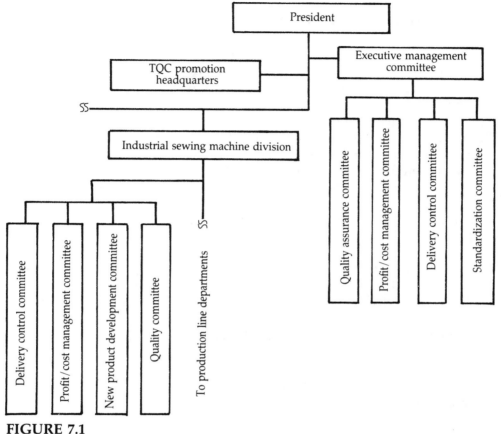

FIGURE 7.1
Cross-functional management committees

were not clearly determined. Full-scale TQC was implemented through policy management in 1978, and cross-functional management the following year. The role of the cross-functional management committee evolved gradually from the time it was introduced. Today, the committee is charged with the responsibilities listed below:

1. Companywide cross-functional management system improvement

2. Horizontal deployment of improvements on a companywide scale

3. Assimilation of valuable learning experiences by every member of the committee.

According to the above description, the committee has undertaken activities to remedy system problems identified as such by the division office and/or to conduct an in-depth study of individual cases.

DELIVERY CONTROL COMMITTEE ACTIVITY AT THE DIVISION OFFICE

The history of the delivery control committee's activities is presented below as an example from the industrial sewing machines division. (See Figure 7.2.)

Improvement activities have been accelerated by delivery control project teams since 1983, and significant progress has been observed. Therefore, activities at the industrial sewing machines division since 1983 have been chosen for detailed discussion in the following section.

Delivery Control Improvement in the Industrial Sewing Machines Division

Delivery control improvement issues in the industrial sewing machines division (hereinafter abbreviated as DCC and ISMD, respectively) were addressed by the delivery control improvement project team and the delivery control committee of the division. The existing situation in the ISMD and its improvement activities are shown in Figure 7.3.

System Improvement by the Delivery Control Project Team

The delivery control improvement project team, under the supervision of the DCC at ISMD, was initiated in 1983 to create an improved, comprehensive system. Improvement activities of this team are listed below.

1. Standardization of classification system for models

2. Improvement of sales predictions

3. Improvement of Order Entry System

4. Improvement of delivery control function in sales and manufacturing (see Figure 7.4)

5. Stabilized manufacturing plan: Lead time for purchase orders, on monthly basis, is too long. Efforts are made to synchronize purchase orders with actual manufacturing cycles by stabilizing manufacturing volume of model group units up to two months in advance.

6. Assembly lead time reduction: Lead time was reduced by using combinations in an improved mixed-production system, with multiple models and small lots, and improved line balancing. The

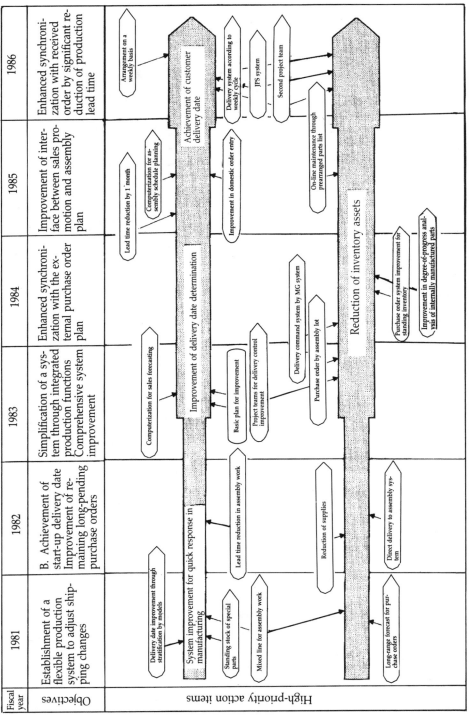

FIGURE 7.2
History of delivery control activities at the Industrial Sewing Machine Division

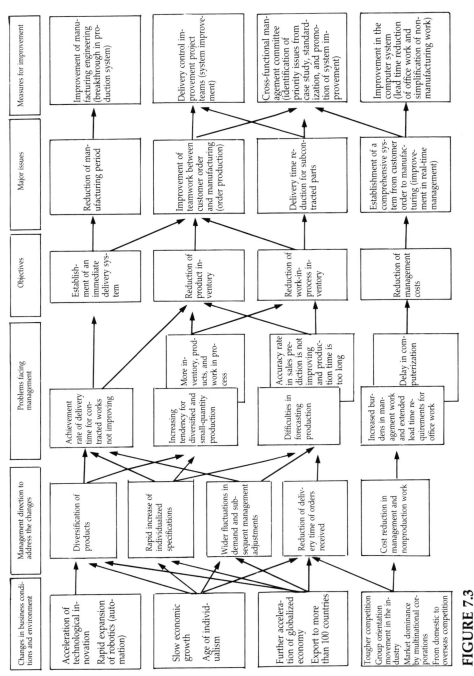

FIGURE 7.3
Delivery control improvement issues in the Industrial Sewing Machine Division

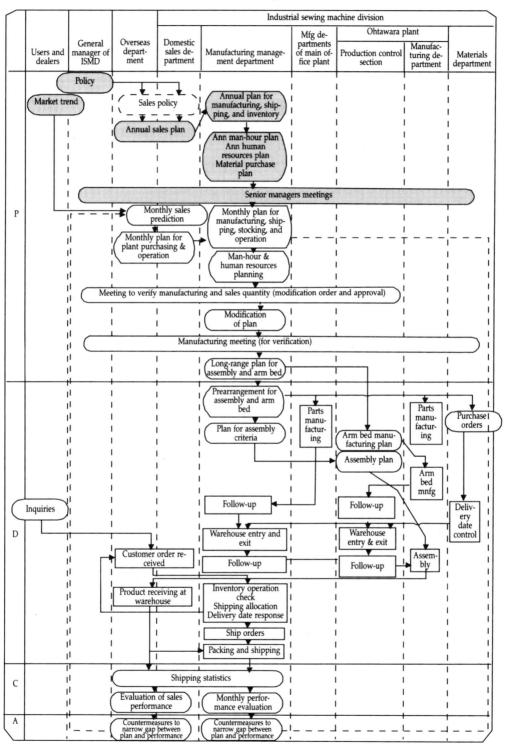

FIGURE 7.4
Delivery control system of the Industrial Sewing Machine Division (ISMD)

relationship between the assembly lead time and the order entry system was assessed, and the customer delivery-response system was improved through computerization of assembly scheduling.

7. Reorganization of prearranged parts list

8. Purchase orders in synchronization with assembly work: In conjunction with the manufacturing stabilization plan, lead time for parts was reduced by one month. A synchronized purchase order for generic parts, used for model group units, was established in synchronization with the assembly plan.

9. Standing stock of exclusively used parts: Detailed specifications for contracted products are often determined just before shipping. Parts used only for certain machines are difficult to order in an organized way. In the past, orders were placed on the basis of prediction. Standing stock levels were now standardized so that orders could be placed on the basis of stocking standards. Also, a maintenance system was established to optimize stock level.

10. Adoption of MG card system in dispatching purchase order for parts to suppliers: The number of delivery lot and processing cards increased at the same time because purchase orders for suppliers' parts are made for each assembly lot. In order to improve the processing work, the "MG stripe method" was adopted for purchase order cards.

Activities of DCC at ISMD

The delivery control improvement project team was formed as a task force to improve the system and to develop a software program. Activities of the DCC at ISMD, as a part of cross-functional management objectives, included the two listed below.

1. Identify key functions in delivery control, implement reorganization and verification of management items, and upgrade delivery control.

2. Improve basic work function of line departments—a prerequisite for system improvement by the delivery control improvement project team.

Reorganization of Management Items and Verification

Reorganization and verification required four main steps.

1. Clarification of the delivery control function (see Figure 7.5)

2. Survey of delivery control status (see Figure 7.6)

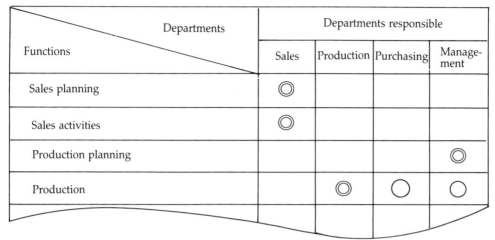

Functions	Departments	Departments responsible			
		Sales	Production	Purchasing	Management
Sales planning		◎			
Sales activities		◎			
Production planning					◎
Production			◎	○	○

FIGURE 7.5
Delivery control function and departments responsible

Control points	Departments						Control status			
	Sales	Management	Purchasing	Production	Plant A	Quality assurance	Data are collected	Control charts are used	Action limits are identified	Abnormal control
User list reorganization rate	○						□			
Rate of delayed deliveries			○				◎	◎	◎	◎
Assembly lead time				○	○		□	□	□	□
Number of months auxiliary parts are stocked		○					□	□	□	□

FIGURE 7.6
Results of survey on delivery control status

3. Improvement themes for delivery control and promotion status (see Figure 7.7)

4. Definition of control items and assigned departments

The committee identifies which department of the division is responsible for specific areas of delivery control. It assesses which department is addressing which improvement theme in routine departmental work and the status of management in each management function. Checking is carried out by the periodic use of control points.

At monthly meetings, the performance of each department responsible is reviewed vis-à-vis control points. The substance of its activities is also reviewed. Concurrently, the improvement status report is reviewed for verification of progress. (See Figure 7.8.)

Promotion of Fundamental Work Improvement

Separately from the project team activities, high-priority improvement activities for the production departments are identified and implemented. These activities are listed below.

1. Improvement in accuracy rate of sales prediction

2. Reduction of delivery lead time for externally produced parts

3. Reduction of assembly lead time

Departments and promotion status / Improvement themes	Sales			Management			Purchasing
	Degree of importance	Plan	Degree of progress	Degree of importance	Plan	Degree of progress	Degree of importance
Establishment of logical demand prediction	△	×		◎			
Reduction of lead time for externally produced parts				◎			○
Improvement in scheduling production plan				◎			◎
Improvement in inventory control	○	○	×	○			

FIGURE 7.7
Delivery control improvement themes and results of survey on promotion status

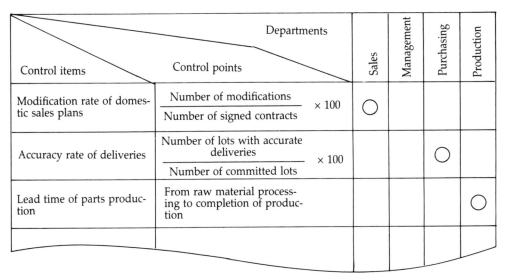

FIGURE 7.8
List of control items

4. Reduction of lead time for internally produced parts

5. Improvement in inventory control

6. Maintenance system improvement, using parts list

Departments and persons responsible are designated to assess and to check the status of improvements of these important items. The delivery control committee conducts its own survey to check the actual situation.

Problems Relating to Improvement Activities

After looking back on overall improvement activities in 1986, greater dispersion in the results was recognized: some results improved while others worsened. Therefore, reevaluation was necessary to determine the future direction of improvement efforts. Some of the problems that surfaced are listed below.

1. Contract acquisition work took up much time, and prolongation of the work slowed down the achievement of delivery rates required by customers.

2. Response time to customer inquiries about delivery time became slower.

3. Work in process became prolonged for materials, parts, and frames. As a result, improvement in overall production lead time became slower. This was a reflection of the strong existing employee review practices conducted on a monthly basis, and implied the presence of an improvement opportunity in this area.

Formation of a New Team for the Delivery Control Improvement Project

Continued foreign exchange rates unfavorable to the Japanese yen forced acceleration of management efficiency. As stated above, existing improvement efforts had proven to be inadequate, and vigorous implementation of the improvement plan was planned. Consequently, a new project team was formed to promote three improvement activities.

1. To reduce production lead time drastically, improve synchronization of contract acquisition with production cycles, and improve accuracy rate of deliveries to customers regardless of demand fluctuations
2. To discontinue the existing monthly review cycle; to establish a daily (for domestic) or weekly (for export) system to facilitate planning and production, not through sales prediction but through synchronizing with contract acquisition (see Figure 7.9)
3. To promote system improvement in an organized way, with the aim of establishing an integrated delivery control system and upgrading the computer system

ACTIVITIES OF THE COMPANYWIDE DELIVERY CONTROL COMMITTEE

The companywide delivery control committee is responsible for promotion of the entire JUKI group's delivery control, whereas DCC at ISMD is responsible for the division office. The companywide DCC focuses on improvement of corporate strategy through its checking and action. (See Figure 7.10.)

Problems in Delivery Control Activities at the Division

Problems in delivery control activities at the division are evaluated from the corporate point of view. (See Figure 7.11.)

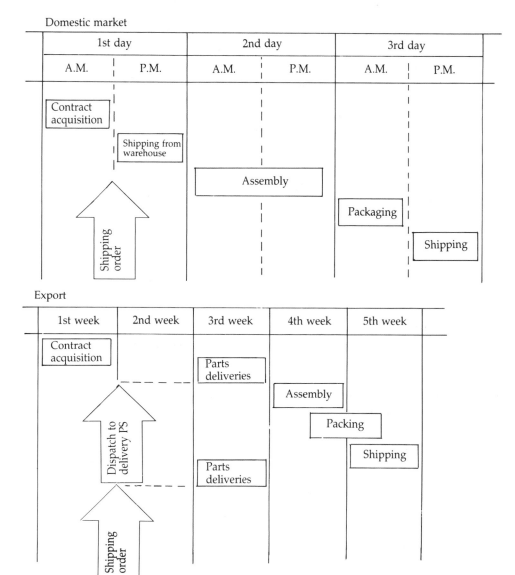

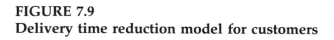

FIGURE 7.9
Delivery time reduction model for customers

Critical Activities of the Companywide Delivery Control Committee

Taking delivery control problems of the division office into consideration, the companywide delivery control committee established basic critical activities. These activities are represented in Figure 7.12.

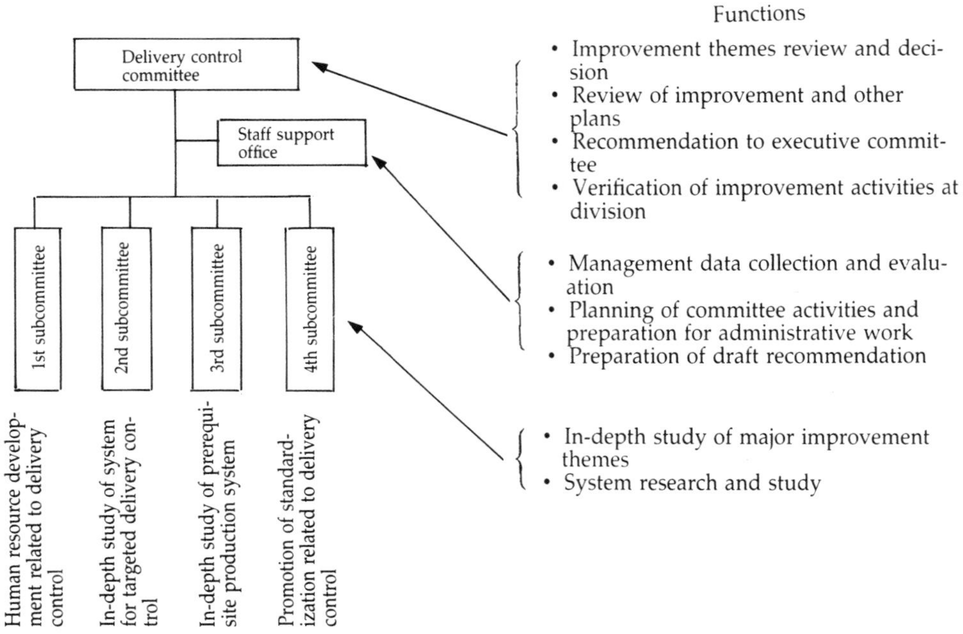

Functions

• Improvement themes review and decision
• Review of improvement and other plans
• Recommendation to executive committee
• Verification of improvement activities at division

• Management data collection and evaluation
• Planning of committee activities and preparation for administrative work
• Preparation of draft recommendation

• In-depth study of major improvement themes
• System research and study

Delivery control committee

Staff support office

1st subcommittee
2nd subcommittee
3rd subcommittee
4th subcommittee

Human resource development related to delivery control

In-depth study of system for targeted delivery control

In-depth study of prerequisite production system

Promotion of standardization related to delivery control

FIGURE 7.10
Structure of the companywide delivery control committee and its function

Structural Organization of the Committee and Subcommittee Activities

The structure of the companywide delivery control committee has been illustrated in Figure 7.10. Subcommittees chosen as professional groups must analyze existing problems selected by the committee, draw an objective, goal-oriented picture based on their analysis, and identify specific improvement opportunities.

First Subcommittee: Human Resources Development

A guide for human resources development has been created by means of which the subcommittee identifies problems relating to human resources and skills for every subfunction of delivery control. Based on this problem identification, the subcommittee draws a model of necessary human characteristics and recommends ways to develop such resources. (See Figure 7.13.)

Second Subcommittee: Search for Targeted System

The subcommittee is responsible for determining what system will best accomplish the basic objectives of delivery control improvement (control

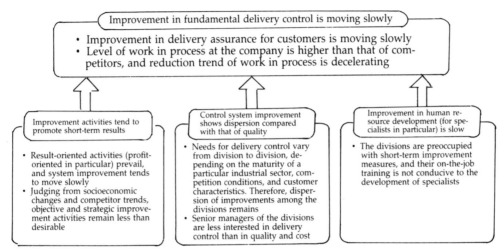

FIGURE 7.11
Problems of division-centered delivery control activities

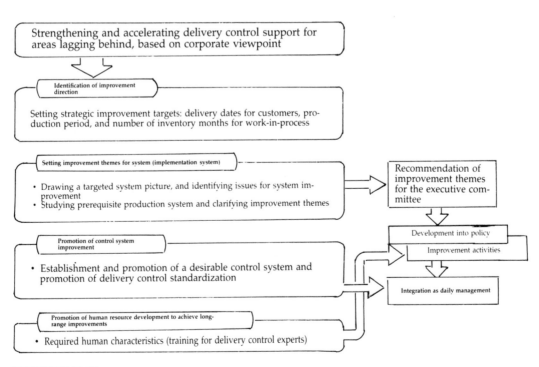

FIGURE 7.12
Activity objectives of the companywide delivery control committee

Survey of needs for human resources guide for delivery control

---

1. Objectives

Evaluate existing status of human resources for delivery control, develop human resources for upgrading delivery control function of JUKI

> (1) Decide on human resources allocation system for every delivery control function
> (2) Identify human resources needs

---

2. Survey contents

(1) Implementation period: December 11 through December 31, 1986
(2) Subject departments: related departments of the company
(3) Return rate: approximately 97%
(4) Survey items:
    ① Information on delivery control-related personnel (name of the employee concerned and his work percentage)
    ② Verification of education level in delivery control (self-evaluation and desired level of education)
    ③ Request for delivery control education

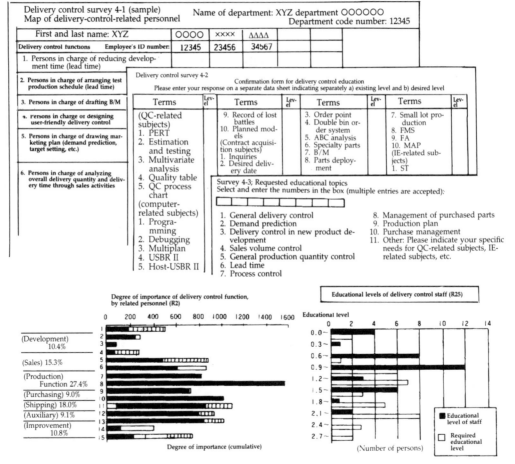

FIGURE 7.13
Sample survey for the human resources guide

points on the results side). It also identifies improvement problems. (See Figure 7.14.)

Third Subcommittee: Search for Prerequisite Improvement System

The primary responsibilities of the subcommittee are to reduce delivery time for customers, to study contributing factors (or prerequisites) to reducing overall lead time, and to improve the production system. (See Figure 7.15.)

Customer delivery problems are divided into two categories for cause analysis: delivery control problems (causal factors in the information system) and production system problems (causal factors in the materials system). Based upon this analysis, the subcommittee suggests directions for improvement.

Fourth Subcommittee: Promotion of Standardization

The subcommittee must promote standardization, improve daily management, and establish a fixed control system. (See Figure 7.16.) After determination of proper delivery control function deployment, a basic QC process chart for delivery control is drawn by the subcommittee. Control items are systematically reorganized, and comprehensive guidelines for delivery control are drawn up.

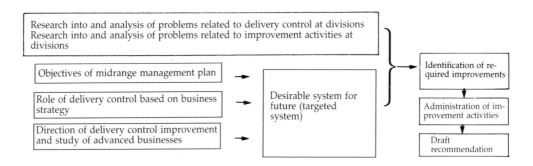

FIGURE 7.14
A targeted delivery control system and improvement problems

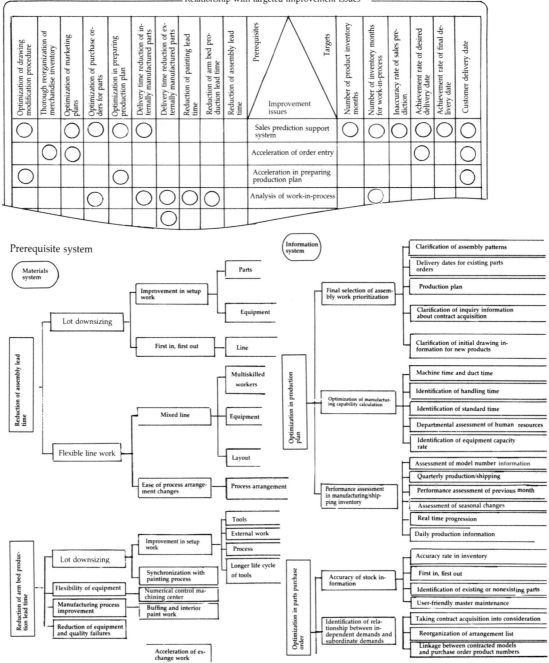

FIGURE 7.15
Prerequisite improvement issues

CONCLUSION

Thus far, we have briefly discussed cross-functional management with a focus on committee activities. We have emphasized the challenge of cross-functional management and the importance of total support and understanding from all employees. We believe that the essentials of cross-functional management lie in the periodic evaluation of activities, vigorous analysis, and continuous improvement efforts.

Load Smoothing and Delivery Control at Toyoda Machine Works, Ltd.
Kenichi Munekata

INTRODUCTION

Toyoda Machine Works was founded in 1941 to manufacture machine tools for mass production of automobiles in Kariya City, Aichi Prefecture, and became a separate entity, totally independent of Toyota Motor Corporation. Later more products were added, including machine tool models, grinding machines, and machining centers. The business has been further expanded to manufacture general-purpose controllers and mechatronics products (robots), which are used to produce auto parts.

As the economic situation changed rapidly in the 1980s, diversified user needs had to be satisfied. In order to respond to customer needs, the company introduced TQC in 1981 to improve quality, but it was slow to solve interdepartmental problems. Therefore, in March 1983, a cross-functional committee was established to explore and implement cross-functional management in quality assurance, cost control, and load smoothing and delivery control. In March 1984, personnel management was added to the existing structure.

SUMMARY OF CROSS-FUNCTIONAL MANAGEMENT AT TOYODA MACHINE WORKS

Cross-Functional and Step-by-Step Management

Three core products of the company are machine tools, mechatronics products, and automobile parts. Since these products differ totally in man-

Appended chart no. 1: delivery control function deployment

Primary	Secondary	Tertiary
1. Setting sales plans	1.1 Predicting demand	1.1.1 Data gathering
		1.1.2 Survey of the market
		1.1.3 Evaluation of prediction methods
		1.1.4 Prediction
		1.1.5 Evaluation of predicted results
	1.2 Target-setting for market share	1.2.1 Current company situation
		1.2.2 Current situation of other companies
		1.2.3 Competitiveness of competitors
		1.2.4 Company market share
	1.3 Target-setting for sales	1.3.1 Sales performance analysis
		1.3.2 Req. sales from management point of view
		1.3.3 From targeted market share
		1.3.4 Sales target-setting
	1.4 Sales promotion measures	1.4.1 Feasible sales quantity

Delivery control and control items system chart

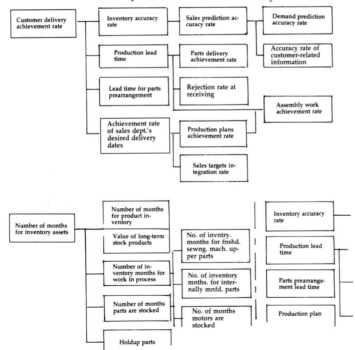

FIGURE 7.16
Delivery control standardization procedure

Basic QC process chart for delivery control

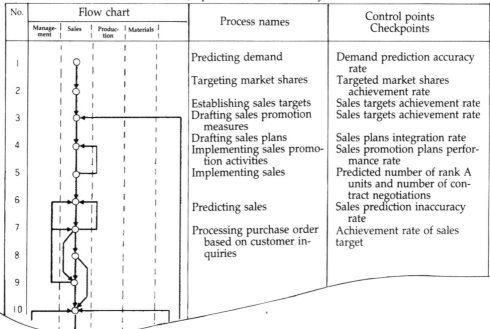

No.	Flow chart				Process names	Control points Checkpoints
	Manage-ment	Sales	Produc-tion	Materials		
1					Predicting demand	Demand prediction accuracy rate
2					Targeting market shares	Targeted market shares achievement rate
3					Establishing sales targets	Sales targets achievement rate
					Drafting sales promotion measures	Sales targets achievement rate
4					Drafting sales plans	Sales plans integration rate
					Implementing sales promotion activities	Sales promotion plans performance rate
5					Implementing sales	Predicted number of rank A units and number of contract negotiations
6					Predicting sales	Sales prediction inaccuracy rate
7					Processing purchase order based on customer inquiries	Achievement rate of sales target
8						
9						
10						

Japanese Standards	Name of standard	Fundamental delivery control regulation	Registration number	Kind— Classification— Grouping— Number
				— — —

1. Objective

The objective of delivery control is to deliver products in the quantity required by customers at the required time and location in an efficient manner

To accomplish the above objective, a fundamental regulation shall be established concerning delivery control for sales and production

2. Scope of application

This regulation is applicable to companywide delivery control

3. Revision or abolition of the regulation

Revision or abolition of this regulation shall be implemented according to the in-house standardization management rule (*Kyo* B 1 001).

4. Delivery control functions

See appended chart 1 for major delivery control functions

ufacturing methods and product format, a divisional management system was adopted.

For purposes of managing three divisions horizontally, four functional areas—quality assurance, cost, load smoothing and delivery control, and personnel—in cross-functional management were deployed. (See Figure 7.17.) For purposes of sales planning, product planning, and purchasing control, step-by-step management of divisions was implemented. The cross-functional and the step-by-step management systems were administered by the executive committee and its subordinate committees. The reporting structure is shown in Figure 7.18.

The current responsibilities of the committees for cross-functional management and step-by-step management are listed below.

1. Establishment and review of five-year plan and annual policy concerning cross functions and steps

2. Reconciliation of departmental policies

3. Total system improvement for cross-functional and step-by-step management.

A summary of the structure and the administrative aspects of the cross-functional management committee is given in Figure 7.19.

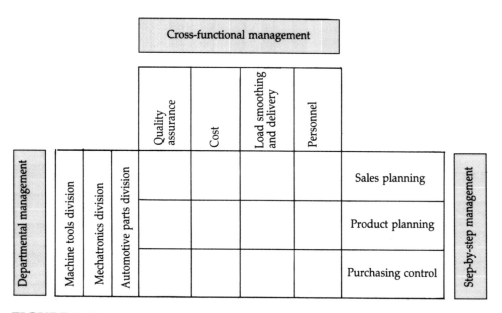

FIGURE 7.17
Cross-functional and step-by-step management systems

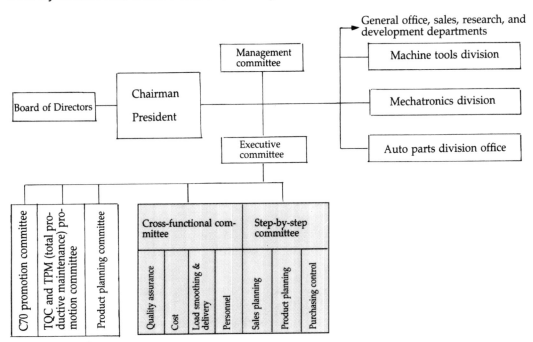

FIGURE 7.18
Reporting structure of cross-functional and step-by-step management

Item	Quality assurance	Cost	Load smoothing & delivery	Personnel
Units	Quality assurance committee	Cost committee	Load smoothing & del. committee	Personnel committee
Scope of responsibilities	As subordinate units of the executive committee, committees provide interdepartmental coordination and advice			
Responsibilities	1. Establishment of 5-year cross-functional management plan and annual policy, and subsequent assignments to departments 2. Review of departmental cross-functional policy and reconciliation of policy 3. Total companywide system improvement of functions			
Structure	Chairman: Executive in charge of total productive maintenance (TPM) promotion office Members: General managers of each division Executive in charge of sales Executive in charge of research and development Staff support office: TPM promotion office	Chairman: Executive in charge of accounting Members: General managers of each division Executive in charge of sales Staff support office: Accounting office	Chairman: Executive in charge of production control Members: General managers of each division Executive in charge of sales Staff support office: Production control department	Chairman: Executive in charge of education Members: General managers of each division Executive in charge of sales Executive in charge of research and development Executive in charge of general affairs Staff support office: General affairs department Education department
Frequency	Generally once a month	Generally once every other month	Generally once every other month	Generally once every other month

FIGURE 7.19
Structure of the cross-functional management committee and its administration

Policy Management

Aspects of the deployment of cross-functional policies and departmental policies in policy management are discussed in this section. A five-year plan is the basis of policy management at Toyoda Machine Works. The fundamental goal is to achieve corporate objectives by making the first-year policy at the five-year plan an annual policy, adopting it for departmental implementation and rotating through a cycle of "plan-do-check-act" with total employee involvement. A system of policy management activity is depicted in Figure 7.20.

Characteristics of policy management are listed below.

1. Basic policy, five-year policy, and annual policy are linked and designed to solve interdepartmental problems through cross-functional committees.

2. Feasibility of implementation plans is upgraded in such a way as to ensure targets and policy deployment. The plans are formulated through a bidirectional consensus-making process from area executives' policy formulation to department managers' implementation.

3. Presidential diagnostic meetings and function checking are carried out to improve accuracy in verifying implementation and to identify and solve problems.

Company policy in 1987 was established and deployed on the basis of issues identified in the five-year plan, changes in the external business environment, and the results of a review of remaining management issues. (See Figure 7.21.)

LOAD SMOOTHING AND DELIVERY CONTROL

History of Load Smoothing and Delivery Control

Gaining customer trust, and contributing to improved corporate performance through timely adjustments of production quantity and achievement of production and shipping plans are the basic goals of load smoothing and delivery control.

1. In order to respond to changes in the business environment, wider fluctuations in supply and demand, and greater production quantity changes, the machine tools division contributed to successful purchasers' production start-ups through timely response to customer needs.

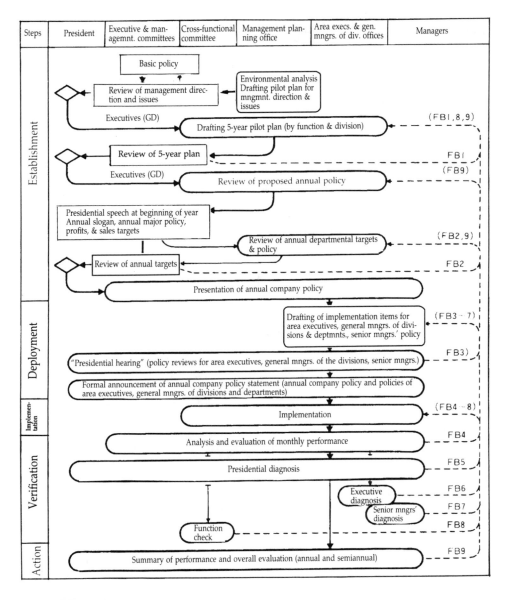

FIGURE 7.20
Policy management activity system

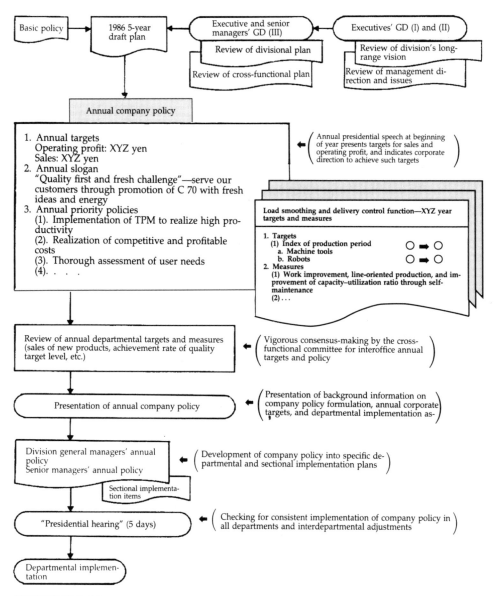

FIGURE 7.21
Establishment and deployment of company policy, 1987

2. The mechatronics division responded to diversified customer needs and constantly streamlined the production system.

3. The auto parts division responded efficiently to load changes required by purchasers' production plans and interfaced directly with purchasers' production lines on an hourly basis, thus succeeding in providing a stable supply of parts.

Diversified needs and ever-increasing demand for a reduced production preparation period in the latter half of the 1980s presented departments with difficulties in spite of their efforts to upgrade the existing load smoothing and delivery control system. Therefore, TQC was introduced and departmental activities were prioritized. Major activities are listed below.

1. Reduction in the manufacturing time from contract acquisition to delivery in the machine tools division
2. Quality improvement of the production quantity control system and increased production in the mechatronics division
3. Quality improvement of production preparation and production planning in the auto parts division

The history of load smoothing and delivery control is shown in Figure 7.22. The activity status of load smoothing and delivery control is discussed in the following section.

Activity Status of the Load Smoothing and Delivery Control Committee

In 1983, the load smoothing and delivery control committee and its subcommittee, the load smoothing and delivery control preparatory committee, were established. The subcommittee members were primarily managers of production control departments. The subcommittee was charged with reviewing departmental problems, drafting improvement measures, and referring these measures to the cross-functional committee for final action. After the committee's final decision, load smoothing and delivery control activities were implemented at the departmental level.

First, a load smoothing and delivery control function deployment chart was drafted after taking certain aspects of load smoothing and delivery control into consideration, including quantity control and load smoothing and delivery time control. (See Figure 7.23.) Companywide interpretation of the basic function of load smoothing and delivery control was standardized by this chart, and implementation items were clarified.

A load smoothing and delivery control process chart was drafted to establish implementation steps and to identify work responsibilities. (See Figure 7.24.) Also identified in the chart were control points and the managers' responsible at every step.

After departmental implementation, the load smoothing and delivery control committee reviewed the performance results, and some detailed modifications were made on the basis of evaluation of the results.

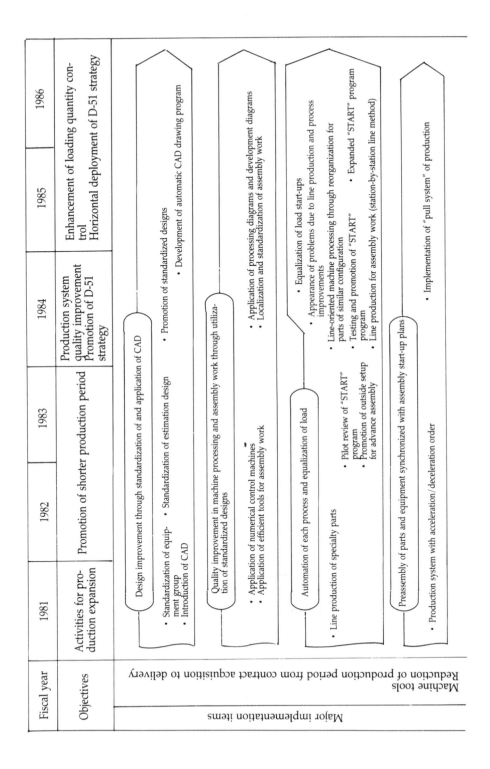

Fiscal year	1981	1982	1983	1984	1985	1986
Objectives	Activities for production expansion	Promotion of shorter production period		Production system quality improvement Promotion of D-51 strategy	Enhancement of loading quantity control Horizontal deployment of D-51 strategy	

Machine tools — Reduction of production period from contract acquisition to delivery

Major implementation items

Design improvement through standardization of and application of CAD
- Standardization of equipment group
- Introduction of CAD
- Standardization of estimation design
- Promotion of standardized designs
- Development of automatic CAD drawing program

Quality improvement in machine processing and assembly work through utilization of standardized designs
- Application of numerical control machines
- Application of efficient tools for assembly work
- Application of processing diagrams and development diagrams
- Localization and standardization of assembly work

Automation of each process and equalization of load
- Line production of specialty parts
- Pilot review of "START" program
- Promotion of outside setup for advance assembly
- Equalization of load start-ups
- Appearance of problems due to line production and process improvements
- Line-oriented machine processing through reorganization for parts of similar configuration
- Testing and promotion of "START" program
- Line production for assembly work (station-by-station line method)
- Expanded "START" program

Preassembly of parts and equipment synchronized with assembly start-up plans
- Production system with acceleration / deceleration order
- Implementation of "pull system" of production

Improved production quantity control system and expansion of production quantity
- Partial pilot implementation of *kanban* system
- Promotion of software program education
- Introduction of production control board
- Promotion of load equalization
- Reorganization of robot assembly process
- Construction of new plants
- Implementation of "pull system" of production

Improvement in production preparation planning
- Standardization of follow-up work on master schedule
- Early start of production preparation
- Delivery control through equipment installation planning schedule

Improvement of production planning
- Optimum allocation of human resources through improved line-by-line load assessment
- Improvement of load capacity assessment method
- Implementation of equalization based on load prediction
- Construction of new plants

Mechatronics Enhancement of control system / **Auto parts** Quality improvement in production preparation and planning					
Results	Increased subcontractors' production quantity significantly contributed to achievement of goals	Production time was reduced gradually	In each department, control points for reducing the manufacturing period have become clearer	Performance by a model work site for the D-51 strategy began to show results	Results of the D-51 strategy began to be replicated
Remaining problems	It became apparent that improvement in management was lagging behind	User needs for short-term manufacturing have become greater	Further quality improvement is necessary to shorten the manufacturing period	Further quality improvement is necessary at the planning stages in machine tool production departments	Improvement measures are necessary to deal with reduced loads

FIGURE 7.22
History of load smoothing and delivery control

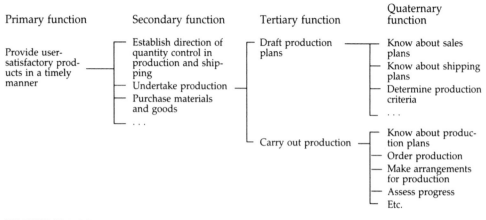

FIGURE 7.23
Load smoothing and delivery control function deployment diagram

Modifications, revisions, and clarification led to the establishment of work responsibilities for load smoothing and delivery control (see Figure 7.25) that in turn led to the load smoothing and delivery control regulation in June 1984.

Figure 7.26 represents a portion of the load smoothing and delivery control regulation. Figure 7.27 shows the load smoothing and delivery control activity system in the machine tools division. The primary responsibilities of today's load smoothing and delivery control committee include the establishment of five-year and annual plans for load smoothing and delivery control, assignments for departmental implementation, and verification activities.

EXAMPLE OF MANUFACTURING TIME REDUCTION IN MACHINE TOOL PRODUCTION

Summary

Demand for machine tools fluctuates widely and thus generates fluctuations in production quantity. Also, individualized customer needs require an individualized manufacturing system for many kinds of products. Therefore, the load at each step of the manufacturing process fluctuates widely, depending upon the kind and model of machines being manufactured. In spite of this difficult business environment, we served our customers' start-up production needs by delivering satisfactory products in a timely manner through achievement of production and shipping

Process	Control points and managers responsible	Control document	When?	Who?	What?
			Actions to be taken under abnormal conditions		
Contract acquisition	1.				
Manufacturing orders	2. Issue dates for manufacturing order • Sales coordination section manager	2. Contract acquisition planning table	In the event that a given machine underperforms by 20% during production period	Departmental managers' conference, representing sales, production control, engineering, casting, machines, assembly, and purchasing departments	Decision whether to accept a contract
Drafting file for full-scale production equipment	3. Delivery dates for full-scale production equipment file • Estimation design section manager				Establishment of agreement on accelerated schedule or adjusted delivery dates
Drawing schedule for manufacturing design	4. Issue dates for coordination meeting minutes on drawing schedule • Production control section manager	3. Control board	In the event that a delay greater than 4 days is expected		
System design	5. Software design completion dates • Senior manager of system department	4. Schedule planning table			
Design	6. Material delivery dates • Senior manager of engineering department Parts drawing delivery dates • Senior manager of engineering department Control drawing delivery dates • Design department manager • Operating manual drawing delivery dates	5. *Kanban* system signboard	In the event that a delay greater than 1 day is expected	Relevant managers of the subsequent processing departments of engineering, production control, machines, assembly, etc.	Call a meeting and come up with action plans
Control design	7. Design department manager • Control design completion dates • Control design section manager	6. *Kanban* system signboard Progress bulletin board for XYZ line production			
Drawing output	8. Drawing output dates • Engineering coordination section manager	7. Table of current status			
		8. Table of current status	In the event that a delay greater than 1 day is expected	Departmental managers from production control, machines, assembly, etc.	Call a meeting, etc.

FIGURE 7.24
Load smoothing and delivery control process chart

239

Steps	Assurance items	Managers responsible for assurance items	Assurance work	Managers responsible for assurance work	Related documents
Production planning	Feasibility of sales plan	Senior manager of production control department	1. Establishment of 5-year production plan 2. Establishment of 5-year plant construction plan, distinction between internal and external manufacturing	Production control department manager Production engineering department manager Production control department manager	Production control regulation Guidelines for long-range policy setting
	Feasibility of manufacturing and production plans	Senior manager of production control department	1. Drafting production plan 2. Selection of internal or external manufacturing of individual products	Production control department manager	
		Senior manager of production planning department	3. Assessment and adjustment for load & capacity	Production planning department manager	
Process planning	Feasibility of production plan	Senior manager of production engineering department	1. Establishment of quality standards 2. Implementation of process arrangements 3. Implementation of FMEA 4. Preparation of equipment plan 5. Improvement and promotion of procedures and processing method deployment	Quality assurance department manager Process estimation department manager Production engineering department manager	Process control procedure Plant liability control procedure Maintenance parts control guidelines
Process reorganization	Feasibility of process plan	Senior manager of manufacturing department	1. Design, manufacturing, and purchasing of tools and equipment 2. Receiving inspection of tools and equipment 3. Drafting equipment operation standards 4. Confirmation of process capability and equipment delivery	Production engineering department manager	Surveying guidelines on process capability Guidelines for formulating QC process charts Guidelines for formulating work procedures
Production preparation	Feasibility of production and process plans	Senior manager of manufacturing department	1. Drafting engineering standards and QC process chart	Production engineering department manager	

Production preparation

FIGURE 7.25

Work responsibilities for load smoothing and delivery control: machine tools

Establishment date: 21 June 1984	Load smoothing and delivery control regulation	Classification number: ST-203-001
Fourth revision: 1 July 1986		Department responsible: production control department

1. Objectives	Prior to companywide deployment of load smoothing and delivery control, this regulation is intended to define basic concepts, policy, and administration. Through deployment in accordance with the regulation, we hope to ensure customer delivery satisfaction and to contribute to corporate prosperity by improving management efficiency

4. Definition of terms	4.1. Load smoothing and delivery control: to ensure customers quantity, quality, and cost-effective deliveries (with a good balance of quality, cost, and delivery); to process efficiently from the time of contract acquisition to material and parts purchasing, manufacturing, and shipment, so as to minimize loss of business opportunities 4.2. Load smoothing and delivery control activity: to realize corporate policy and plans through assurance of predetermined management goals by persons responsible at each step of load smoothing and delivery-control-related work 4.3. Assurance item: an assurance item for the next process that is predetermined at each step of load smoothing and delivery control; person responsible for such items is referred to as "a person responsible for quality assurance" 4.4. Assurance work: work necessary to achieve "assurance items"; a person responsible for its execution is referred to as "a person responsible for assurance work"

5. Load smoothing and delivery control policy	5.1. Load smoothing and delivery control policy:
	Demand for our products fluctuates widely, which generates a wide range of production changes. In this business environment, we must achieve plans for production and shipping through minimum work in process and timely adjustments to the fluctuation of production quantity, and must implement the follow key activities
	  1. Reduction of manufacturing period to facilitate rapid changes in production plans
	  2. Implementation of flexible equipment utilization, multiple-capacity processing, and load equalization so that equipment and load factor changes can be adjusted to rapid production plan changes
	  3. Improved productivity through continued development of production engineering and improvement in the production control system
	5.2. Load smoothing and delivery control

FIGURE 7.26

Load smoothing and delivery control regulation (excerpts)

plans. However, increasingly diverse customer needs and customer pressure for shorter production preparation time were apparent in the latter half of the 1980s. Customer demand led to a reduction of time between contract acquisition and delivery.

Activity History

Two key activities were promoted in response to the conditions mentioned above: (1) production efficiency, including design; (2) manufacturing

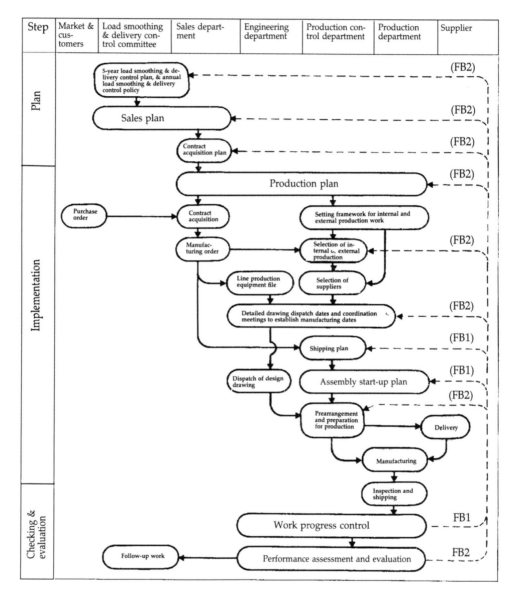

FIGURE 7.27
Load smoothing and delivery control activity system

time reduction through the application of a new production system, the "pull system."

Production Efficiency, Including Design

- Efficiency in design through standardization and application of CAD

An individualized production system, necessitated by contract acquisition, required many individualized designs. Standardization of design by instrument unit and introduction of CAD greatly facilitated standardization of estimation design. Application of standardized design contributed to the improvement of overall design efficiency.

- Improvement of machine processing and assembly work by application of standardized design

Production efficiency has been upgraded by using standardized designs that include numerical control, manufacturing diagrams, and development charts. Improvement efforts were made in the areas of parts processing and assembly work through decentralization and standardization of assembly plants.

Manufacturing Time Reduction through Application of Pull System

- Elimination of bottlenecks at each step in the work process, and load equalization

Machine manufacturing for specialty parts used to be impeded by bottlenecks in the line production process. A specific line was designated for such products in order to reduce the machine manufacturing time and to advance outside set-up for advance assembly. In addition, machine processing of like-configuration parts was automated during line production, permitting the assembly of parts in a timely manner. Elimination of bottlenecks was achieved by developing a system in which workers traveled from one work station to another in the overall assembly process.

Furthermore, the "START" program—a total production management system based upon the "source-respect" management concept—was developed, and load equalization was maintained from the beginning of the contract acquisition phase. Quality in planning was improved through accurate assessment of load time—both actual and estimated—as a result of an improved feedback system to gather and analyze data for time estimation.

• Arrangement of parts and equipment in synchronization with the assembly start plan

First, a three-month shipping plan was drafted. The plan was subdivided into weekly plans, and plans for necessary parts and equipment were made by calculating backward from the subsequent process so that the assembly start date could be synchronized with the shipping date. The assembly period was reduced by half after the development of the pull system of production for individualized manufacturing. A specific example of improvement is discussed in the following section.

Manufacturing Time Reduction in Machining Center Production

Summary

This is an example of manufacturing time reduction in which customer needs for delivery time reduction were addressed, work in process was reduced, and a new production system was developed.

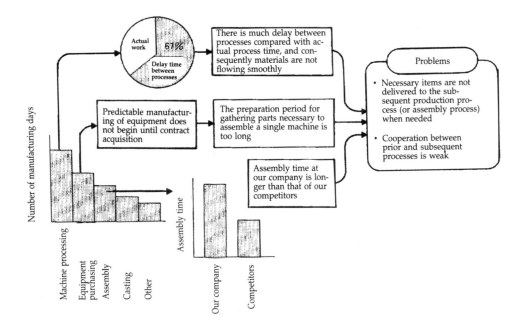

FIGURE 7.28
Manufacturing time of machining centers, and existing problems

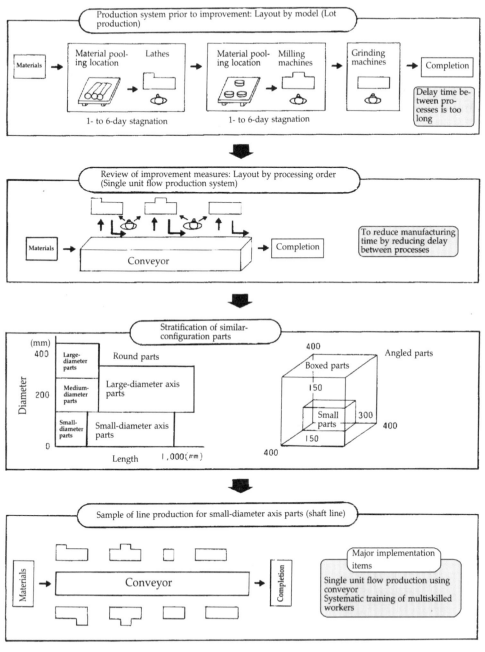

FIGURE 7.29
Line production by similar configuration

*The Current Situation and Problems Concerning Manufacturing
Time Reduction of Machine Centers*

Manufacturing time of the machining centers can be roughly divided into two categories: preparatory manufacturing time for standard parts and manufacturing time for line-produced parts after contract acquisition.

Preparatory manufacturing time does not impact directly on customer delivery time requirements, but it does on the amount of work in process. Therefore, reduction of both manufacturing times needs to be addressed because reduction of line-produced parts would definitely impact on deliveries.

A step-by-step analysis of the current situation and of manufacturing time problems is given in Figure 7.28. Individualized problem-solving activity as well as a cross-functional system to solve interdepartmental and interstep problems needed to be developed.

Implementation Status of Improvement Activities

The existing manufacturing system in the machine manufacturing process, based on layout by model and by processing unit, was partially converted into a line production system to accommodate layout by processing order and the streamlining of production of similar-configuration parts. With this conversion, machine manufacturing time was drastically reduced to approximately one third. (See Figure 7.29.)

The existing system encompassing all processes in the overall assembly work called for two or three workers. A revised production system called for line production requiring 22 separate processes with 1 dedicated worker assigned to multiple processes.

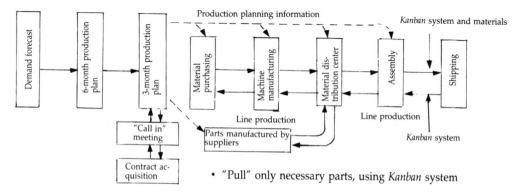

FIGURE 7.30
Conceptual diagram for "pull system" of production

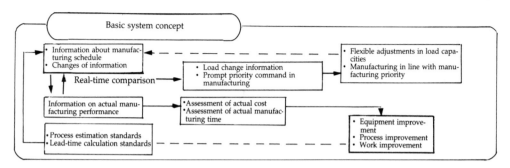

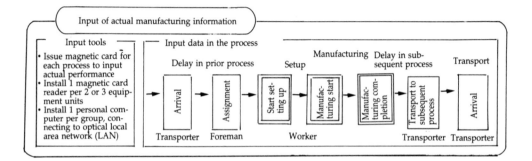

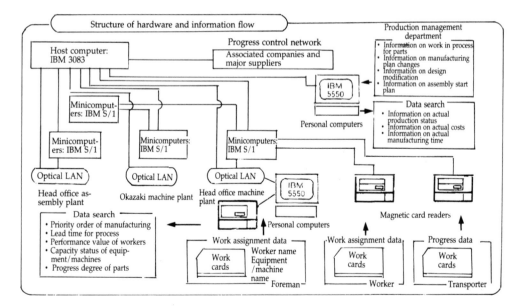

FIGURE 7.31
START at Toyoda

In developing a line production system, the "station-to-station" production system was devised, allowing workers to move instead of materials, resulting in cost reduction and acceleration of the assembly process.

As a result of line production of assembly work, all necessary manufacturing schedules were clearly identified by parts and equipment. This made it possible for workers to place advance orders for supply parts, using a *Kanban* system. Consequently, the company succeeded in creating the unique pull system of production. (See Figure 7.30.)

Development of a Production Management System for Single Unit Products

The reduced life cycle of products and changes in the manufacturing system created gaps between the standard time specified by planning departments and the actual time required at the production site. This gap inhibited the attainment of profit targets. On the other hand, diversified customer needs, cost reduction requirements, and pressures for delivery time reduction increased information needs in cost management and production management. Upgraded information quality was also required, and needs for a new system of production management surfaced.

START—short for "Schedule on Time and Accurate Recording System at Toyoda"—was developed as an answer to problems in the production management system for single unit products. (See Figure 7.31.) Thanks to the deployment of START, delay time between processes was reduced, manufacturing time was reduced to one third, and work in process was consequently reduced drastically.

Accurate determination of actual setup time and manufacturing time by process and by products facilitated the determination of actual costs, which in turn stimulated activities for process improvement and for evaluation of external/internal manufacturing needs.

RESULTS OF CROSS-FUNCTIONAL MANAGEMENT AND KEY POINTS TO REMEMBER

The introduction and deployment of cross-functional management at the company brought about significant changes, promoting companywide employee unity, system improvement, and the successful horizontal deployment of positive results.

Based upon experience, certain key points have been identified that promote cross-functional management.

1. Top managers must recognize the importance of cross-functional management and demonstrate their commitment.

2. The chairman of the cross-functional management committee should be an executive with the rank of vice president or higher, and the head of the manufacturing department closely related to the function for which improvement is being sought.

3. Members of the cross-functional management committee include executives of related departments. Members should represent two interests concurrently: that of their own departments and that of the company as a whole.

4. A plan-do-check-act cycle must be followed in conjunction with cross-functional management diagnosis and implementation status checks in the production departments.

5. Decisions of the cross-functional committees and results of the checking must be reported to the executive committee, and cross-functional management must be deployed with the complete approval of all executives.

CONCLUSION

The company still faces rapid changes in the business environment, including fluctuations of foreign exchange rates and trade frictions. Competition in quality due to diversified customer needs is intensifying rapidly. To weather the crisis and to build Toyoda Machine Works in the future, the company intends to improve continuously in the areas of quality assurance, cost, load smoothing and delivery, and human resources development.

Index